Bofton Evening-Poft.

Monday, July 8. 1745.

BOSTON.

As the Surrender of the City of Louisburgh *on* Cape Breton, *is at prefent the Subject of moft Converfations, we hope the following Draught will be acceptable to our Readers, as it may ferve to give them an Idea of the Situation and Strength of the Place, and render the News from thence more Intelligible.*

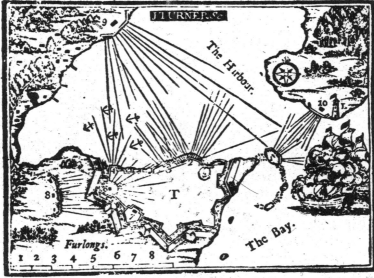

EXPLANATION.

(1.) The Ifland Battery, at the Harbour's Mouth. 28 Guns, ———Pounders.
(2.) The Town North Eaft Battery, 18 Four pounders, on two Faces.
(3) Three Flanks, with two Guns each, eighteen pounders.
(4.) A fmall Battery of Eight Guns, Nine Pounders.
(5.) Demi Lune, or Circular Battery, of 16 Guns, 24 pounders.
(6.) The Magazine.
(7.) The Fort or Citidel, fortified diftinctly from the Town, in which the Governor lived.
(8.) Three Fafcine Batteries, erected by our People againft the Weft Gate, &c.
(9.) The Grand Battery, of 36 Guns, 42 pounders, right againft the Harbour's Mouth, &c.
(10.) A Fafcine Battery erected by the *Englifh* near the Light-Houfe, oppofite to the Ifland-Battery, and not quite half a Mile from it. From this Battery our People play'd fo fuccefsfully upon the Ifland-Battery, both with their Cannon and Mortar, that the Enemy abandoned it with the utmoft Precipitation, and ran up to their Necks in Water, to fecure themfelves.
T The Center of the Town. L The Light-Houfe.

YANKEES
AT
LOUISBOURG

THE STORY OF
THE FIRST SIEGE
1745

George A. Rawlyk

Breton Books

Yankees at Louisbourg originally appeared as part of the University of Maine Studies, Series 2, Number 85, in the *University of Maine Bulletin* (Volume 69, Number 19, April 1967).

"The Plan of the Town and Harbour of Louisburgh" (page i) appeared in Benjamin Franklin's *Pennsylvania Gazette,* June 6, 1745, in James Parker's *New York Weekly Post-Boy* and, at least, in the *Boston Evening-Post.*

The following three maps are in the collection of the Beaton Institute, University College of Cape Breton, and published with their kind permission: N. Bellin's map (pages ii-iii), "A New Chart of the Coast of New England...," *Gentlemen's Quarterly,* 1745; "A Plan of the City & Harbour of Louisburg; shewing that part of Gabarus Bay in which the English landed, also their Encampment during the Siege in 1745" (page vi); "Town and Fortifications of Louisbourg in 1745" (after page 76).

The cover is a painting of the landing of the New Englanders at Louisbourg in 1745, said to be by John Stevens. Several engraved versions have been located, including work by Brooks, Bowles, and Stevens himself. It is a rare example of contemporary portrayal of the event, but it contains inaccuracies, including the emphasis on British uniforms rather than New England dress. We have reversed the painting for design purposes.

Our thanks to staff at Fortress of Louisbourg National Historic Park for encouragement to publish *Yankees at Louisbourg,* and for help in locating information. As always, it should be understood that any errors discovered are the sole responsibility of Breton Books.

Editor: Ronald Caplan
Production Assistance: Bonnie Thompson

THE CANADA COUNCIL | LE CONSEIL DES ARTS
FOR THE ARTS | DU CANADA
SINCE 1957 | DEPUIS 1957

We acknowledge the support of
the Canada Council for the Arts for our publishing program.

We also acknowledge support from Cultural Affairs,
Nova Scotia Department of Tourism and Culture. NOVASCOTIA

Canadian Cataloguing in Publication Data

Rawlyk, George A., 1935-1995

  Yankees at Louisbourg

  1st ed.

  Includes bibliographical references and index.
  ISBN 1-895415-45-4

1. Louisbourg (N.S.) — History — Siege, 1745. I. Title.

FC383.R38 1999   971.6'95501   C99-950234-4
E198.R38 1999

Acknowledgements

I AM DEEPLY INDEBTED to Professor Mason Wade of the University of Western Ontario who not only first suggested that I should write about New England and Louisbourg in the 1740's but who also perceptively and constructively criticized the manuscript. The manuscript was also read by Professors Alice Stewart and James Henderson of the University of Maine, and by Mr. Fred Thorpe, Senior Historian of the Human History Section of the National Museum of Canada. I have implemented many of the suggestions made by these scholars who have rescued me from numerous pitfalls. But I, of course, am solely responsible for the errors of fact and interpretation that may remain in this book.

Generous financial assistance from the Canadian Studies Programme of the University of Rochester as well as from Dalhousie University greatly facilitated my research and writing. I am also grateful for the assistance given to me by numerous archivists and librarians in the United States and in Canada.

Finally, I would like to thank my wife Mary for her noteworthy contribution to the writing of this book.

G. A. Rawlyk
Kingston, Ontario

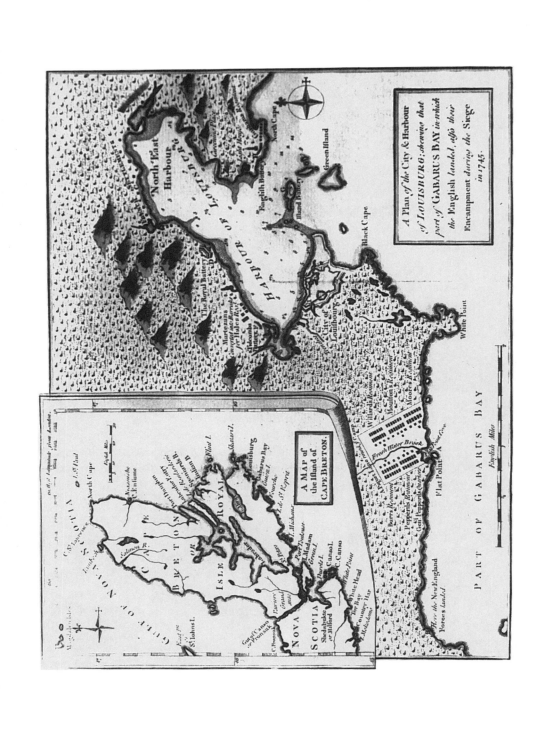

Contents

MAPS ON PAGES i-iii AND vi

MAP AND PHOTOGRAPHS BETWEEN PAGES 76 AND 77

Introduction

THROUGHOUT THE 17TH CENTURY and the first half of the 18th century it was Nova Scotia's misfortune to be the "eastern outpost and flank for both the French and English in North America."[1] Many New Englanders regarded Nova Scotia, which for them also included Cape Breton Island, as their northeastern frontier and as a vitally important stepping-stone to the valuable North Atlantic fisheries and to the St. Lawrence region. The French, on the other hand, tended to consider Nova Scotia as well as Cape Breton Island as the eastern base of their military and commercial empire in North America.[2] Both Frenchmen and Englishmen in the New World were convinced that the possession of Nova Scotia and Cape Breton Island was the strategic key to eventual control of the vast interior of the northern half of the continent, as well as the key to the control of the "Empire of the North Atlantic."

The Louisbourg expedition of 1745 really had its origins early in the 17th century when Acadia, or Nova Scotia, was founded by De Monts and Champlain, and Massachusetts by the Puritans. For whenever war broke out between France and Britain, and at least once during a prolonged period of peace, the capture of Nova Scotia became the primary concern of Massachusetts and of almost all New England. In 1654, when France and Britain were at peace, the Massachusetts leaders were largely responsible for sending an expedition under the command of Major Robert Sedgwick to capture Port Royal. It was not until 1670 that the French regained possession of Nova Scotia. Soon after the outbreak of King William's War, the New Englanders struck once again against Nova Scotia. In 1690 Port Royal was captured by a New England force, this time under the command of a former shepherd and ship's carpenter, Sir William Phips. Then, in 1710, during Queen Anne's War, after two previous unsuccessful attempts, another New England force, this time supported by some British warships, and commanded by Francis Nicholson, seized Port Royal. Unlike the Treaty of Ryswick of 1697, the Treaty of Utrecht of 1713 did not restore the *status quo ante bellum.* Cape Breton Island—Isle Royale—remained in French hands, but the rest of Nova Scotia became British territory.

The ease with which the New Englanders had been able to capture Port Royal, not only in 1710 but also in 1690 and 1654, finally convinced the French colonial authorities of the vital need to build a strong fortress on Cape Breton Island. In 1720 the French began to construct their North American Dunkirk at Louisbourg. It was hoped that Louisbourg would become the centre for the expanding French fishery in the North Atlantic. In addition, Louisbourg was to protect the St. Lawrence region from Anglo-American encroachments, serve as an entrepôt of trade between the French West Indies and New France, and also be a base for future offensive thrusts against Nova Scotia and New England.

The expeditions of 1654, 1690 and 1710 had much in common, and the latter two especially had something in common with the Louisbourg expedition of 1745. In these expeditions the New Englanders revealed—to use Henri Pirenne's interesting phrase— "the craving for adventure and the love of gain which are inherent in human nature."[3] Moreover, these expeditions can be considered to be excellent examples of New England economic and territorial expansionism as well as the area's natural defensive response to the threat of French encirclement. New England's penetration into Nova Scotia was neither purely offensive in nature nor defensive; it was both. Of course there were other factors involved, notably the prevailing English antipathy toward Roman Catholics and toward Frenchmen. There was also the widely held view that the Indian threat on the northern and eastern frontiers of New England could be eradicated only if the French forces were driven out of Nova Scotia. After the signing of the Treaty of Utrecht, some New Englanders eagerly awaited the outbreak of new hostilities between France and Britain so that the French could be driven from Cape Breton Island. These men would not be satisfied until the Island as well as the peninsula became "New England's Outpost."

Soon after Louisbourg was selected in 1720 as the site for a substantial French fortress, New England merchants began their economic penetration into the area. These merchants "supplied

Louisbourg with building materials, with food, with planks and oaken staves" and received in exchange rum and molasses from the French West Indies and from France "the cloths of Carcassone, the wines of Provence, sailcloths and linens."[4] Peter Faneuil, "the greatest of the Boston merchants of his time,"[5] had his own agents at Louisbourg. It has been estimated that in 1733, of the 158 vessels arriving officially at Louisbourg, forty-six were from New England and Nova Scotia, seventy from France, seventeen from New France and twenty-five from the French West Indies. Ten years later, in 1743, of the 175 vessels, seventy-eight were from New England and Nova Scotia, only fifty-eight from France and seven from New France, and thirty-two from the French West Indies.[6] Thus two years before the Louisbourg expedition, the number of New England vessels trading with Louisbourg was not only greater than those from France but also greater than the number from New France and the French West Indies combined. In the economic sense only, Louisbourg had become "New England's Outpost."[7] These economic ties only prepared the way for the New England expedition of 1745.

The walls of Louisbourg enclosed an area of less than 100 acres. On the landward side, the defences were dominated by three bastions of varying strength. The King's Bastion which also included the Citadel or Chateau St. Louis was flanked to the northwest by the West Gate or Dauphin Bastion and to the southwest by the Queen's Bastion. On the northeast seaward side were to be found the *Batterie de la Grave* and the Maurepas Bastion.

The narrow entrance to Louisbourg Harbour was defended by two powerful batteries. The Island Battery was located on a tiny island to the northeast of the fortress and the Royal or Grand Battery was situated on the northeast shore of the inner harbour approximately one mile by sea from both the town of Louisbourg and the Island Battery. These two batteries together with Dauphin Bastion were regarded by the French of Louisbourg as their key instruments of defence since the probability of an attack by land was not apparently seriously considered. And Louisbourg was vulnerable to a land assault. The Royal Battery was dominated by a nearby hill, and the guns of the Island Battery could easily be silenced by a battery built at Lighthouse Point. Furthermore, largely because the stones were inadequately dressed and laid and the mortar made of unsuitable sea sand, the landward walls of the fortress as well as the Royal Battery were in a dangerous state of disrepair in 1744 and 1745. To make matters even more serious, the fortress was defended by fewer than 600 soldiers most of whom had never fought in a military engagement.

Most historians would agree with L. E. DeForest's statement that the "capture of Louisbourg in 1745 was the most important military achievement of the American Colonists prior to the War of the Revolution."[8] The purpose of this book is to account for and to describe this colonial achievement. Not all of the emphasis, however, will be placed upon the New England aspects of the affair. Some attention will also be devoted to the policies and actions of the two European powers involved, as well as to the French in Louisbourg, New France, and Nova Scotia. London and Paris were just as much involved in the outcome of the Louisbourg expedition as was Boston; the regional conflict was merely one aspect of a broader imperial conflict. This is a point that many American historians, especially, find very difficult to grasp. But unless the Louisbourg expedition is seen in its proper context, its essential North Atlantic context, a distorted picture is bound to emerge.

An examination of a single significant historical event in considerable depth and detail requires no long justification. It was William Blake who wrote: "He who would do good to another must do it in Minute Particulars." This volume is primarily concerned with the "Minute Particulars" of New England-Louisbourg relations in 1744 and 1745.

The work of two historians has greatly influenced the general approach taken in this study: J. B. Brebner's *New England's Outpost*, and C. P. Stacey's *Quebec, 1759.* Brebner's perceptive analysis of New England's penetration into Nova Scotia has been extended to include Louisbourg, while some of Stacey's techniques have been applied to another crucial battle in North America's history.

1

The French Attacks Upon Canso and Annapolis Royal (May-October, 1744)

ON THE WHARVES of Louisbourg a crowd gathered on May 3, 1744,[1] as a tiny French ship that had sailed from St. Malo on March 27 made its way carefully into the sheltered harbour.[2] In the crowd, no doubt, was Jean Baptiste Louis Le Prévost, Seigneur Du Quesnel, the elderly governor of Isle Royale, as eager as anyone for the first European news of the year. To his enemies, he was "whimsical, changeable, given to drink, and when in his cups knowing no restraint or decency."[3] It is to be expected that the popular Port Captain Morpain, and François Bigot, the enigmatic Commissaire-Ordonnateur, also were among the townfolk.

As the ship rubbed along the wharf, excited sailors shouted the news. War against Great Britain had been declared by the French monarch on March 18. Most people in Louisbourg had long anticipated such a declaration. Many in the crowd were desperately concerned with discovering whether the ship carried badly needed food supplies. These people included the poorer inhabitants of Louisbourg, who were largely dependent upon the coastal cod fishery. Since the middle of April these unfortunates had been on the verge of starvation, eating little else than shell fish.[4] They faced starvation because the Basque fishing entrepreneurs, who had regularly supplied many of the Cape Breton fishermen with food and fishing supplies in early spring in return for dried cod at the end of the season, refused to sail for Cape Breton in the early months of 1744 because they had been warned of the impending declaration of war against Britain.[5] These close-fisted Basques did not relish the thought of losing their defenceless ships to English privateers.

While the Basques stayed home, the coastal fishermen from

Louisbourg and the neighbouring settlements of Baleine and the Lorambecs suffered, but not in silence. Early in May fishermen from the latter settlements, with the full support of their Louisbourg friends, openly threatened to seize provisions by force in the town.[6] The frightened Du Quesnel responded quickly by ordering his troops to stamp out the flames of revolt;[7] the discontented fishermen were forced to retreat, but not before they had made everyone in Louisbourg and its environs fully aware of the fact that unless they soon received a sufficient supply of food, there would probably be a bloody insurrection.

It was only a few moments after the ship had docked on May 3 that Du Quesnel and Bigot began to read the letters sent to them by the Minister of Marine, the Compte de Maurepas. After informing them of the declaration of war, Maurepas clearly laid down two broad principles regarding the general role that he expected Louisbourg to play during the early months of the war. First, since "the first moments of war will be the most important ones,"[8] for privateers, Du Quesnel and Bigot were to encourage as many inhabitants of Isle Royale as possible to send out vessels to prey upon the unsuspecting British ships.

It should be pointed out that Britain did not declare war upon France until April 9, and that news of the British declaration of war did not reach Boston until May 23.[9] However, since the French in Louisbourg lacked a sufficient supply of "small cannon with their ammunition, pistols, swords, and axes for these expeditions,"[10] only two privateers were immediately properly outfitted. *Le Succès* was placed under the command of Morpain, who had made his reputation as an amazingly successful privateer during Queen Anne's War, and the other ship was captained by Doloboratz, an experienced Louisbourg seaman.[11] Second, Du Quesnel and Bigot were instructed to concert "all the necessary arrangements in order to protect and to maintain the fishery and commerce."[12] In other words, the two French officials were to do all in their power to destroy British commerce and the British cod fishery in the North Atlantic. Such destruction was considered to be concomitant of the expansion of the French fishery and commerce. Two ships, *L'Ardent* from France and *Le Caribou* from Quebec, were to be sent to Louisbourg to implement Maurepas' policy;[13] Bigot was asked to recruit some 100 men from Louisbourg to man the latter, which had been constructed recently in New France.[14]

Bigot received another rather startling command. He was ordered to supply the *Compagnie des Indes* treasure fleet from the East

Indies, which was expected to stop briefly at Louisbourg sometime in June or early July, with "fresh meats...the supplies that they might find necessary for their crossing from there to France."[15] Bigot found himself on the horns of a dilemma. Where could he obtain the necessary supplies in the required time? New England and New France were considered to be out of the question. Furthermore, the Louisbourg garrison's provisions, which had been expected to last until the spring of 1745, were disappearing at an unanticipated rate because of the general scarcity of foodstuffs. After carefully considering the various ramifications of Maurepas' order, Bigot came to the conclusion that only from the Acadians of Nova Scotia could he obtain the necessary supplies, especially the fresh meat. Bigot's conclusion is not a surprising one; it was estimated that the Acadians illicitly shipped yearly to Louisbourg "6 or 700 Head of Cattle, and about 2000 Sheep."[16] There was, however, one serious stumbling block in Bigot's path—the presence of a small British guard sloop at the island fort of Canso, at the northeastern extremity of Nova Scotia.

Realizing that most of the illicit trade between the Acadians and Louisbourg took place either before the arrival at Canso of the British warship in the early summer or after its departure in the autumn, Captain Young of the *Kinsale* had decided in 1743 to leave a guard sloop under the command of a Lieutenant Ryall to winter at Canso.[17] It was hoped that Ryall's presence would reduce substantially the volume of the illicit trade, whose main avenue was by sea from the Chignecto-Tatamagouche region, through the Gut of Canso, and then northeastward to the French fortress town.

In order to facilitate this traffic, Bigot wished to drive the British troops from Canso and to destroy or capture the guard sloop. By the middle of May, Du Quesnel had arrived at a similar decision, but not necessarily for the same reasons.[18] A number of factors help to account for the governor's decision, and some of these factors cast light upon Louisbourg's relations with the Acadians in 1744. Du Quesnel saw in his instructions from Maurepas of March 18 a clear justification for an attack upon Canso.[19] The capture of what many Frenchmen still regarded as one of the most important British fishery posts in North America could only benefit the French fishery and seriously weaken that of the enemy. The governor could not forget his first instructions received from Maurepas in September 1740:

> The King's intention is not that, once the war has broken out
> you remain simply on the defensive. You will find in M. de

Forant's letters that he had proposed an expedition against Accadie, and that he had demanded only two frigates to carry it out. His Majesty wishes that you obtain all the necessary information not only about this project; but also about the attack on Plaisance, Newfoundland.[20]

Would not the capture of Canso prepare the way for a French offensive against peninsular Nova Scotia—the area that Maurepas particularly wanted to regain from the British? Furthermore, Du Quesnel was of the opinion that the seizure of Canso would open wide the trading lanes between Nova Scotia and Louisbourg, thus providing the much needed food supplies for the ships of the *Compagnie des Indes* as well as for the starving inhabitants of Louisbourg. It was also hoped that the excitement generated by the expedition and the expectation of booty would persuade a number of the discontented fishermen in Louisbourg to join the expedition, while keeping the minds of the less adventurous from being too absorbed with the problem of hunger. Finally, the governor felt that the capture of Canso would encourage the Indian allies of the French and perhaps even win over a few wavering Acadians.[21]

Du Quesnel selected Captain Joseph Dupont Du Vivier to lead the attack upon Canso.[22] Du Vivier had never before seen active military service, but he was regarded as an excellent officer,[23] intimately familiar with the general situation of the tiny British fort and fishing settlement some sixty miles to the south of Louisbourg. Poupet De La Boularderie, a retired French officer who had served with the illustrious Richelieu Regiment at the battles of "Kel, Philisbourg and Clauzen,"[24] was asked to accompany the expedition because, in his own words, "the officers who were appointed had no experience, never having served in time of war."[25] A small fleet, made up of the two privateers commanded by Morpain and Doloboratz, a supply sloop owned by Du Chambon, the commanding officer on the Isle St. Jean (Prince Edward Island), and fourteen "fishing vessels for making the assault landing," was to carry twenty-two French and Swiss officers, eighty French soldiers, thirty-seven Swiss soldiers, and 212 sailors—a grand total of 351 men.[26] On May 23 the flotilla sailed south from Louisbourg, and in the early morning hours of the following day the men on board the ships found themselves in Canso harbour.[27]

Canso had seen much better days; in English eyes it was no longer an important cod-fishing centre.[28] During the early months of 1744, the British government had finally come to take it "for granted that there is no Fishery now at Cancea."[29] How the great had fallen! For in the 1720's Canso had been New England's cod capital.[30] There were four incomplete companies of Lieutenant-General Richard Phillip's regiment stationed on Canso Island in 1744 under the command of Captain Heron. Of the eighty-seven soldiers "one third was sick or lame,"[31] and the others were poorly armed and badly trained. These men, their sizeable families, and a small number of fishermen-settlers were housed in rude shelters on the various islands in the harbour and along the nearby rocky mainland. Canso's only defence work was a totally inadequate blockhouse built of timber donated by grateful fishermen.[32] Heron's troops were in no condition to resist any enemy attack.[33]

In preparation for a landing at dawn on May 24, the two French privateers began to bombard the Canso blockhouse with cannon-shot.[34] The first shot sailed through the thin blockhouse walls and almost immediately Heron rushed out with a flag of truce, thinking "it advisible to capitulate in time to obtain the better terms."[35] Lieutenant Ryall in the guard sloop provided some belated opposition, "but was oblig'd to strike to the superior Force, after having one man kill'd and three or four wounded."[36] Capitulation terms were readily arrived at. The wives and children of the troops were to be sent to Boston as soon as possible, but the troops were not to be free to return to New England or Annapolis Royal until May 1745.[37] After loading the not inconsiderable booty[38] on to the ships, together with the prisoners, the French put to the torch all the buildings at Canso harbour.[39]

As the British prisoners disembarked at Louisbourg, Du Quesnel and Bigot were confronted by another major problem; they now had over 100 new mouths to feed. Even though by the closing days of May some supplies had been received from France, there was still a scarcity of food in Louisbourg. Nevertheless, it is clear that most of the discontent regarding the very real possibility of starvation had completely disappeared. Because of the shortage of food, Bigot was compelled to limit the daily rations of the Canso prisoners to "a pound of bread...four ounces of cod and four of pork."[40] Completely dissatisfied with their totally inadequate rations, the prisoners early in June sent one of their own number to obtain food and other supplies from Boston.[41]

As a result of the food situation and also because of the absence of suitable prison accommodations, Du Quesnel was eager to rid himself of the Canso prisoners, as well as of those "Englishmen" later captured by French privateers. The presence in Boston of a small number of French fishermen and sailors captured by New

England privateers facilitated somewhat the governor's task. It was not, however, until August and September that satisfactory arrangements were made with Governor William Shirley of Massachusetts regarding the exchange of prisoners. During the intervening period Du Quesnel had persuaded Heron to accept new capitulation terms.[42] Heron promised that his troops would not serve in any capacity against the French until September of the following year.[43] Du Quesnel's insistence upon these new terms is of some consequence. By the early days of September 1774 the governor, expecting a major French offensive against Annapolis Royal to take place in the spring and early summer of 1745, did not want Heron's troops to be used to reinforce the British garrison there. Late that month 350 English prisoners, including the healthy Canso soldiers[44] (but not their wives and children and the "invalid soldiers and five old cripples"[45] who had been sent to New England weeks earlier) sailed for Boston.

With Canso destroyed, Du Quesnel, enjoying the heady effect of military victory, began to envisage a much grander project—an attack upon Annapolis Royal and the eventual repossession of Nova Scotia. Believing that the arrival of the 64-gun *L'Ardent* from France was imminent, he decided to combine two previously formulated plans for an attack upon Annapolis. One of these had been advocated by Du Vivier in 1735, and the other by a former governor of Louisbourg, Isaac Louis de Forant, in 1739. Du Vivier, a descendant of the La Tours of Acadia, maintained:

> The inhabitants [Acadians] are entirely devoted to [the French Crown]...this enterprise would be accomplished, provided advantage was taken of the first moments. One may reckon on the zeal of the inhabitants and of the greater part of the savages. The English have...few troops there. So that with 100 men only from the garrison of Louisbourg, and a certain quantity of arms and ammunition to distribute to the inhabitants, [he]...would pledge his head to make the conquest of this part of North America.[46]

Du Vivier appears to have expected the Louisbourg troops to land on the north shore of the Chignecto Isthmus, then march to Minas and from thence through the Annapolis Valley to the British fort. He hoped that as the Louisbourg force advanced it would gather Micmac and Acadian recruits like a rolling snowball and would easily "drive out the English without any help from France."[47]

On the other hand Forant was of the opinion that since a formal siege operation against Annapolis Royal was probably necessary, two well-armed French warships, with two hunderd regular troops and siege materials, should sail from Louisbourg after war had been declared. Following the disembarkation of the troops with their artillery, "the frigates should put a stop to the help coming by sea from New England to the besieged."[48]

Du Quesnel was certainly no military genius; he nevertheless came to the conclusion that if an invading land force made up of Micmacs, Acadians, and Louisbourg troops was supported by two French warships, the expedition against Annapolis Royal was far more likely to succeed. However, his proposed two-pronged offensive demanded unusually careful planning and delicate timing, two requisites that the governor could in no way guarantee. Disregarding tactical realities and wishing to take further advantage of the element of surprise, Du Quesnel resolved to take a military gamble. He would instruct the Abbé Le Loutre, the missionary to the Micmacs of Nova Scotia, to lead his parishioners, who detested the British, in an attack upon Annapolis.[49] Du Quesnel appears to have promised the Micmacs that they would be reinforced shortly by Louisbourg soldiers and further supported by French warships.[50]

Le Loutre, who Parkman unfairly described as being a "man of boundless egotism [possessing] a violent spirit of domination, intense hatred of the English and a fanaticism that stopped at nothing,"[51] unquestioningly obeyed. The priest had become a military commander. N. McL. Rogers, in an excellent study of Le Loutre's career, accounted for the latter's significant decision thus:

> It may also be urged in Le Loutre's defence that he was not at this time a parish priest to the Acadian French, but missionary to a people who had never recognized the sovereignty of the British crown. He received his directions from Paris and Louisbourg, and it was in accordance with instructions sent by Du Quesnel...that he accompanied the expedition against Annapolis. No doubt he realized the delicacy of his position, for he was permitted to remain in Nova Scotia by the courtesy of the English governor. He was obliged to choose between this obligation to Mascarene and the explicit orders received from Louisbourg, strengthened in all probability by his own strong desire to serve his country in a time of war. Under these circumstances, it was impossible to remain neutral without disobedience to his instructions. His loyalty to France impelled him to commit a breach of good faith against Mascarene. This decision, once made, was irrevocable.[52]

On July 12, 1744, Le Loutre with two French inhabitants of Nova

Scotia and 300 Micmacs began to besiege Annapolis Royal.[53]

In July 1744 the fortifications of Annapolis were inadequate, but the place was obviously not "still in such a state of dilapidation that its sandy ramparts were crumbling into the ditches, and the cows of the garrison walked over them at their pleasure,"[54] as Francis Parkman declared. Since late in October 1743, after receiving instructions from Britain "to prepare against any surprise by putting the colony into a proper position of defence,"[55] the commander of the fort had diligently directed the considerable repairs hurriedly made to the fortifications.[56] Consequently, by July 1744 it was impossible for a Micmac, let alone a cow, to walk over the ramparts.

It was indeed fortunate for the British cause in North America that Paul Mascarene was the commanding officer at Annapolis Royal. Having spent all of his adult life in the New England-Nova Scotia region, he regarded Annapolis as a vitally important outpost of New England. To Mascarene, "Acadia" was New England's northeastern frontier and Boston was Nova Scotia's true capital. By carefully following an extremely conciliatory policy towards the Acadian inhabitants, he hoped to keep them neutral in case war broke out with France.[57] He feared that if the Acadians were alienated in any major way in time of peace, most of them would probably join the French and Micmacs in driving the British out of Nova Scotia in time of war.

On July 12, 1744, Mascarene had only approximately one hundred troops in his garrison and twenty or thirty of these he considered to be "utterly invalides."[58] Indeed, Canso and Annapolis Royal had almost become pastures for aged and infirm soldiers. But Mascarene himself was equal to one hundred typical 18th-century British regulars serving in North America. He was supremely confident that his small force, supported by the men in the employ of the Ordinance Department, could easily repel any land attack made without regular siege weapons. J. B. Brebner judiciously assessed Mascarene's policies and character in 1744 thus:

> He set himself, therefore, to rouse and train and discipline his elderly warriors, to repair as best he could, handicapped by insufficiency of funds and lack of materials, the most serious breaches in his fort, and to reach a practical understanding with the Acadians.
>
> He seems to have been in many ways very different from other contemporary officers. He possessed real judgment, a power of seeing situations clearly, of analysing them simply,

and of making shrewd and practicable recommendations for their solutions; and yet he revealed the gentleness, reasonableness, and patience which military men can seldom afford to practise.[59]

On May 29 panic had swept the homes of the families of soldiers and artificers located outside of the fort, in the wake of alarming rumours that a French-Micmac raid was imminent.[60] The panic caused an unprecedented exodus of woman and children "in shoals to New England."[61] It was not, however, until June 15 that Mascarene received reliable information regarding the fall of Canso. He anticipated that the "French do not intend to stop there...but they will come and pay us a visit."[62] The fort hummed with feverish activity; guns and bayonets were repaired and the artificers were quickly armed and work on the fortifications was greatly accelerated.

It was on July 11 that Mascarene discovered that 300 Indians were poised for an attack not more than two leagues from the fort.[63] On hearing of the impending assault, the Acadians from the Annapolis region who had been assisting in the repair work at the fort suddenly fled to their homes. In the presence of the much feared Micmacs, the Acadians were determined to walk the knife-edge of neutrality. Mascarene's men were tense but confident as they awaited the first enemy onslaught; it came on the following morning, July 12.

Early that morning, the Indian invaders were surprised to see two British soldiers in one of the gardens outside the fort. The two men, who had acted contrary to Mascarene's orders, were easily killed by the Micmacs who then made a half-hearted attack upon the fort.[64] British artillery and musket fire quickly dispersed the undisciplined mob of Micmacs who, after setting fire to some buildings in the lower town, were quite satisfied to retreat to a hill about a mile from the fort.[65] Here most of them decided to await the arrival of the promised reinforcements from Louisbourg; they were in no mood to mount a frontal attack upon the fort, a manoeuvre they correctly considered to be suicidal.

The following day, July 13, the disorganized invaders had the effrontery to ask Mascarene to surrender the fort. He replied the next day to the impertinent request:

> Gentlemen: The first shot you heard fired from the Fort was according to our custom when we think we have enemies. Afterwards your people killed two of our soldiers who were in the gardens without arms. I am resolved to defend this Fort

until the last drop of blood against all the enemies of the
king of Great Britain, my master, whereupon you can take
your course.[66]

The course of the enemy was to burn some of the remaining buildings outside the fort, to fire a few harmless volleys against the fort,
and on July 16 to retreat unexpectedly to Minas.

Why was the "siege" not prolonged until the arrival of the expected force from Louisbourg? On July 16 seventy reinforcements
from Boston reached Annapolis on board the Massachusetts "Province Snow," the *Prince of Orange*.[67] New Englanders were convinced
that the arrival of these reinforcements frightened off the
Micmacs:

> Upon Captain Tyng's arrival, the Indians seeing the Ham-
> mocks in the Netting of the Ship, took them for Indians; and
> being informed by a French woman that he had a great num-
> ber of Mohawks on board, and had landed several hundreds
> of Men to cut them off, they ran into the Woods in such
> haste, that their Priest left his Crucifix and other religious
> Trinkets behind him.[68]

The arrival of reinforcements was not in itself responsible for
the retreat of Le Loutre's force. There is some evidence to suggest
that by July 16 Le Loutre had been informed by Du Quesnel that
L'Ardent was not expected until the end of July and that his scheme
to capture Annapolis Royal had been unavoidably delayed.[69] It is interesting to note that *L'Ardent* did not arrive in Louisbourg until
August 16.[70] Realizing the hopelessness of their situation because of
the lack of French reinforcements and the arrival of British reinforcements, Le Loutre's Micmacs resolved to return to Minas. Du
Quesnel's gamble had resulted in a miserable fiasco. His Indian allies were understandably discontented and disillusioned, the Acadians unimpressed by French power, and the British were more
confident in their military potential.

Despite the embarrassing retreat of Le Loutre's force, Du
Quesnel stubbornly insisted on a second dubious plan to obliterate
Britain's last vestige of military power in Nova Scotia. He decided
to gamble once again with a combined land and sea assault on An-
napolis Royal. What had this dying old man to lose? He had nei-
ther a military reputation nor an administrative career to protect.
By the last week of July *Le Caribou* had arrived in Louisbourg and
L'Ardent was expected daily. On July 29 Du Vivier was dispatched to
Minas by way of the Chignecto region with about fifty soldiers and
an undetermined number of Indians. It was hoped that they would

combine forces at Minas with Malecites from the St. John River and other Micmacs for a final thrust against Mascarene's fort.[71] A simultaneous naval assault was to have been carried out by *Le Caribou* and the long overdue *L'Ardent*.

It was August 8 before Du Vivier's troops landed at Chignecto.[72] They were delayed by contrary winds and a prolonged stay on Isle St. Jean. Proceeding from Baie Verte on the north shore, they spent five days crossing the narrow Chignecto Isthmus to Beaubassin on Chignecto Bay.[73] Here Du Vivier pleaded for recruits and supplies, arguing that the Acadian people could be redeemed by his success. The response was disappointing. A few Acadians volunteered to bear arms on condition that they could choose their own officers and remain in the Isthmus area—a safe distance from the conflict.[74] Du Vivier felt compelled to accept these unusual terms.

Although for decades anti-British feeling had been strongest in the Chignecto region, by 1744 neutrality was the policy that the vast majority of these and other Acadians found most expedient. They were bound by certain emotional ties to France, but they were reluctant to risk expulsion from their prosperous farms by allowing Du Vivier to purchase supplies from them.[75] In addition, they considered the French incapable of recapturing Nova Scotia.

Finding no more enthusiasm for his cause at Minas, Du Vivier finally made threatening demands that did little to endear him to the Acadians:

> The whole of the above [supplies and draft animals] must be brought to me at ten o'clock on Saturday morning at the french flag which I have had hoisted, and under which the deputies from each of the said parishes shall be assembled, to pledge fidelity for themselves and all the inhabitants of the neighbourhood who shall not be called away from the labours of the harvest. All those for whom the pledge of fidelity shall be given will be held fully responsible for said pledge, and those who contravene the present order shall be punished as rebellious subjects, and delivered into the hands of the savages as enemies of the state, as we cannot refuse the demand which the savages make for all those who will submit themselves.[76]

This disappointment at Minas was further increased by the small number of Micmacs who proved willing to join Du Vivier.[77] At the most, there could have been only 160 Micmacs, since his total force numbered 280 men, fifty of whom were Louisbourg troops and seventy of whom were Malecites from the St. John Valley.[78] Micmac support was weak for two reasons. First, the French had lost face by their previous failure to capture Annapolis Royal. Second, Le Loutre, the leader of the Micmacs, took no part in the renewed attempt.[79]

The Acadians in the regions around Minas, Piziquid and Cobequid were even more apathetic than those at Chignecto.[80] Du Vivier held the two priests of the general area responsible for this attitude, charging Father Chevreux with pronouncing excommunication against French supporters and Father Miniac with surreptitious actions "to cause the wreck of the enterprise."[81] But the policy of neutrality so fervently preached by the priests had long been accepted by their parishioners.

On August 30 Du Vivier led his men out of Minas and marched towards Annapolis Royal. Apparently awaiting further news from Du Quesnel, Du Vivier appeared to be in no hurry to reach Mascarene's fort. On September 5, while still at a considerable distance from the fort, he finally received intelligence from Du Quesnel that the French warships were expected to be in the vicinity of Annapolis on September 8.[82] The jubilant Du Vivier decided not to attack the fort until that date; he also resolved to attempt to trick the British into believing that he had at least twice the number of troops that he actually had. His ruse was a brilliant success. He carefully arranged his men as they marched towards the fort but not too near it with outer ranks complete but the centre absolutely devoid of troops,[83] so that Mascarene was persuaded that Du Vivier had at least "Six or Seven hundred men."[84] Mascarene thus described the affair:

> The next morning (8th) when they march'd down to us under the cover of some hedges and fences, with Colours flying, a Gunn was pointed att their Colours, and graz'd as we heard since between Monsr. Duvivier their Commander and his Brother.... They did not then think fitt to proceed further, butt soon return'd to their Camp beyond the Mill.[85]

Between July 6 and September 8, Mascarene had received fifty-three additional reinforcements from Governor Shirley of Massachusetts.[86] Thus when the second siege commenced, the fort was defended by over 250 men with cannon, muskets, bayonets and huge logs at their disposal. These logs had been placed at the top of the ramparts by John Henry Bastide, the fort's engineer, who had instructed the defenders to roll them on the invaders if they attempted to use ladders to scale the walls of the fort.[87]

In order to protect his troops from the superior British fire power and to conceal the small numbers of his invading force, Du Vivier launched a series of night "attacks."[88] Usually Indians stole silently to the foot of the glacis, uttered a few blood-curdling yells and took a number of badly aimed shots at the parapet. Then, pleased with their evening's labour, they returned to their camp. It was hoped that these raids would unnerve the defenders and lead them to believe that a large invading force including hordes of fierce Indians surrounded them. In preparation for his major assault, Du Vivier demanded supplies from the neighbouring Acadians—ladders, shovels, pick-axes and wagons.[89]

On September 15 Du Vivier tried a new approach which he hoped would prevent the needless shedding of French blood and would add to his reputation as a military leader and strategist. Under a flag of truce he boldly demanded the capitulation of the British fort. He declared that "he expected a Seventy, a Sixty and a Fourty gunns Shipps, mann'd one third above their compliment, with a Transport with two hundred and fifty men more of regular Troops with Cannon, mortars and other implements of warr; that as he knew [the British] could not resist that Force and must then surrender [they] could expect no other terms than to be made prisonners of Warr."[90] He suggested the drawing up of preliminaries to a capitulation that would come into force the moment the French ships arrived in the Annapolis Basin. In the intervening period a truce would be carefully administered.[91]

Mascarene was disappointed to find "all the officers except three or four very ready to accept of the proposal, the dread of being made prisoners of warr having no small influence with most."[92] DuVivier's suggestion was accepted on terms extremely favourable to the British. All eyes now turned seawards. As time passed, Du Vivier slowly realized that the warships were not coming and that the truce was only benefitting the enemy. A messenger was dispatched to Du Quesnel requesting the sending of two privateers in the hope that they would frighten the disillusioned British troops into surrender.[93] Du Vivier cancelled the truce and resumed hostilities sometime before September 23.[94]

The British troops received this news with "three chearfull Huzzas,"[95] delighting Mascarene with their spirit. They found the renewed nightly forays "more and more contemptible" and resulting in "little more harm...than the disturbance in the night."[96]

Finally, two vessels were sighted in the Basin on September 26. The French and British strained their eyes to see the colours of the armed brigantine and sloop. As the ships edged closer, jubilation swept through the British fort—the ships were from Boston, carrying fifty Pigwacket Indians under Captain Gorham and much needed supplies. Du Vivier sadly noted in his journal:

> The British yelled out many hurrahs. I had them carefully watched during the night. They were singing and enjoying themselves thoroughly they probably spent the whole night drinking.[97]

The morale of the invading force had been shattered; nevertheless, the stubborn Du Vivier refused to withdraw. On October 2, however, De Gannes, an officer from Louisbourg, arrived at Du Vivier's camp with word that "The King's vessels were not coming"[98] and that Du Quesnel expected the invading force to raise the siege. Two or three days later the retreat towards Minas began.[99]

It was not until August 16 that *L'Ardent* with a broken bowsprit had limped into Louisbourg.[100] Her captain, Meschin, informed Du Quesnel that the ship would not be ready to sail for Annapolis Royal until September 5 or 6.[101] The governor immediately sent word to Du Vivier that *Le Caribou* and *L'Ardent* would definitely be at Annapolis on September 8. However, sometime before this date Du Quesnel suddenly changed his mind. He decided that it would be unwise to send the two warships to Annapolis and that Du Vivier should winter at Beaubassin "in order to prevent the British from spreading discontent among the Accadiens."[102]

There were two main reasons for this unexpected *volte-face*. First, probably at the beginning of September, Du Quesnel received instructions from Maurepas not to mount an attack upon Annapolis. *L'Ardent* and *Le Caribou* were to be used to protect "the fishery and commerce of his Majesty's subjects at Isle Royale" as well as to interrupt "the navigation of the enemy in these waters."[103] Second, by August 1744 New England privateers were playing havoc with French shipping to and from Louisbourg, and Bigot and the influential Louisbourg merchants urged the governor to use the two warships to keep the trade lanes open and to drive the New England privateers from the coasts of Cape Breton. It was argued that if the expected supply ships from New France were captured, Louisbourg would be faced with the dreadful prospect of starvation by the new year.[104]

Along with the news of the change in Du Quesnel's policy, De Gannes brought orders for Du Vivier to return immediately to Louisbourg, so that he could sail for France to make preparations for a large-scale assault upon Annapolis Royal now proposed for the spring of 1745. De Gannes, with a company of fifty men, was expected to winter in Nova Scotia. But because of open Acadian opposition to the plan, De Gannes felt compelled to go back to Louisbourg with his troops.[105]

Du Quesnel died on October 9;[106] he was succeeded by Louis Du Chambon, the former commanding officer on Isle St. Jean. Obviously totally ignorant of his predecessor's instructions to De Gannes, but having noted Du Vivier's urgent demand for some naval help, Du Chambon decided to send two privateers, one described as a "30 or 40 Gun Ship"[107] and the other a smaller brig, to Annapolis. The ships arrived off Annapolis on the evening of October 25.[108] Bitterly disappointed at not finding the expected besieging force, the two ships returned to Louisbourg.

In October 1744 the Acadians remained content to live under the existing "mild and tranquil government"[109] of the British at Annapolis Royal. The devastation of Canso had secured, at a most crucial time, the major avenue of commerce between Nova Scotia and Louisbourg and also had prepared the way for the French offensive against Annapolis. But the abortive attempts to seize Annapolis Royal revealed that Louisbourg was of doubtful military value as an offensive base without reliable sea power and an adequate system of communications with France, New France, and the Micmacs of Nova Scotia.

2

Massachusetts Response to French Aggression (May-October, 1744)

ON MAY 23, 1744, a merchantman from Glasgow arrived at Boston with intelligence that war had been declared by Britain upon France.[1] Governor Shirley had long anticipated the outbreak of hostilities and had laboured diligently, after his appointment as governor of Massachusetts in 1741, to strengthen the colony's defences. He greatly feared possible attacks by Indian allies of the French upon the exposed western, northern, and northeastern frontiers of Massachusetts, as well as French naval assaults upon the eastern seaboard. As early as October 1743, he had issued the following orders to the militia commanders along the frontiers:

> Having received advices from Great Britian that there is great
> danger of a rupture with France, I think it necessary and ac-
> cordingly direct you forthwith, to advertise the exposed towns
> and settlements hereof, and to take proper care that the in-
> habitants secure themselves and families against any sudden
> assault from the Indians, and that they do not expose them-
> selves by being too far from home in this time of danger, and
> that the companies in your regiment that are not much ex-
> posed, be in readiness to relieve any of the neighbouring
> places in case there should be any occasion for it.[2]

Furthermore, Shirley adopted a conciliatory policy towards the traditionally pro-French tribes, the Penobscots, Pigwackets, Norridgewocks, St. Francis, and Malecites. By giving them presents and by carefully regulating their trade with the English merchants, he courted their favour and support, or at least their neutrality, in case of a rupture with France. But since Shirley could not count upon the success of this policy, he encouraged the construction of small forts, especially in Maine where the French-Indian threat was greatest.[3]

Governor Shirley's ambition went far beyond his earnest desire to protect Massachusetts from French aggression. He wished to see the French driven from North America and supplanted by the British, and he also coveted personal political power. Not wishing to remain a puppet in the hands of the leading members of the General Court, Shirley was eager to manipulate that body. In short, he proposed to be not only governor of Massachusetts, but also its prime minister. His clever plan for gaining control began with an ambitious defence policy which would result in a significant increase of patronage for him to dispense as commander-in-chief. The careful distribution of military appointments, supply contracts and other favours would lead to the desired control of the General Court.[4]

On June 11, the day after the first meeting of the General Court in Boston for the year 1744, Shirley clearly enunciated his defence policy in a speech to the members of the House of Representatives and the Council.[5] In this most significant address Shirley advocated six measures which he was convinced would ensure the safety of the colony. First, he endeavoured to deal with the mercurial Indians residing on the frontiers of the colony. Shirley observed that he had notified them of the declaration of war and "insisted on their obligations of Fidelity to us by Treaty, assuring them of our Protection and Friendship, so long as they shall keep good Faith with us." He emphasized that the Massachusetts government was obliged to refrain from all acts of hostility towards the Indians "'till their Breach of Treaty shall discharge us from those Obligations." Second, because of his refusal to trust the Indians, Shirley urged the members of the General Court "to provide for the immediate Defence of our Frontiers both in the Eastern and Western Parts." He argued that the implementation of such a policy would not only protect the isolated frontier settlements from "any sudden Surpize from the Indians," but would also probably persuade the Indians of the utter foolishness of their attacking the settlements. Third, to protect the maritime commerce of the colony as well as the eastern seaboard from possible French naval attacks, the governor urged the General Court to arm and man an adequate number of guard vessels. Fourth, he demanded that the various forts throughout the colony, especially Castle William in Boston, be properly garrisoned and be put "forthwith...in a Condition to make a more vigorous Defence against any Attacks of our Enemies." Fifth, Shirley maintained that the successful defence of Annapolis Royal was depen-

dent upon immediate reinforcements from Massachusetts and that
its defence was absolutely essential for the well-being of the colony:

> As the Acquisition of the Country of Nova-Scotia, and more
> especially of the Fortress of Port-Royal [now Annapolis Royal]
> has been always thought by this Government, ever since it's
> first settlement by the French, to be a Point of the greatest Im-
> portance to the Welfare and Safety of this Province; and many
> Designs have been form'd, and Expeditions fitted out for re-
> ducing that Place, and recovering it out of the Hands of the
> French, so I cannot but hope you will think it of equal Neces-
> sity to preserve it for his Majesty at this Juncture, from any At-
> tempts of the Enemy: And as it appears highly probable that
> the French will make some Attempts upon that Place before
> the Garrison there can have a Reinforcement from Great-
> Britain, I believe you will judge it a Piece of Service that will
> be highly acceptable to his Majesty, and tend to secure some
> of the most valuable Interests of this Province, to send some
> Recruits for that Garrison to continue there for a few months,
> or 'till it be sufficiently reinforced from Great-Britain—the
> Expense of this will not be very great (as we may suppose the
> men will have both Pay and Subsistence from his Majesty:)

Finally, Shirley asked the members of the Council and House of
Representatives "to pass a Law, prohibiting upon great Penalties all
Trade with our Enemies, and more especially the supplying of
them with Arms, Ammunition or Provisions of any Kind whatsoever."[6] He did not wish to see French invading forces supplied by ava-
ricious Massachusetts merchants.

Most of the members of the General Court realized that the
governor's speech proposed an increase in his control over them,
and their resentment was bitter. The colony was in no financial position to fight a defensive war. However, to ignore or to refuse Shirley's six demands was to expose Massachusetts to possible French
aggression.

Throughout June the inhabitants of Massachusetts and New
Hampshire, especially those living in the northern and northeastern frontier regions, were terror-stricken, daily expecting a mur-
derous French-Indian assault. Women and children were not permitted to stray from the relative safety of their homes and
settlements, while the men and older boys kept a sharp lookout for
the treacherous enemy. A Boston correspondent for the *Pennsylvania Journal*, writing on June 29, 1744, described cogently this atmosphere of fear:

On Tuesday some men who had been out upon the Scout, coming into Dover (at the Eastward) imprudently fired off their Guns, which alarmed the Town, and before the Cause could be known, the Alarm was communicated to several other Towns; upon which 700 men were raised, who marched to the Assistance of their Friends tho' (as it happened) they stood no need of their Help. This Account of The Affair is publish'd, to prevent those Fears and false Reports which are two (sic) often raised in such Times as these. The Indians, so far as can be observed, appear desirous to live in Peace with us.[7]

Not unexpectedly, therefore, on June 13 the House of Representatives gave Shirley the authority to send 500 men, impressed from various militia companies, to defend the more vulnerable frontier areas. The House also decided to seek additional reinforcements from New York, Rhode Island and New Hampshire.[8] But the somewhat imperious letters sent to these governments brought only negative responses. These three colonies had serious defence problems of their own, and they were in no mood to take orders from the Massachusetts House of Representatives.[9] Therefore, on June 24 the House of Representatives voted for an additional 500 men to serve on the frontiers.[10]

Shirley was convinced, and rightly so, that the raising of 1,000 troops to defend the colony's frontiers, the construction and manning of the frontier blockhouses, and his conciliatory Indian policy had kept the Penobscots, Pigwackets, Norridgewocks, and St. Francis Indians at peace in 1744, in spite of the declaration of war. In a letter to the Lords of Trade, written on August 21, Shirley proudly patted himself on the back; he pointed out that his policies:

...had the Effect not only to keep the Bordering Indians, who upon other Occasions of a French Warr ever broke out into sudden Hostilities upon our Settlements before, quiet; But has produced the most strong Professions of Peace from 'em and made 'em really Sollicitous to prevent a Rupture with us at present; And this has very much encourag'd our people upon the Exposed part of our Frontiers to stand their Ground, and saved some young settlements.[11]

It was not until October 28, 1744, that Shirley considered it necessary to declare war on the Malecites, and upon the Micmacs of Nova Scotia.[12] These distant tribes had joined Du Vivier in his abortive attempt to capture Annapolis Royal during the early autumn.

On July 27 the House of Representatives enacted a measure designed "to prevent all traiterous Correspondence with the French

King or his Subjects, or those who are in alliance with him, and supplying them with Warlike or other Stores."[13] Five days earlier the House had agreed to add a tiny ship, armed with eight 4-pound carriage guns and eight swivel guns, and manned by some fifty seamen, to the colony's magnificent fleet of two insignificant vessels.[14] Confronted by a serious shortage of funds, the Massachusetts government had decided to rely largely upon New England privateers to keep the sea lanes to the colony clear and also to protect the eastern seaboard from French naval assaults. The vital role played by the New England privateers during the early months of the war with France should not be underestimated. The privateers had a considerable impact upon the French in Louisbourg and were in part responsible for Du Quesnel's abandonment in early September of his projected attack by sea upon Annapolis Royal. If *L'Ardent* and *Le Caribou* had arrived at Annapolis in the early part of September, all the available evidence suggests that Mascarene would immediately have surrendered the fort.

The French in Louisbourg had first heard about the declaration of war on May 3, some three weeks before the news reached Boston.[15] As would be expected, French privateers had been quick to take full advantage of the element of surprise. From May 31 to June 12, at least ten Massachusetts fishing vessels, ranging in size from twenty-eight to fifty tons, were captured by two enterprising French privateers, armed only with muskets.[16] These vessels were captured on the Sable Island Bank and on the Canso Bank. The ease with which the New England fishing vessels were taken persuaded the French privateers based at Louisbourg to move their operations futher south, where they could tap the busy shipping lanes to and from Boston.[17]

The Boston merchants were first informed of the French policy in early July by some Massachusetts fishermen who had been captured by the French privateers in June. These fishermen, enjoying immensely their unexpected importance and fame, spun exaggerated yarns regarding the privateering strength of the French.[18] They informed the already frightened Massachusetts inhabitants that Morpain, the "noted Commander, famous for his Exploits on this Coast in the last War," had threatened to lead a fleet of French privateers to "take the Vessels out of Nantasket Harbour."[19] The fears of the Boston merchants were realized during the first week of July, when a French privateer under the command of Beaubassin captured three Massachusetts vessels within twelve leagues of Boston.[20] During the same week a French privateer commanded by

Doloboratz, who had played an important part in the French seizure of Canso, was captured by Captain Tyng of the Massachusetts government's snow *Prince of Orange* approximately fifteen leagues from Cape Cod.[21]

In early July there were only three French privateers in New England waters, but these had almost paralyzed the maritime trade of Massachusetts. The New England merchants, however, refused to be intimidated for long. Privateers were hurriedly fitted out in Rhode Island, Massachusetts, and New Hampshire; it has been estimated that by August no fewer than eight Rhode Island privateers were under sail against the French, five from Boston[22] and one from New Hampshire.[23] During the same period six privateers sailed from New York and four from Philadelphia;[24] but most of these ships headed south towards the Caribbean. By early August French privateers were no longer an immediate threat to Massachusetts. Instead, the New England privateers had boldly forced their way into the French waters about Cape Breton and by September were playing havoc with French shipping to and from Louisbourg.[25] Apparently dissatisfied with the lack of suitable French shipping, at least one privateering captain landed his crew on Cape Breton and "plundered some villages, and had the good fortune to surprise some Traders, from whom he took Gunpowder and other Goods to a great Value."[26] Some other enterprising New England privateers began to prey upon French shipping in the Gulf of St. Lawrence. The aroused Intendant of New France, Gilles Hocquart, requested that Maurepas send "two frigates to escort commercial vessels from Canada and Isle Royale."[27]

The 1744 privateering war between Louisbourg and Boston was in one sense won by the French. Some thirty-six prizes were declared in Louisbourg, of which twenty-six were in all likelihood Massachusetts vessels.[28] The number of Cape Breton prizes taken by Massachusetts privateers and those from Rhode Island[29] was only a small fraction of the French number. In controlling the seas, however, New England numbers were eventually more than a match for Gallic audacity; by the autumn of 1744 French privateers had been virtually driven from North Atlantic waters into their Louisbourg nest. The element of surprise had given the tiny fleet of Louisbourg a valuable windfall of British prizes in June and July. However, superior numbers had given the New England privateers a distinct advantage by August. In this sense, therefore, Boston had defeated Louisbourg's naval aggression.[30]

Though Shirley considered his various measures to protect

Massachusetts from Indian and French attacks to be of great consequence, he was nevertheless convinced that the successful defence of Annapolis Royal was the keystone of his policy to resist French aggression.[31] He believed Annapolis Royal to have considerable symbolic and strategic importance. Mascarene's fort represented British military power in Nova Scotia, whose vast expanse was often asserted to stretch from the Penobscot to Canso. If Annapolis fell to an invading French force, Shirley was sure that the tenuous ties binding the thousands of Acadian inhabitants to the British Crown would be permanently severed. Furthermore, he feared that the fall of Annapolis Royal would immediately destroy the delicately balanced neutrality of the Indian tribes along Massachusetts frontiers and throw them into the welcoming arms of the French. To these Indians, Shirley insisted, Annapolis had become a symbol of British military might, and as such, an important reason for their succumbing to his blandishments. If the fort were captured, their respect for British military power would disappear, and they would do everything in their power to ingratiate themselves to the French. What better expressions of their loyalty to the French could they offer than a string of Massachusetts scalps and a number of devastated frontier settlements?

Like Mascarene, Shirley considered Annapolis Royal to be an outpost of New England. He wished to see it used to consolidate the British position in Nova Scotia and also to serve as a stepping-stone for extending the boundaries of the British Empire to Cape Breton and eventually to New France. In French hands, however, the place would become a nest for French privateers, as in the days of Subercase forty years earlier. These ships, it was contended, would without doubt completely undermine Massachusetts' valuable cod fishery as well as the colony's thriving export of masts from Maine. Moreover, there was always the possibility that the French military authorities might consider the time propitious for mounting an invasion from Annapolis in order to appropriate the northeastern part of Massachusetts. Thus it is not surprising that Shirley placed so much emphasis upon the retention of Annapolis Royal.

Sometime between June 15 and June 22 news of the fall of Canso reached Boston.[32] Shirley was not alone in realizing that Annapolis Royal would be the next target for French aggression. In a letter to the Lords of Trade, the governor further commented on the loss of the tiny British outpost:

> ...the late surprize of Canso will not only give the French the
> Advantage of the Sole Fishery there, but has also open'd a

free Communication between Louisbourg and the Inhabitants of Menies [Minas] and Schenecta [Chignecto], which Tract is not only the Granary of those Parts but abounds with plenty of live Stock...not to mention that they thereby have freed themselves from Annoyance, which any British Ships station'd there might give to the Trade and Privateers of that Port [Louisbourg] during the Warr.[33]

But the economic importance of Canso had declined as already noted, and by the early 1740's its role in the Massachusetts cod fishery was insignificant. Since Massachusetts had ceased to regard Canso as an outpost of New England, its fall was not as alarming as the fall of Annapolis Royal would have been.

Fearing an attack upon Annapolis, the House of Representatives on June 23 finally decided to act upon Shirley's demand for the despatch of reinforcements to the British stronghold in Nova Scotia.[34] The House asserted that since the successful defence of Annapolis Royal was "an Affair of great Importance to the Crown, and in particular to the respective Governments of New England" it was imperative to send "some immediate relief." It was agreed:

That his Excellency the Captain General be desired to give orders for raising two independent Companies of Voluntiers, consisting of sixty Men each, exclusive of Officers, to be sent to Annapolis Royal, as soon as may be, at the Charge of the Province: And for Encouragement to good and effective Men to inlist in this Service, that there be and hereby is granted to be paid out of the Province Treasury to each Man that shall inlist twenty Pounds old Tenor...and that they be freed from all ordinary Impresses within this Province for the space of three Years after their Return.[35]

The House further emphasized that after the troops had arrived at Annapolis Royal they were to receive neither wages nor supplies from the Massachusetts government. The governor was urged "to use his good offices with the Commander of that Fortress in obtaining Pay and Subsistence for the said Companies from the Crown until they return home."

At first, few men volunteered to serve at Annapolis in spite of the offer of the seemingly attractive bounty of £20, and in spite of Shirley's promise that the British government would provide the reinforcements, once they were in "Acadia," with "both Pay and Subsistence." It is interesting to note that the bounty offered to the men volunteering for the Louisbourg expedition in the following year was only £4.[36] Realizing the strength of their bargaining position, interested Massachusetts inhabitants demanded even more bounty money before they would enlist for the Annapolis expedition. However, until July 1, the House of Representatives adamantly refused to increase the bounty money and as a result the recruiting campaign was a miserable failure.

On the last day of June Shirley informed the House that he had just received a letter from Mascarene,[37] "representing the Danger they are in, of being speedily attacked by the Enemy, and the present Weakness of the Garrison there, and requesting that we would send speedy Succours to them of at least two Hundred Soldiers well arm'd and victualled for some Months." He appealed to the members to deal immediately with Mascarene's request so "that no Disaster may happen."[38] On the following day the House acted, but not in the way Shirley wished it to act. It adopted the following resolution:

> ...Ordered, That each able body'd effective Soldier on his Inlistment for Annapolis Royal receive five Pounds old Tenor, for their Encouragement, and that the Sum of twenty Pounds old Tenor be paid them on their being muster'd in the Town of Boston, or such other place as his Excellency shall appoint, under their proper Officers complete in their Arms at their own Charge.[39]

The House had stubbornly refused to increase the number of reinforcements to 200 men, and had also refused to provide the two companies with supplies for an indefinite period of "some months." The members of the House contended that their main concern should be the defence of the immediate boundaries of the colony; they had serious misgivings about defending inadequately armed outposts of British imperialism.

Shirley was dissatisfied with the response of the House of Representatives; he continued to apply steady pressure on the members to raise at least an additional company of reinforcements and also to provision the Massachusetts troops during their sojourn in Nova Scotia. On July 3 he stressed to the members that he was certain another company of reinforcements was needed, "for rendring the Succours already voted effectual for the Preservation of the Garrison, and without such an addition to it, what is already done may probably prove ineffectual."[40] He firmly implied that if the House decided to raise another company, he would promise not to ask for any additional troops or funds for Mascarene. The House agreed to grant "a Bounty of twenty-five Pounds old Tenor...for an Encouragement to one Hundred and eighty Soldiers to inlist...for the Defence of Annapolis Royal."[41] However, the House continued to refuse to supply the troops with provisions.[42] The members of the House had made their last concession to the governor regarding his cherished project.

The extra £5 of bounty money aided the recruitment drive, but not sufficiently to fill all available openings. On July 12 some seventy men sailed for Annapolis Royal, and their arrival four days later was perfectly timed to raise the sagging morale of Mascarene's force. The day of their disembarkation witnessed the retreat of Le Loutre's Micmacs who had been besieging the fort. All the British regulars shared Mascarene's thoughts as he wrote to Shirley on July 18, "I can hardly find expressions to thank you for the seasonable succour you have sent us."[43] On July 31, a further fifty-three reinforcements, a score of whom were probably Pigwacket Indians, sailed for Annapolis.[44]

The sending of the Pigwacket Indians marked a definite change in Shirley's thinking regarding the Annapolis Royal reinforcement problem. By the closing days of July it was clear to Shirley, as it was to most officials, that the available supply of Massachusetts men who were willing to serve in Nova Scotia had completely dried up. A new source had to be found; all eyes turned to the friendly Pigwackets.

On July 29 Shirley had announced to the General Court that the Pigwacket Indians had recently decided to settle within the colony:

> Since your last adjournment (July 11) divers Families of the Pigwacket Indians, who have relinquished the French Interest, and cast themselves upon this Government for Protection, are arrived here: And as those People are desirous to live amongst us, I think it of great Importance, that, in this first Instance of the Eastern Indians quitting their Dependence on the French in a Time of actual War between us and them, we should so treat and manage them, as to convince them and other of those Tribes, how much they will find their Advantage in our Friendship and Protection. I must also desire you to consider in what Manner these Indians may be best disposed of to save Charge to the Province, and to make them in some Measure useful to us.[45]

What better way was there to make the Pigwackets useful to Massachusetts and to "save Charge to the Province," than to send them to Annapolis Royal? Furthermore, had not Mascarene asked for "20 or 30 bold and warlike Indians...to keep in awe the Indians of this Peninsula who believe all the Indians come from New England are

Mohawks of whom they stand in great fear?"[46] It is not surprising then that Shirley was sure that "Providence has, in so extraordinary a Way, cast them among us."[47] The remaining openings in the second incomplete company and in the third company were offered to the Pigwackets and eagerly accepted; the £25 bounty was an enticing inducement for the Indians.

Believing that Mascarene was in no position to provision adequately the new Pigwacket recruits, Shirley resolved to have those who did not sail on July 31 remain in Massachusetts, supplied with food and other necessities by the government, until they were needed in Annapolis Royal. They were not sent to Mascarene until the latter part of September, and their arrival coincided with Du Vivier's siege of the fort.[48] Shirley was certainly gifted with the "Nelson Touch" in the timing of the sending of his reinforcements to Annapolis.

Shirley's Annapolis Royal policy did not go unnoticed in Whitehall. On September 17, 1744, the Lords of Trade reported to King George II:

> ...That your Majesty's said Governour of the Massachusetts'
> Bay hath acted as became a Dutifull and Zealous Servant to
> your Majesty in obtaining the aforementioned Succours for
> the assistance of your Majesty's other Province of Nova Scotia
> and that therefore it may be adviceable for your Majesty not
> only to enable him to make good the engagement he hath
> entred into for the pay of the said forces but also to Signify
> your Royal approbation of his conduct in this affair.[49]

Shirley's promise, made on July 11, that the British government would eventually reimburse Massachusetts for any money spent on the defence of Annapolis Royal, had been fulfilled. On being informed of the favourable development, the members of the House of Representatives on October 24 heaped praise upon their governor:

> ...nor should we be just to your Excellency, or to the present
> Sentiments of our own Minds, to let your Excellency's early
> Care and Concern for his Majesty's Honour and the Safety of
> his Subjects, in first leading us into this Method of raising Re-
> cruits for the Defence of that Fortress, and then of your un-
> wearied Care and Diligence after express'd, in order to ren-
> der them effectual, pass without our most publick and
> thankful acknowledgements.[50]

The successful defence of Annapolis Royal added greatly to Shirley's reputation; he had become a much respected governor in whom the inhabitants of Massachusetts and the British Lords of Trade were willing to place increasing confidence.

3

Plans for the Capture of Louisbourg (1744-45)

THROUGHOUT THE CLOSING MONTHS of 1744, Governor Shirley's concern persisted for the "Preservation of his Majesty's Interest at Annapolis Royal."[1] In December he urged the capture of Louisbourg, primarily with the defence of Annapolis in mind. What more effective way to protect the keystone of his military policy than to eradicate the French threat in the Atlantic region?

A report of the arrival of the large *Compagnie des Indes* fleet at Louisbourg had reached Shirley sometime in September.[2] He feared that the enlarged French fleet would in all probability attack Annapolis before late autumn and he knew that Mascarene's fort was vulnerable, lacking the naval force so vitally necessary for its defence. As a result and almost as a last resort, Shirley felt compelled to adopt a defensive policy based almost completely upon outright guile. He therefore arranged matters so that the commander of the first French flag of truce arriving at Boston with New England prisoners in September returned to Louisbourg with what the latter considered to be most valuable intelligence. The commander reported that a "secret Expedition" against Louisbourg was being organized in Boston and that "a very considerable Reinforcement of men"[3] had been recently sent to Mascarene.

The authenticity of this report was not doubted. The Louisbourg officials were particularly concerned with the unexpected increase in Mascarene's force. Annapolis Royal would be even more capable of successfully resisting a French attack. But the French officials apparently did not anticipate any immediate threat from the so-called "secret expedition" against Louisbourg because of the reassuring presence of the *Indes* fleet and the lateness of the season. They concluded that a joint Anglo-American land and sea assault was being planned for the spring of the following year.[4] There is no evidence to suggest that Shirley's ruse was responsible for the abandonment of any large-scale French naval assault upon Annapolis Royal. It must also be emphasized that there had been no consideration by those in power in Whitehall and the New England colonies in September and October, 1744, of an attack on Louisbourg.

French fears of an Anglo-American attack in early 1745 were further confirmed by the highly respected and influential Louisbourg privateer Doloboratz.[5] He had been captured by the Massachusetts government's snow, *Prince of Orange*, and had returned to his home port in early November after spending several months as a prisoner of war in Boston. He reported that the governments of Massachusetts, New Hampshire, Rhode Island and Connecticut had offered the British Government no less that £800,000 if a fleet of fifteen warships was sent to capture Louisbourg. Doloboratz expected the British fleet to arrive at Boston sometime in December to make final preparation for a spring attack. Moreover, the French privateer declared that the New England colonies had promised to raise 6,000 troops to take part in the expedition. He questioned, however, whether such a force could be raised in New England without "*des grandes promesses et récompenses.*"[6]

Doloboratz probably received some of his information in the same way and for the same reason as the commander of the French flag of truce received his false intelligence in September. The deliberate misleading of Doloboratz can be considered to be a further elaboration of Shirley's September policy. It must be remembered that Shirley believed that the false report carried by the French commander of the flag of truce was largely responsible for nipping in the bud a proposed large-scale French naval assault upon Annapolis Royal. Was there not an equally good chance that false intelligence concerning a planned Anglo-American attack upon Louisbourg early in 1745 would keep the French from mounting an attack upon Annapolis at least until the arrival at Annapolis in the early spring of 1745 of "one or more of his Majesty's Ships"?[7]

Shirley, however, was not content to rely completely upon spurious reports carefully planted in the minds of gullible French officers to protect Annapolis Royal. He also bombarded his patron, the Duke of Newcastle, and the Lords of the Admiralty, with requests for warships to patrol the North Atlantic from Cape Sable to Boston. Fully aware of the vital importance of sea-power, Shirley was of the opinion that a few British warships could easily protect Massachusetts commerce as well as Annapolis from French encroachments. On November 25 he wrote to the Lords of the Admiralty:

> ...by [Spring 1745]...it is scarcely to be doubted but that the Enemy will send such a Naval force against it [Annapolis Royal], as will make 'em masters of it, if it is not protected against 'em by a Naval force from England. I need not observe to your Lordships how heavy the loss of the Garrison and Province of Nova Scotia would be on the one hand to his Majesty's northern Colonies, and how much it would affect the British Trade and Navigation to these parts.[8]

Shirley's persistence bore fruit; the formerly indifferent British government began to show some genuine concern for the defence of Nova Scotia. On January 14, 1745, the Duke of Newcastle wrote the following circular to the governors of the American colonies:

> His Majesty having thought it necessary for the Security of the Collonys in North America, and particularly of the Province of Nova Scotia, (which has been already invaded by the French, & upon which there is great reason to apprehend that they will early in the Spring renew their attempts by the attack of Annapolis Royal) to employ such a strength of Ships of Warr in those Seas under the Command of Comodore Warren as may be sufficient to protect the s^d Province, and the other neighboring Collonys in North America, and the Trade and Fishery of His Majesty's Subjects in those parts and may also as Occasion shall offer, attack and distress the Enemy in their Settlements, and annoy their Fishery & Commerce.[9]

It was not until the latter part of November that Shirley began to consider seriously "the great consequences of the acquisition of Cape Breton."[10] He wanted to see Cape Breton in British hands in order to make Annapolis Royal safe from possible French attacks. Shirley's rather vague theorizing regarding the capture of Cape Breton was galvanized into definite expression on December 14, 1744. On that day he was informed by reliable witnesses, who had been prisoners in Louisbourg, that Du Vivier, who had led the successful attack upon Canso and the unsuccessful assault on Annapolis Royal, and three Louisbourg pilots intimately familiar with the coasts of Nova Scotia and Massachusetts had recently sailed for France. They were expected to return in February with "Some Ships with Stores and Recruits for the Garrison at Cape Breton and also some Ships of Force to proceed to the coasts of Cape Breton, Nova Scotia...With a design...To make a Descent on Annapolis Royal and to cruise on the Coasts of New England."[11] Shirley's worst fears had apparently been realized. The aroused governor immediately sent a letter to the Lords of the Admiralty in which he enunciated the broad outlines of his plan to drive the French from Cape Breton.

Shirley simply wanted British warships to intercept the French fleet, thereby dealing "a killing blow to the Enemy." Without reinforcements and supplies, the "extremely ill mann'd" and "exceedingly discontented"[12] Louisbourg garrison was expected to surrender without any resistance to a blockading naval force.

Shirley was not the first colonial governor to advocate the capture of Cape Breton. In 1741[13] and again in 1743[14] Lieutenant-Governor Clarke of New York had urged the British navy, in time of war with France, to "block up the harbour of Louisbourg before any ships from France can arrive there" and prepare the way for a land force made up of "four or five thousand men...raised in New England."[15] It is highly unlikely, however, that in December 1744 Shirley was even aware of Clarke's proposals.

The plan to capture Louisbourg had gradually evolved in Shirley's mind during the closing months of 1744; it was the natural outgrowth of his Annapolis policy. Four major factors appear to have influenced his thinking regarding Louisbourg during this period: first, the difficulty he had experienced in obtaining reinforcements and supplies for Annapolis Royal; second, the news about conditions in Louisbourg brought to him by returning prisoners of war; third, the views of Robert Auchmuty, Judge of the Vice-Admiralty Court in Boston; and fourth, the policies advocated by Christopher Kilby, London agent of the Massachusetts government.

The vast majority of Massachusetts residents had reacted indifferently to Shirley's urgent appeals for reinforcements to serve at Annapolis Royal. He therefore expected an even more apathetic response to the call for volunteers to join an expedition against Louisbourg. Furthermore, the Massachusetts government, already in serious debt, was bound to oppose such a scheme if it involved the spending of any significant sum of money. Consequently Shir-

ley was at first of the opinion that any expedition against Louisbourg should be carried out by the British fleet.

The returning New England and Canso prisoners reported that
Louisbourg was a ripe fruit ready to be plucked by an enterprising
invading force.[16] The walls of the fortress were in disrepair; the
troops, badly disciplined and inadequately supplied with arms,
clothing and foodstuffs, were on the verge of open revolt. More
than any other single factor, this information supplied to the governor by the returning prisoners was responsible for his decision to
advocate enthusiastically a naval assault upon Louisbourg.

In April 1744, while acting as a special agent of the Massachusetts government in London, Judge Auchmuty presented to the
British government a memoir entitled "The Importance of Cape-
Breton To The British Nation."[17] In all likelihood, Shirley was sent a
copy of the memoir and carefully studied it. Auchmuty claimed
that once Cape Breton was captured, Britain would immediately
obtain a monopoly over the valuable North Atlantic cod fishery,
"which annually will return to the English nation two millions sterling...and constantly employ thousands of families, otherwise un-
serviceable to the public, and greatly increase shipping and navigation and mariners." In addition, Auchmuty argued, but not very
convincingly, that the acquistion of Cape Breton would "in the run
of very little time" lead to the fall of New France.

Believing that his arguments had conclusively proved that the
"expense and danger in taking this place [Cape Breton] will bear
no proportion to the advantage and profits thereby resulting to the
English nation, and her plantations," Auchmuty concluded the memoir by describing in some detail his plan to capture Louisbourg.
He proposed that by the beginning of April 1745, a force of 3,000
men be raised in the colonies north of Virginia "under the spe-
cious pretence that [they]...are raised to defend the governments
from invasion, or the surprise of an enemy." Not until the last possible moment were they to be told that they were to be used to attack
Louisbourg. By "concealing the real design" Auchmuty hoped to
take full advantage of the element of surprise and also to facilitate
recruitment. Many men might be expected to volunteer to defend
their own soil from the enemy but few to take part in an assault upon "The Dunkirk of North America." He further proposed:

> ...that a squadron of six sail of the line, with two thousand reg-
> ular troops, and all things necessary for a formal siege, should
> take their departure from [Britain] the beginning of March
> next, so as to anchor in Gabaron [Gabarus] bay, within four

miles of the rampart of Louisbourg, by the middle of April following; there to be joined by the American troops under convoy of the station ships. This may be executed without loss of men, no cannon commanding the entrance of this harbour, and where the navy of England may safely ride. It may be conceived advisable there to land the troops, and from thence to march and make regular approaches to the rampart.... It is judged by connoisseurs that the fire of their own cannon will shake down the works, and that they will not stand a battery.[18]

As early as 1741 Christopher Kilby had shown some interest in the capture of Cape Breton. In that year he sent a "kinsman"[19] to Louisbourg to investigate the strength of the French fortress. The information Kilby received[20] persuaded him that Louisbourg, because of inadequate "Fortifications and Garrison" was vulnerable to a combined land-sea assault.[21] On April 14, 1744, only a few days after Britain had declared war upon France, Kilby submitted to the Board of Trade a detailed statement of what he considered to be the best policy for Britain to adopt immediately regarding Louisbourg.[22] Kilby's statement was remarkably similar in content to Auchmuty's memoir presented to the Board one week later. This similarity was no coincidence. These men were associates, and both were especially concerned not only with the general welfare of Massachusetts but also with the success of their own ambitious commercial schemes. Would not their proposed expedition mean a considerable number of supply contracts which they could profitably help to fill? In order to protect Nova Scotia and New England commerce from French encroachments, Kilby advocated an immediate British assault upon Louisbourg. He argued that the information he had received made it abundantly clear "that the reduction of the Island is not only practicable but easy, and that in the present conjuncture which brings the war upon them in the midst of a famine, a well-conducted and vigorous attempt would entirely subdue all their possessions on the continent of North America."[23]

After the British government had declined to organize a naval assault upon Louisbourg at the outbreak of hostilities, Kilby proposed in October 1744 that in the early part of 1745 "Six Ships of the line—three or four smaller ones, and a Bomb ship, with a compleat Regiment of Experienc'd Land forces, a proper Train of Artillery, and 4000 Troops to be raised in America"[24] should attack Louisbourg. Kilby's proposal was sent to the Duke of Newcastle, the Earl of Winchelsea, the Earl of Harrington, as well as to Shirley.[25] Kilby also informed Shirley that if a colonial force was raised it would be "Effectually supported"[26] by the British government. In actual fact, however, Kilby had received no official assurance of any support. He apparently hoped that if Shirley began to organize an expedition against Louisbourg, the British government would be quickly goaded into action.

But despite Auchmuty's and Kilby's emphasis upon a joint Anglo-American assault upon Louisbourg, Shirley in early December stubbornly insisted that any expedition against Louisbourg should be the sole responsibility of the British government.[27] Shirley was probably reflecting the majority opinion in Massachusetts and throughout the British North American colonies at the time. Only a small but vociferous minority led by William Vaughan of Damariscotta in Main and John Bradstreet, a returned Canso prisoner, pressed for a New England invasion of Cape Breton independent of any support from Great Britain.

Bradstreet was born in Nova Scotia, or else emigrated there from Britain while still a youth.[28] In 1735 he had purchased an ensign's commission in General Phillip's foot regiment and was stationed at Canso, where he almost immediately became actively engaged in numerous illicit commercial ventures with the French at Louisbourg.[29] Captured at Canso in May 1744, he was imprisoned at Louisbourg until his release in October of the same year. While a prisoner he had come to the conclusion that the French fortress could be easily captured by a small New England force.[30] The response, however, on the part of most Massachusetts inhabitants to whom he made his daring proposal was largely negative. They were not eager to prove the validity of his hypothesis. Nevertheless, Bradstreet was able to make at least one important convert, William Vaughan.

A Harvard graduate and a successful fishing and lumbering entrepreneur at Damariscotta and Matinicus in Maine, Vaughan in 1744 was dissatified with his lot in life.[31] Always a restless man, he was eagerly looking for new worlds to conquer. He coveted fame, glory, and increased riches. In Bradstreet's proposal he saw an extraordinary opportunity to achieve his desired goals. If he could only organize and participate in such an expedition, he argued, he was bound to become a popular hero. Moverover, he could be almost certain that the British government would reward him, perhaps with colonial governorship. Had not his father been appointed Lieutenant-Governor of New Hampshire in 1715 largely because of the important role he had played in the capture of Port Royal from the French in 1710?[32]

Vaughan was gifted with boundless energy and a "daring, enterprising and tenacious mind."[33] Once decided upon a course of action, he refused to permit any obstacle to prevent him from achieving his desired goal. A contemporary described an example of his persistence and temerity thus:

> [Vaughan] had equipped a number of small vessels at Portsmouth to carry on his fishery at Matinicus. On the day, appointed for sailing in the month of March, though the wind was so boisterous that experienced mariners deemed it impossible for such vessels to carry sail, he went on board of one, and ordered the others to follow. One was lost at the mouth of the river; the rest arrived with much difficulty, but in a short time, at the place of their destination.[34]

In December 1744, Vaughan began to travel extensively throughout Massachusetts and New Hampshire "Day and Night,"[35] enthusiastically advocating a secret New England expedition against Louisbourg. Here was a saddle-preacher with a new gospel. He sought to convince his sceptical audiences that Louisbourg could be captured by a "force consisting of 1500 raw militia, some scaling ladders, and few armed craft of New England."[36] The scaling ladders would not be needed, Vaughan contended, if the expedition sailed immediately. If a secret landing were made during the winter months, the invading force could easily enter the fortified town by scrambling up the snow that usually drifted up over the ramparts.[37] When he was not talking about his proposed expedition, Vaughan was listening to observations made by men who had recently been in Louisbourg.[38] Vaughan's enthusiasm, confidence and persistence won him a surprising number of supporters, especially in eastern Massachusetts, including Maine, where he was well known and where the fishing interests had suffered most from French privateering raids.

Confident of considerable support in eastern Massachusetts, Vaughan, probably sometime in December, approached Shirley with a "regular Scheme"[39] to surprise and capture Louisbourg. Vaughan claimed sole authorship of the plan, as did Bradstreet.[40] In all likelihood, the plan placed in Shirley's hands by Vaughan was originally drafted by Bradstreet and then revised by Vaughan. Vanghan realized that his plan would never be implemented unless Shirley vigorously endorsed it.[41] Shirley was impressed with Vaughan's somewhat exaggerated account of "The General Spirit of the people in the eastern parts of the Province for undertaking"[42] the assault upon Louisbourg. He listened attentively to Vaughan's arguments of why it was essential to organize the expedition immediately without waiting for assistance from Britain. To Vaughan and to Bradstreet the timing of the expedition and the element of surprise were of far more consequence for its eventual success than the support of the entire British fleet.

Shirley had firmly opposed the idea of an independent New England expedition largely because he had believed that it lacked the support of an appreciable number of Massachusetts residents. But on hearing Vaughan's report of the mood of the people in eastern Massachusetts and after carefully weighing the political risks of supporting such an expedition, Shirley reluctantly decided to ask the General Court to finance and to organize the expedition. If it succeeded, and there was strong evidence to suggest that it would, Shirley's position in Massachusetts would be almost unassailable. If it failed, the governor could always argue that he had been pushed into the Vaughan-Bradstreet proposal by irresistible popular pressure. Regardless of whether it eventually failed or succeeded, Shirley would have a vast new reserve of patronage to dispense.

On January 20, 1745, in an unprecedented secret session of the General Court, Shirley stunned those present by strongly urging an expedition against Louisbourg. The audacity of the governor's proposal lay in the recommendation, not that the French fortress town should be attacked, but that it should be attacked by raw New England militia. After a brief, trenchant introductory paragraph in which he commented upon Louisbourg's "utmost annoyance" of Massachusetts commerce, Shirley presented his proposed plan of action:

> From the best information that can be had of the circumstances of the Town and of the number of the soldiers and Militia within it, and of the situation of the Harbour, I have good reason to think that if Two Thousand men were landed upon the Island as soon as they may be conveniently got ready (which as I am credibly informed may be done in the proper part of the Island for that purpose with little or no risque) such a number of men would, with the blessing of Divine Providence upon their Enterprize, be masters of the field at all events, and not only possess themselves of their two most important batteries with ease, break upon their Out Settlements, destroy their Cable and Magazines, ruine their Fishery Works, and lay the town in ruines, but might make themselves masters of the Town and Harbour...I would earnestly

recommend it to you to make a suitable provision for the Expences of such an expedition, which, if it should succeed no further than with respect to laying open the enemies Harbour and destroying their Out Settlements and Works, must greatly overpay the expence of it, by its consequences to this Province, and if it should wholly succeed, it must bring an irreparable loss to the enemy, and an invaluable acquisition for this Country.[43]

Shirley considered it unnecessary to discuss in "Detail...The manner of executing such an attempt." He was primarily concerned with winning the support of the General Court for the idea of the expedition.[44] Details regarding its implementation could be worked out later.

Most members, "struck with amazement at the proposal," were of the opinion that the undertaking had "no rational prospect of success."[45] However, in deference to Shirley's earnest plea, on the following day, January 21, a committee made up of members of the House of Representatives and of the Council was appointed to consider the Governor's proposal.[46] For two days the committee members vigorously debated Shirley's recommendation. His supporters argued that unless the French fortress were captured, the Massachusetts cod fishery would be destroyed, Nova Scotia would be lost, and Louisbourg "would infallibly prove the Dunkirk of New-England." They asserted that the time was propitious for a successful assault. The Louisbourg garrison was openly mutinous; provisions were scarce and "the works mouldering and decayed, the governor an old man unskilled in the art of war." It was therefore necessary to launch an attack immediately, since it was believed that in "another year the place would be impregnable." A gamble had to be taken. If the expedition failed, the Massachusetts government would have "to grapple with the disappointment" of bearing the brunt of the entire cost of the expedition. However, if it succeeded:

> ...not only the coasts of New England would be free from molestation, but so glorious an acquisition would be of the greatest importance to Great-Britian and might give peace to Europe, and [the Massachusetts government] might depend upon a reimbursement of the whole charge.

On the other hand, those who opposed the scheme declared that some kind of arrangement could be made with the French whereby "both sides would be willing to leave the fishery unmolested." Had not Louisbourg's commanding officer Du Quesnel make such a proposal to Shirley a few months earlier? Moreover they argued:

that the accounts given of the works and the garrison at Louisbourg could not be depended upon, and it was not credible that any part of the walls should be unguarded and exposed to surprise, that instances of disaffection rising to mutiny were rare and but few instances were to be met with in history where such expectation has not failed. The garrison at Louisbourg consisted of regular experienced troops, who, though unequal in number, would be more than a match in open field for all the raw unexperienced militia which could be sent from New-England...that if only one 60 gun ship should arrive from France, or the French islands, she would be more than a match for all the armed vessels [New England] could provide.

It was also pointed out that it was highly unlikely that a sufficient force of volunteers could be raised in New England, let alone supplied with arms, ammunition and provisions and transported to Cape Breton. Furthermore, the Massachusetts government was in no position to finance such an expedition. In conclusion, whose who attacked the scheme gloomily predicted that if the expedition failed, and they expected it to fail, "such a shock would be given to the province that half a century would not recover us to our present state."[47]

The committee members were almost unanimously opposed to Shirley's scheme.[48] On January 23, their report was quickly endorsed by the General Court and sent to the governor. Shirley was informed that the members were "fully convinced that all the Sea and Land Forces that can possibly be raised [in New England] will be insufficient...in reducing the said French Settlement."[49] It was further emphasized that it was solely the responsibility for the British government to organize and to finance any assault upon Louisbourg. In the last sentence of its message to the governor, almost as an after thought, the General Court vaguely promised "as far as they are able to exert themselves in conjunction with the other [colonial] Governments on such an occasion."[50]

Shirley had experienced a bitter rebuff, but he immediately decided to accept the Court's recommendation. On January 25 he wrote to the Duke of Newcastle and vigorously supported the Court's request for British initiative in attempting "the Reduction of Cape Breton."[51] Furthermore, he maintained that the General Court's promise to support any British expedition was to be taken seriously.[52] After finishing his letter to Newcastle, Shirley, like the members of the House of Representatives and of the Council, appeared content to sit back and to wait for the British government to make the next move. But William Vaughan had other ideas.

The irrepressible Vaughan, who regarded the Court's action as a personal affront, pledged that he would be personally responsible for the Court's reversing its decision. He swiftly executed a three-pronged campaign to achieve this end. First, he went to Marblehead and persuaded over 100 leading fishermen to send a strongly worded petition to the General Court in which they promised "to furnish Vessels in 14 Days for 3500 men"[53] if Vaughan's plan for a surprise assault upon Louisbourg was accepted. He also urged "more than 200 principal Gentlemen in Boston" to petition the Court to accept his scheme. Second, Vaughan assiduously fanned the dying embers of Shirley's enthusiasm for the plan. He induced the Governor to "make one push more at this time in the affair."[54] Third, to strengthen Shirley's position in his renewed attempt to have the plan accepted by the Court, Vaughan urged that a detailed plan of the proposed attack should be presented to the members and defended in person by Bradstreet and Captain Loring, who had returned from Cape Breton the preceding month.[55] Vaughan confidently expected that in such a confrontation the opponents of his scheme would be immediately placed upon the defensive and eventually routed.

The plan[56] that was finally presented to the Court envisaged a surprise assault upon Louisbourg early in the spring by a volunteer force of 3,000 New Englanders. These troops were to sail in fishing vessels to Canso, the "place of Rendezvous"[57] and from Canso the fleet was to proceed to Gabarus Bay arriving there "by Dusk." Whaleboats, each equipped with two ladders, fifteen feet long, were to be used to land the troops by cover of darkness. Then a simultaneous assault was planned on the Grand Battery and at various strategic points along the walls of the fortress:

> ...it will be Absolutely Necessary to appoint a time to strike the Blow all at Once which can be done by Agreeing upon a certain hour just before Day which is the Sleepiest time, and to the Commanding Officer of each Detachment to know the time, and when the time comes, by his Watch to begin without any further Ceremony, The enemy finding themselves Attack'd at so many different places at Once its probable that it will breed such Confusion among them that Our Men will have time to get in Unmolested.

If for some unforeseen reason the original assault was repulsed, the attacking force was to bombard the fortress with the "12 Nine

Pounders and Two Small Mortars" in order "to make Breaches in their Walls and then to Storm them." If the bombardment with such heavy artillery failed to breach the walls, the besiegers were to be satisfied with capturing the Grand Battery and with awaiting "an attack by Sea from England."[58]

The petition of the Marblehead fishermen which was sent to the General Court on January 30 was accompanied by a brief message from Shirley.[59] The governor asserted that since the Marblehead fishermen were clearly reflecting the general mood prevailing throughout the maritime regions of the colony, the Court was under an obligation to reconsider the proposal to surprise Louisbourg. A committee of both houses was therefore appointed to take another look at the matter.[60] Four days later, on February 3, accompanying the petition of "a great number of merchants, traders and other inhabitants of Boston...praying that an Expedition...may be undertaken,"[61] Shirley sent another message to the General Court. After considering the main feature of the Vaughan-Bradstreet plan for the execution of the assault, Shirley emphasized that any such expedition would be supported by the neighbouring governments of New York, New Hampshire, Connecticut and Rhode Island and that in all probability the British government would gladly reimburse the Massachusetts government for much of the expense involved in the expedition.[62]

After examining the plan of action and questioning Bradstreet and Loring and other Massachusetts residents who had been traders at Louisbourg, the committee that had been formed on January 30 presented its eagerly awaited report on February 5. It was recommended:

> ...that it is incumbent upon this Government to Embrace this favourable Opportunity to Attempt the reduction thereof; And they humbly propose that His Excellency the Captain General be desired to give forth his Proclamation to Encourage the Enlistment of Three Thousand volunteers under such Officers as he shall appoint; That there be delivered to each man a blanket, that one month's pay be Advanc'd & that they be entitul'd to all the Plunder;
>
> That Provision be made for the furnishing of necessary Warlike stores for the Expedition...That a Committee be appointed to procure & fit Vessels to serve as Transports to be ready to depart by the beginning of March...That Application be forthwith made to the Governments of New York, the Jerseys, Pensylvania, New Hampshire, Connecticut & Rhode Is-

land to furnish their respective Quotas of Men & Vessels to Accompany, or follow the Forces of this Province.[63]

The committee's resolution was hotly debated in the House of Representatives until late in the evening on February 5. When the roll was finally taken the resolution passed by the narrowest margin of one vote.[64] It was rumoured that the resolution passed only because "of the absence of several members who were known to be against it."[65] Vaughan's "mad scheme" was to be implemented. Vaughan's tenacity had been rewarded; Shirley had a vast new reservoir of patronage to dispense, and Annapolis Royal was safe. The Boston merchants had the pleasant prospect of large supply orders to fill, and the Massachusetts fishermen, driven from the codfishing grounds by the French, had the opportunity to transport troops and supplies to Cape Breton—of course for a price.

By the joint efforts of Vaughan and Shirley the proposal to mount a New England assault upon Louisbourg had been accepted by the General Court. Without Vaughan's enthusiasm and persistence and the governor's active support the plan would never have been accepted in February 1745.

4

Organizing
the Expedition
(February-March, 1745)

PREPARATIONS FOR the expedition against
Louisbourg began on February 5, 1745. After reluctantly agreeing
to send the expedition, the General Court of Massachusetts out-
lined the broad framework of policy within which it expected the
governor to work.[1] Shirley was instructed to raise a force of 3,000
volunteers and to appoint all necessary officers. Each noncommis-
sioned volunteer was to be paid 25 shillings per month and was to
be given one blanket. To facilitate recruiting, the governor was empowered to offer the volunteers one month's pay in advance, as
well as to promise that they would be "entital'd to all the Plunder."
In addition, unspecified arrangements were to be made "for the
furnishing of necessary Warlike Stores for the Expedition" and for
the securing of four months' provisions. A committee of the General Court was to be appointed to procure and to fit out vessels to
transport troops and supplies to Louisbourg and it was hoped that
these vessels would be ready to sail by March 12. Moreover, the governor was to write to the "Governments of New York, the Jerseys,
Pennsylvania, New Hampshire, Connecticut & Rhode Island to furnish their respective Quotas of Men & Vessels to Accompany or follow the Forces"[2] of Massachusetts. Finally, to prevent the enemy
from learning of the expedition, Shirley was to place an embargo
upon all Massachusetts shipping, presumably until the expedition
finally sailed from Boston.[3] Furthermore, all French nationals and
other "suspected persons" were to be arrested and special "Watch-
men" were to be stationed on various roads throughout the colony
"to search suspected passengers."[4] Once put into force the embargo
not only proved successful in keeping the French ignorant of the

projected expedition until after it sailed, but also made available numerous vessels to transport men and supplies to Louisboug.

It was clear to Shirley and to many of the members of the General Court that few men would volunteer to serve in the expedition until an unusually popular commander-in-chief was appointed. One critical observer went so far as to maintain that:

> Fidelity, resolution and popularity must supply the place of
> military talents;...It was necessary that the men should know
> and love their General, or they would not enlist under him.[5]

Even though Shirley possessed the power to appoint such an officer independently, he nevertheless preferred to consult the General Court before making his final decision. He realized that if the General Court was to maintain its enthusiasm for the Louisbourg venture its approval of the commander-in-chief was imperative.

Four men eagerly offered their services to Shirley—William Vaughan, Samuel Waldo, Lieutenant-Governor Benning Wentworth of New Hampshire and John Bradstreet. Vaughan's offer[6] was never taken seriously by Shirley, who like many members of the General Court regarded Vaughan as a "whimsical wild projector"[7] and as an ambitious "outsider." Shirley did not wish to see Vaughan receive all the credit and the reward for originating and carrying out the expedition. As far as Shirley was concerned, Vaughan had served his purpose and now could be discarded.

Samuel Waldo was an active member of the General Court and one of Shirley's closest friends.[8] A land speculator on a grand scale, Waldo had purchased the questionable Alexander land rights to Nova Scotia in 1730.[9] In 1745, confronted by serious financial difficulties, Waldo saw in the Louisbourg project an excellent opportunity to have his claim to much of Nova Scotia recognized by the British government.[10] However, Waldo lacked the required popular appeal, and his close association with Shirley was resented by the General Court. Shirley probably resisted a temptation to accept Waldo's offer, realizing that such an appointment would result in violent criticism and lack of support in the General Court and throughout the colony. Waldo had to be satisfied with a brigadier-general's commission.

Wentworth, apparently temporarily dissatisfied with his position as Lieutenant-Governor of New Hampshire, considered himself to be admirably qualified to lead the expedition. When the gouty governor informed Shirley of his willingness to sail to Louisbourg, the startled Shirley immediately shattered Wentworth's dream:

> Upon communicating y[r] offer of your taking the Command of
> the Expedition and proceeding in it, to two or three Gentle-
> men in whose prudence & judgm[t] I most confide, I found 'em
> clearly of opinion y[t] any alteration of the present command
> would be attended with great risque, both with respect to our
> assembly and soldiers being intirely disgusted.[11]

John Bradstreet, who had had some limited military experience
at Canso, regarded himself as a military strategist and leader of
considerable note. Shirley was evidently impressed with Bradstreet's ability and, if Bradstreet's journal is to be taken seriously,
offered him the command of the expedition.[12] However, "finding it
would be difficult to raise a Sufficient Number of Men Unless under the Command of one of their own Country Men,"[13] Shirley was
forced to withdraw his offer. In all likelihood Shirley's offer was not
made in good faith.[14] He realized that Bradstreet did not have the
necessary qualifications. But in order to cajole Bradstreet into join-
ing the expedition, Shirley felt compelled to offer him the command with one hand and then immediately take it back with the
other. Shirley was an astute judge of character; Bradstreet eventually joined the expedition as the commander-in-chief's special military advisor.[15]

One man, William Pepperrell, towered above all possible candi-
dates, but he showed little enthusiasm at first to lead the expedition. Shirley soon came to realize that Pepperrell, who had been a
member of the General Court since 1727 and who in 1745 was
president of the Council and colonel of the Maine militia, was the
only man with the necessary qualifications to serve as commander-
in-chief. Pepperrell was an unusually successful merchant "of un-
blemished reputation, of engaging manners, extensively known
both in Massachusetts and New Hampshire, and very popular."[16]
His military experience, however, had been limited to the none too
exacting inspection of frontier defences and to the general organization and training of the Maine militia.[17] But there were very few
Massachusetts residents who had more military experience than
Pepperrell, and there was certainly no one who had any satisfactory
training or experience in the technical side of warfare.

Almost immediately after the General Court accepted the resolution of the special committee under chairmanship of Pepperrell
to undertake the Louisbourg expedition, Pepperrell was approached by Shirley and leading members of the General Court "to
head ye forces."[18] Pepperrell politely yet firmly refused—"Mrs. Pepperrell being in an ill state of health & my business unsettled."[19]

Pepperrell's refusal spurred Shirley and the Court members into increasing their pressure upon the reluctant Piscataqua merchant. They emphasized that unless he acceded to their request, there would be no expedition.[20] Instead the French from Louisbourg would probably invade "ye eastern part of New England, & Newfoundland would have stood but a poor chance, so that ye greatest part of yᵉ codd fishery in a short time would have been in yᵉ French hands, and great part of our trade to New England, Verginia, etc. interceptᵈ by yᵐ."[21] Pepperrell found himself on the horns of a dilemma. He did not want "to undertake so dangerous and fatiguing an Enterprize,"[22] but he also did not want to jeopardize the sending of the expedition. Thoroughly confused and burdened by the fear that his refusal might in fact lead to the destruction of Massachusetts, Pepperrell sought the advice of a close friend, the evangelist George Whitefield who was in Boston conducting "a hopeful Revival of Religion."[23] Whitefield assured Pepperrell that:

> ...if he did undertake it, he would beg of the Lord God of armies to give him a single eye; that the means proposed to take Louisbourg, in the eye of human reason, were no more adequate to the end, than the sounding of rams' horns to blow down Jericho; but that, if Providence really called him, he would return more than conqueror.[24]

After much prayer and after receiving the "free consent" of his wife, Pepperrell on the following day, February 11, declared that he would accept Shirley's offer to lead the expedition and was commissioned Lieutenant-General and Commander-in-Chief of all land and sea forces.[25]

Pepperrell's appointment "paid enormous political dividends to Shirley."[26] By gaining the wholehearted support of the powerful Pepperrell faction in the General Court, Shirley had at last been able to unite formerly warring factions under his own firm leadership. In February 1745 Shirley's position in Massachusetts had never been stronger. To consolidate his position further, Shirley appointed his friends and allies—men such as Joseph Dwight, Robert Hale, John Choate, Shuball Gorham—to the vitally important and financially remunerative colonelcies in the expedition force.[27]

With Pepperrell's acceptance the recruiting campaign began in earnest. The campaign was carefully planned by Shirley and his supporters. A concerted propaganda barrage was intended to prepare the way for the recruiting officers. Across the length and breadth of Massachusetts, supporters of the expedition led by the energetic Vaughan[28] proclaimed that the capture of Louisbourg was simply a matter of sailing there. The French fortress was "slenderly Fortified"[29] and its garrison was eager to surrender to an invading force. Moreover, it was stressed that the Louisbourg merchants and officers possessed vast sums of money and other valuables—readily obtainable plunder that would doubtless make each volunteer a rich man.[30] Some ministers of the gospel, but not all, joined the propaganda chorus. By giving the expedition the motto '*Nil desperandum Christo duce*'[31] Whitefield tried to transform it into a Protestant crusade. One poetic divine declared:

> For Zion's Sake hold not your Peace
> While She's in such Distress,
> Compressed by Vast Thousands of
> The Sons of Wickedness....
>
> 'Tis nothing less than Christ himself,
> These Anti-Christians fight,
> And if it were but in their Power
> They'd ruin his Kingdom quite....
>
> Ev'n so, Lord Jesus, quickly come,
> In thine almighty Power,
> Destroy proud Antichrist, O Lord,
> And quite consume the Whore.[32]

Another pious Calvinist exclaimed:

> ...And how sweet and pleasant will it be...to be the person under God that shall reduce and pull down that stronghold of Satan and sett up the kingdome of our exalded Saviour. O, that I could be...in that single church [in Louisbourg] to destroy ye images their sett up, and ye true Gospel of our Lord and Savior Jesus Christ their preached.[33]

To other ministers, the Louisbourg expedition was imperative to see clearly whether their God was pleased with the spiritual growth of the Massachusetts Church.[34] The capture of Louisbourg would be convincing proof that their God was still their "great Preserver and Benefactor."[35]

From the beginning of the campaign there was "a considerable readiness in many to enlist,"[36] especially in the Maine region. Many men sought commissions for other reasons than their anti-Roman Catholic feeling or their fear of a possible French invasion. They wanted commissions because of "a hope, well or ill grounded, that if the place be taken they may have their commissions confirmed at home, and so have either a full sterling pay, if they are employed, and if they are dismissed a half-pay."[37] One frank father wrote Pepperrell:

> The Prospect of Profit either by Wages or Plunder had no Weight in ye Scale to induce my Son to engage in the expedition...what he principally aimed at is a Capt.[s] Commission in the King's Pay. I have been told the Company of Voluntiers who went to Annapolis last summer were (as soon as advice of it got home) put in the British Pay and if that be true, I suppose Cape Breton if it be reduced will be garrisoned in part by New England Voluntiers upon the Same Establishment and the Officers have commissions from the Crown, as it should be so.[38]

After receiving their commissions from Shirley authorizing them "to beat...Drums" within a certain militia regiment "for the enlisting of Voluntiers,"[39] some officers went to great lengths to persuade volunteers to enlist:

> [Captain Sewell] called his men to his own house & generously entertained them all with a dinner & much encouraged them to engage in the present expedition, promising to as many...as would go that he w[d] give them out off his own pocket so much as with the Province pay they sh[d] have 8£ p[r] month. And that if any of their familys were in want he would supply them so that they sh[d] not suffer.[40]

James Gibson, a Boston merchant and former officer in the Royal Regiment of Foot Guards in Barbados, raised "some hundreds" of volunteers at his own expense.[41] Vaughan was so successful in raising men that the jealous Shirley eventually ordered him "to stop enlisting."[42] A few audacious individuals recruited volunteers without first receiving commissions from Shirley.[43] After they had collected together a regiment of volunteers, they demanded commissions. Usually Shirley gladly met their demands.

The rank and file had various reasons for enlisting. The desire for plunder was probably the most important single reason. Only a few years earlier, hundreds in Massachusetts had rushed to volunteer to participate in the Carthagena expedition to the Caribbean.[44] So many volunteered in Massachusetts, in fact, that a large number had to be turned away. These men were not primarily interested in driving the Spanish from the West Indies; they were concerned with filling their empty pockets with Spanish gold. The Louisbourg expedition was regarded in a similar light, though some men were motivated by "The Expectation of Seeing Great things, etc." and others were convinced that unless the French were driven from Louisbourg the French fortress "was Like to prove Detremental if not Destroying to our Country."[45] It seems that only a relatively small number of men volunteered solely because of their strong anti-Roman Catholic feeling.

To stimulate further the recruiting campaign the General Court on February 18 adopted a wage list for volunteers serving in the land force and also clarified certain details regarding bounty payments and subsistence and other allowances. Colonels were to receive £15 new tenor monthly, Captains £4, 10 shillings, Lieutenants £3, Chaplains £4, 10 shillings, Corporals £1, 8 shillings. Ordinary soldiers were to be allowed, in addition to their monthly pay of 25 shillings, £1 bounty money on enlisting and a weekly subsistence allowance of 5 shillings.[46] Also they were to be given "a Gill and half of Rum pr Day for the first Month and one Gill pr Day afterwards."[47] There is evidence to suggest that the General Court went even further "to Incourage men to Inlist" by proposing:

> ...that the Widows or nearest relatives of any officer or soldier that is slain or shall otherwise loose his life in the service, shall be entitled to four months pay.
>
> And that the wives of any officer or soldier in the Expedition or any other person that appears with a power of Attorney duly authenticated, shall at the end of every month receive out of the Treasury half or all the wages of such officer or soldier.[48]

There may have been good financial reasons therefore for the women of Massachusetts supporting the Louisbourg expedition with such unusual vigour![49] Two days later the Court resolved to give each captain "two Shillings and six Pence for the Charge of inlisting each effective Man."[50] Two weeks earlier the Court had agreed "That half a Pound of Ginger, and one Pound and an half of Sugar, be allowed each Soldier that proceeds in the intended Expedition against Louisbourg."[51]

The recruiting campaign met with vigorous opposition in certain quarters, and this opposition was partly responsible for preventing the Expedition from sailing on the intended date, March 12. There were three main centres of opposition in Massachusetts. First, an undetermined number of fishing entrepreneurs discouraged their workmen from volunteering, in the hope that when the embargo on shipping was lifted they would be able to fish on the Sable Island Bank and elsewhere without any immediate fear of French attacks. Would not the French in Louisbourg be far more concerned with the New England invading force than with a few harmless fishing vessels? Second, a small number of clergymen vociferously argued that those who volunteered "would dye there [at Louisbourg] and be dammn'd to[o]."[52] The souls of too many of the potential volunteers were still unregenerate and thus death would open wide the gates to everlasting torment. Third, frontier inhabitants, fearing possible Indian attacks, did all in their power "to keep the people at home."[53] In spite of the concerted opposition to the expedition, by April 4 over 3,000 Massachusetts residents had volunteered to serve in the land force and some 1,000 to man the expedition's ships.[54]

The unexpected delay in the sailing of the expedition—the first Massachusetts contingent did not sail until April 4 and the second until two days later[55]—was only partly the result of the persistent opposition to the scheme. The delay was also caused by the unexpected difficulty in obtaining supply and transport ships and sailors to man them, by the belated and often negative response of the other colonial governments to Shirley's urgent appeal for aid, and by Shirley's decision to wait until the last possible moment to see whether British warships from the Caribbean would join the expedition.

Apparently the General Court accepted without question Vaughan's wild claim that the Marblehead merchants themselves would supply a sufficient number of ships to transport 3,500 troops and the necessary provisions to Louisbourg by the middle of February.[56] As a result, the Court concentrated upon the raising of a land force and did very little to encourage owners to offer their vessels and sailors to volunteer to man them. By early March, however, the complacency of the Court about the naval aspects of the expedition was shattered by the realization that unless transports were immediately found, the expedition could not sail in time to take advantage of Louisbourg's weaknesses. On March 10 the Court resolved to pay each captain of a transport vessel sailing in the expedition £3 monthly, each mate £2, 10 shillings, and each ordinary seaman £2.[57] It is interesting to note that the ordinary seaman received a higher monthly wage than the ordinary volunteer in the land force. If such an arrangement had been made at the start of the recruiting campaign, it is highly doubtful that very many men from the coastal areas of Massachusetts would have volunteered to serve in the land force. By March 10, however, the recruiting of land forces had advanced so favourably that the Court could offer sailors more pay, especially since there was a greater need for seamen. In order to obtain ships, the Court decided on March 12:

> ...That the several Vessels that are or shall be taken up in the
> Service of the Province in the intended Expedition, be and
> they hereby are insured by the Government, according to the
> several Apprizements taken by Persons under Oath.[58]

Eventually the money the shipowners were undoubtedly promised
for the use of their vessels and the inability of the owners to make
profitable use of their vessels in any other way because of the embargo, induced a sufficient number of them to come to the aid of
the Court, but not until after the original departure date.

In his circular letter of February 9, sent to all the colonial governors north of and including Pennsylvania, Shirley requested
"Land & Sea" assistance for the Louisbourg expedition. He argued
that such an expedition would provide for "the safety of the trade
and navigation" of all the colonies north of Pennsylvania. Shirley
further promised that the British government would dispatch a sizeable fleet of warships to "Support us in our Design."[59] Shirley's letter
was carried to the various governors by members of the Massachusetts General Court chosen because of their persuasive powers.[60]

The New Jersey government brusquely rejected Shirley's request. Seeking a scapegoat, Governor Lewis Morris declared that
the powerful Quakers were responsible for his government's refusal to support the expedition.[61] He would have been closer to the
mark if he had maintained that there was really no concern in New
Jersey about the Louisbourg threat and consequently little interest
in the proposed expedition.

Governor George Thomas of Pennsylvania laid Shirley's request before the Assembly during a special session, which was not
called, however, until March 8.[62] Thomas urged the Assembly to
send Shirley a "Provision of Money." He pointed out that:

> The Conquest of Louisbourg, which is the only French Port
> of Consequence in this Part of the World, either for Strength
> or the Accommodation of large Ships, will banish all appre-
> hensions for the future of Maritime Attempts upon the Colo-
> nies, or their Trade upon this Coast,...Dispatch, you will see,
> is the life of the undertaking.[63]

But the Quaker-controlled Assembly refused to accept Thomas'
recommendation. One member declared:

> We have often been importun'd to do something in our own
> Defence, and have always refus'd: therefore it will not be-
> come us to raise Men and Money to go and disturb those that
> neither meddle nor make with us; People with whom we have
> nothing to do.[64]

Some members who did not share *"the religious Principles* of the Majority"[65] agreed with Benjamin Franklin when he wrote to his brother in Massachusetts:

> Fortified towns are hard nuts to crack; and your teeth have not been accustomed to it. Taking strong places is a particular trade which you have taken up without serving an apprenticeship to it. Armies and veterans need skilful engineers to direct them in their attack. Have you any? But some seem to think forts are as easy taken as snuff.[66]

The consensus of the Assembly members was that since they had not been consulted beforehand regarding the expedition, and since there were no instructions from Whitehall, it would be extremely imprudent "to unite in an Enterprize where the Expence must be great, perhaps much bloodshed, and the Event very uncertain."[67] Pennsylvania's money could be spent on much more worthwhile projects.

In spite of a ringing appeal to the New York Assembly to provide men and ships for the expedition, Governor George Clinton had to be satisfied with lending Shirley ten 18-pound cannon with their carriages and other equipment.[68] The Assembly refused to support the expedition in any other manner because its members wished to concentrate New York's military effort on its exposed northern frontier. Moreover, the Assembly was locked in bitter dispute with the governor and stubbornly refused to adopt his Louisbourg policy largely because he had advocated it.[69] Shirley was overjoyed on hearing on March 13 of Clinton's offer to lend the ten cannon. Up to that date Shirley had serious reservations regarding whether the expedition should sail with what he considered to be totally inadequate artillery.[70] Clinton's offer drove all doubts from Shirley's mind and the Massachusetts governor quickly abandoned his uncharacteristic procrastination.[71]

On February 16 the Rhode Island Assembly considered Shirley's request for assistance.[72] "After a long and Tedious Debate" the Assembly decided to raise 130 seamen to man the colony sloop *Tartar*.[73] The *Tartar*, after being "equipped with all necessary warlike stores," was to join the Massachusetts expedition "at the place of rendezvous."[74] The Assembly, however, refused to raise a land force since there was no guarantee that the expedition would be supported by the British government or even by the Massachusetts people. Had not the resolution favouring the expedition been "carry'd but by one single Vote"? Furthermore, most of the members of the Assembly resented the fact that the Massachusetts government had undertaken "the Conquest of Cape Breton, without previously consulting their Neighbours."[75]

Shirley was totally dissatisfied with what he considered to be Rhode Island's miserable response to his reasonable request. He was grateful for the promise of the *Tartar* and also pleased that two Newport merchants had consented to have two of their privateers, the *Fame* and *Caesar*, chartered by the Massachusetts government.[76] But the governor wanted some Rhode Islanders to join the land force. He therefore wrote to Governor William Greene of Rhode Island on March 15 and insisted that Rhode Island supply at least a token land force for the Louisbourg expedition.[77]

On receiving Shirley's letter, which promised among other things that the expedition would definitely be supported by "some of his Majesty's Ships of War from the West Indies and Great Britain,"[78] the Rhode Island Assembly completely reversed its former Louisbourg policy. One hundred and fifty men were to be "enlisted as soldiers" and nine men as commissioned officers. Apart from the bounty of 30 shillings new tenor, 10 shillings more than the Massachusetts bounty, the wages to be paid the volunteers and other arrangements were exactly patterned after those of Massachusetts. Furthermore, the assembly empowered Shirley to enlist up to 350 Rhode Islanders to serve in the Massachusetts contingent, offering 10 shillings bounty, in addition of course to the Massachusetts bounty, to those who volunteered.[79]

There were probably two main reasons for the Assembly's reversal of policy. First, the bitter boundary controversy between Rhode Island and Massachusetts had not as yet been settled by the British authorities.[80] The Rhode Island Assembly members feared that if the Louisbourg expedition succeeded and there were no Rhode Islanders in the land force, inevitably the British government would support the Massachusetts claims in the boundary question. Second, on hearing that Connecticut and New Hampshire had decided to send sizeable land forces to Louisbourg, pride compelled Rhode Island to do likewise.[81]

To enunciate a policy was one thing; to implement it successfully was another. Rhode Islanders refused to volunteer;[82] many hurried off instead to man the large number of privateers. Only some ninety men served on the *Tartar*, which was destined to play an important role in the expedition.[83] Eventually the government was forced "to impress Men to compleat the Companies;"[84] but before the Rhode Island force could sail Louisbourg had already fallen.

Unlike its sister "Old Charter"[85] government, the Connecticut

Assembly, on first being informed of Shirley's Louisbourg scheme resolved "(relying on the blessings of Almighty God) to joyn...in the intended expedition." It was agreed that a land force of 500 men was to be raised under the command of the deputy-governor of the colony, Roger Wolcott. Wolcott more than any other man was responsible for this decision. He wanted to see the French driven from Louisbourg and he vigorously asserted the importance of sacrificing "domestic ease and...private interests, to the more important concerns of the public."[86] The Connecticut volunteers were to receive higher bounties and wages than those in Massachusetts. In addition, the colony's guard sloop, the *Defence*, was to be "equipped and manned with her full complement of officers and men"[87] to convoy the Connecticut transports from New London to Canso.

Armed with the Assembly's Louisbourg resolutions, two of its most prominent members, "Jonathan Trumble and Elisha Williams," made their way to Boston fully prepared for some hard bargaining with Shirley. They demanded that Wolcott be appointed second-in-command to Pepperrell. Only if this were done would they guarantee that 500 volunteers would be raised in Connecticut. After consulting Pepperrell, who regarded Wolcott as "a Gentleman of...Wisdom & Experience,"[88] Shirley gave Wolcott "the Second Command over the Forces raised for the Expedition against Cape Breton."[89] When news of Shirley's decision reached Connecticut, probably on March 20 or 21, the recruiting campaign began in earnest. Eventually 516 men, including commissioned officers, were enlisted largely because of Wolcott's unusual popularity. But the scarcity of guns, ammunition, supplies,[90] and transport vessels,[91] and generally bad organization,[92] prevented the Connecticut fleet from sailing from New London until April 25,[93] some three weeks after the Massachusetts fleet left Boston. The Connecticut fleet consisted of seven transports and two armed vessels, the *Defence* and the *Tartar*.[94]

Shirley had confidently expected that Benning Wentworth could persuade the members of the New Hampshire House of Representatives to provide men and supplies for the expedition. By so doing, the New Hampshire government would serve as an excellent example for the other colonies. Shirley, however, had underestimated the growing independence of the New Hampshire House and overestimated the political power of Wentworth.

After carefully examining Shirley's request for aid, the members of the House of Representatives, on February 13, declared that they were in favour of raising at least 250 volunteers but only "if proper methods may be concluded on for defraying the charge." By "proper methods" they meant the printing of £4,000 of new money.[95] Three days later the House further clarified its policy. They asked Wentworth to have £10,000 printed "towards the Defraying the charge of the said Expedition for the Reduction of Louisbourg & the further carrying on the warr against his Majesty's Enemies & for the necessary support of this his Majesty's Governement."[96] Special taxes to be levied during the period 1755 to 1765 were to provide funds "for Drawing in and Sinking the said Bills."[97] In advocating such an inflationist policy, the New Hampshire House was following the example of the Massachusetts House of Representatives which had had £50,000 printed, "for putting the Province in a better Posture of Defence."[98] The New Hampshire House of Representatives was controlled by paper-money advocates who saw in the Louisbourg affair an extraordinary opportunity to force their inflationary views upon a hitherto hostile Council and lieutenant-governor. The House stressed that unless Wentworth acceded to their request regarding the issue of paper money, they would refuse to pass the necessary legislation for the recruiting of Louisbourg volunteers. By February 16 the battle lines were clearly drawn and neither side contemplated surrender or even compromise. The stubborn Wentworth maintained that he had received definite instructions from Whitehall not to print "any more money than what is now Extant."[99] On the other hand, the members of the House vehemently argued that unless money was printed there would be no New Hampshire contingent in the Louisbourg expedition and in all probability the "naked and defenceless"[100] frontiers of the colony would be overrun by Indian allies of the French. To the House the capture of Louisbourg was of great significance, but the successful defence of the immediate frontiers of the colony was considered to be of far greater consequence.

Confronted by the unexpected New Hampshire impasse, the disconcerted Shirley proposed to Wentworth that five or six companies of volunteers be raised in New Hampshire to serve in the Massachusetts force and to be paid by the Massachusetts government.[101] Shirley also tried to persuade Wentworth to "consent to the Emission of a further sum in bills" because of the "extraordinary Emergency."[102] Shirley was not the only one who was disappointed with New Hampshire's refusal to support the Louisbourg expedition. Many New Hampshire residents, stirred by Vaughan's vision[103] and encouraged by Pepperrell,[104] began to exert considerable pressure upon Wentworth.[105] Finally on February 23 and 24, after the House of Representatives had resolved to raise 350 volunteers and pay them according to the Massachusetts scale, Wentworth agreed to the emission of £13,000.[106] It should be noted, however, that the House intended to spend less than one half of the £13,000 on the Louisbourg expedition.[107] The new Hampshire House of Representatives had indeed won a notable victory.

On hearing of the resolution passed by the New Hampshire House and agreed to by Wentworth, Shirley decided that only 150 men should be raised in New Hampshire and paid by the Massachusetts government.[108] Furthermore, he ordered these men to serve under the officer in charge of the New Hampshire-paid volunteers, Colonel Samuel Moore. When the New Hampshire fleet of transports sailed for Canso on April 3, only 456[109] volunteers were on board, including the thirty-odd men who manned the colony guard vessel.[110] The number of New Hampshire volunteers had fallen some fifty short of the desired goal.

Since he had serious reservations regarding the strong emphasis placed upon the element of surprise in the plan to capture Louisbourg accepted by the Massachusetts General Court, Shirley on February 9 wrote to Sir Chaloner Ogle, commander of the British squadron stationed at Jamaica, and to Commodore Peter Warren, commander of the Leeward Islands squadron, asking for naval assistance.[111] In his letter to Ogle, Shirley stressed that the success of the expedition depended to a considerable degree upon the arrival in Louisbourg waters by at least May of some British warships. By blockading the French fortress with British warships, Shirley hoped to prevent the landing of the expected French reinforcements and supplies and thus provide "the finishing hand to this important Enterprise." He was confident of naval aid:

> [since] the success of this affair will be attended with such Advantages to the Crown and the Trade, not only of all the Northern Plantations in America, but even of Great Britain itself, by securing to his Majesty the Fortress of Annapolis Royal, and the whole province of Nova Scotia, and by preserving that valuable Branch of our Trade which depends on our Fishery...I doubt not but you will contribute everything in Your power to Our Assistance.[112]

Ogle did not receive Shirley's letter until March 25 when his command was at an end. He forwarded it to his successor Admiral Davers with a trenchant remark—"I am of opinion that it is not in Your power to comply with Mr. Shirley's request."[113] Ogle's advice to Davers was undoubtedly correct, since Davers in the early months of 1745, with few ships at his disposal, was in no position to send naval aid to anyone.[114] However, there was no good reason for Ogle's own refusal to come to Shirley's aid. Ogle was about to sail to England with one small and four large warships, all of which had been recently refitted. He could easily have sailed to Cape Breton but he lacked the necessary initiative.

Warren, on the other hand, regarded Shirley's request in an entirely different light. He was unable to treat it with the superciliousness of Ogle. For in September 1744, Warren had proposed to the Lords of the Admiralty that it was of vital importance for the British cause in North America to drive the French from Louisbourg.[115] Shirley's scheme, therefore, struck a responsive chord in Warren.

In 1745 Warren was only 42 years old, but he had received his captain's commission eighteen years earlier. Having spent some years stationed in North American waters and having married a resident of New York, Warren tended to look at strategic problems in the same way as Shirley did.[116] In addition, Warren was an unusually ambitious man who in 1744 and 1745 desperately wanted to be appointed governor of one of the northern colonies, preferably New York.[117] He believed that if he could carry out successfully some brilliant military stroke against the French, he would receive this desired reward.

Shirley's letter reached Warren at Antigua on March 5.[118] The Massachusetts governor used all of the persuasiveness at his command in urging Warren to send warships to support the proposed expedition. Shirley even offered Warren "the command of the expedition...a most happy event for his majesty's service and your own honour."[119] Warren immediately called the captains of his squadron together to discuss Shirley's letter. After a prolonged discussion, it was decided that it would be extremely unwise to send ships to Cape Breton without first receiving instructions from the Admiralty. Nevertheless, it was decided to send two ships, the *Launceston* and the *Mermaid,* to Boston and New York respectively where they were to await further "directions from the Lords of Admiralty."[120]

But the *Launceston* and *Mermaid* were never sent to Boston and New York. For on March 19[121] Warren received instructions from the Admiralty to proceed immediately "either to the Relief & Succour of Annapolis Royal...or for making any Attempts on the enemy."[122] The only brake on Warren's desire to support Shirley had been removed. Warren called together his captains once again and informed them of the instructions he had just received from the

Admiralty. The captains, together with the Governor and Assembly of Antigua, pleaded with Warren not to sail to Cape Breton. They had heard rumours about a large French squadron making its way towards the Caribean.[123] Warren refused to be intimidated and he refused to be tied to the decision made by the council of war:

> Warren was prepared to take the risk that the French were
> not coming, or that if they were a British force equal to them
> would follow. Realizing that in war risks must be taken, he
> was sure that this was one that was justifiable.[124]

On March 24 Warren sailed from Antigua with the *Superbe*, 60 guns, the *Launceston*, 40 guns, and the *Mermaid*, 40 guns. He also sent orders to the *Eltham* at Piscataqua and the *Bien Aimé*, a prize at Boston, to join him off Cape Breton.[125]

Shirley knew nothing about Warren's departure until after the Massachusetts troops had left Boston for Canso.[126] On April 4, having in his possession Warren's negative response to the request for naval assistance, Shirley had no good reason to delay the sailing of the expedition any longer. However, he kept the volunteers ignorant of the potentially explosive intelligence, and consequently when they sailed from Boston they were convinced that "Commodore Warren is coming to our assistance, which with the blessing of God will be of great advantage."[127]

Without question the departure date of the expedition was delayed more by Shirley's decision to wait for Warren's answer to his request than by any other single factor. Nevertheless, the procrastination of the other colonies and the difficulty in obtaining transports also caused delay.

Before the expedition sailed, Shirley sent six armed colonial vessels "to cruise before the harbour of Louisbourg in order to intercept any intelligence, Recruits or Supplys, which might be sent to the Enemy before the arrival"[128] of the invading army. *The Prince of Orange*, 14 guns, the *Boston Packet*, 12 guns, and the *Fame*, 24 guns, sailed for Cape Breton waters sometime before March 24. The *Molineux*, 24 guns, the *Caesar*, 14 guns, and the *Massachusetts*, 22 guns, followed on March 27.[129] The *Prince of Orange, Boston Packet* and the *Massachusetts* were owned by the Massachusetts government, while the other vessels were hired by it.[130] On March 28, to prepare the way for the expedition, the *Resolute*, 10 guns, and *Bonetta*, 6 guns, were sent to Canso.[131]

At four o'clock in the afternoon on Sunday, April 4, the first Massachusetts contingent of some 2,800 men, in fifty-one transport vessels under the convoy of the *Shirley*, 24 guns, sailed from Boston.[132] Two days later, the second contingent of 200 sailed.[133]

The selection of Sunday for the sailing date for the main body of the expedition was significant. It was a public declaration by the Massachusetts residents of their belief that without the direction and blessing of the Almighty the expedition would be a failure. As the ships slowly vanished out of sight, an unprecedented campaign of prayer began in Massachusetts to ensure the success of the Louisbourg expedition. This prayer campaign was caustically criticized by Benjamin Franklin in a letter to his brother in Massachusetts:

> You have a fast and prayer day for that purpose [fall of Louisbourg]; in which I compute five hundred thousand petitions were offered up to the same effect in New England, which added to the petitions of every family morning and evening, multiplied by the number of days since January 25th (O.S.) make forty-five millions of prayers; which, set against the prayers of a few priests in the Garrison, to the Virgin Mary, give a vast balance in your favor....in attacking strong towns I should have more dependence on works, than on faith; for, like the kingdom of heaven, they are to be taken by force and violence; and in a French garrison I suppose there are devils of that kind, that they are not to be cast out by prayers and fasting, unless it be by their own fasting for want of provisions.[134]

5

Canso
(April–May, 1745)

IN SPITE OF THE FERVENT PRAYERS of the pious Massachusetts inhabitants, Pepperrell's fleet was soon buffetted by strong "contrary...east-south east"[1] winds. On April 7 those persistent winds forced the fleet to seek shelter in the mouth of the Kennebec River at the eastern extremity of Massachusetts.[2] While impatiently waiting for a favourable wind, Pepperrell was able to scrutinize the instructions[3] he had received from Shirley before the fleet's departure from Boston. These instructions had been drafted by Shirley in close consultation with two "astute" military men. One of these was John Bastide, the military engineer responsible for the rebuilding of Annapolis Royal, and the other was Captain Philip Durell, commander of the British man-of-war *Eltham*.[4] The starting point of their detailed instructions to Pepperrell was the plan of operations against Louisbourg adopted by the Massachusetts General Court in February. They refined somewhat this original amateurish plan of operations proposed by Bradstreet and Vaughan and added some directives in military strategy. These directives were based upon a remarkable grasp of the geographical features of the Louisbourg region and took into consideration the need for flexibility. The final product, though much more sophisticated than the original plan, still left a great deal to be desired.

Pepperrell was unquestionably impressed with the detailed nature of his instructions. Immediately on landing at Canso, he was to build "a block house frame, on the hill of Canso, where the old one stood, and hoist English colours upon it; enclosing it with pickets and pallisadoes." The blockhouse was to be manned by eighty volunteers and their officers and was to be defended by eight 9-pound cannon. Furthermore, before the fleet finally sailed for Gabarus Bay, a largely sheltered bay and excellent anchoring place, only a few miles west of Louisbourg, 200 men were to be sent to capture the strategically located French fishing settlement at Port Toulouse, or St. Peter's as it was known to the New Englanders, a short distance north of Canso.

The instructions stressed that only if Pepperrell was sure that Louisbourg was unaware of the New England invading force was he to "prosecute the design of surprize." The fleet was to sail from Canso at such a time that it would anchor in Gabarus Bay at nine o'clock in the evening, shielded by darkness from the unwary French.

Three "separate divisions," one consisting of 400 troops and the other two of 600 each, were "to be immediately, by the whale boats, landed in the best manner that the necessary haste can allow" at Flat Point Cove. The cove, situated at the mouth of Landing Cove Brook on the eastern side of present-day Simon Point, possessed not only a fine landing beach and excellent fresh water supply but was also less than two miles from the walls of Louisbourg. These three "divisions" were to march quickly overland in the general direction of the Grand Battery, which was situated across the western reaches of Louisbourg harbour from the fortress town. While the two larger "divisions" kept a "profound silence," the force consisting of 400 troops was to begin its thrust against the isolated Grand Battery "entering at a low part of the wall, that is unfinished at the east end." The attack upon the Grand Battery was to be accompanied by a simultaneous assault upon "the west gate of the town" by only one of the other "divisions." The other was to "post themselves behind...a hill about south west from the town wall...to secure, if need be, the retreat of the attacking party.

An additional force of 600 men was to be landed at White Point, one mile southwest of the fortress. These man were:

> ...to proceed along shore, till they come to the low wall of the town, that is close into the sea on the south-easterly Part of the town.... Here this party are to scale the wall, and enter the town if possible; proceeding as fast as can be towards the citadel.

It was hoped that at least one of the attacking forces would enter the fortress, but if both of them were driven back, they were "to retreat to the back of the hill, where the other party is posted to cover and receive them." The unsuccessful attackers would then await the arrival of the train of artillery from Gabarus Bay, and when the artillery arrived a regular siege would commence.[5]

To be carried out successfully the proposed surprise assault demanded not only extraordinary timing and swift disciplined movements on the part of the inexperienced invaders, but also almost perfect weather conditions and the total absence of any observant Frenchmen from the Gabarus region.[6] It was possible, but highly unlikely, that these conditions would exist when the New England fleet anchored in Gabarus Bay.

In for any reason, however, Pepperrell believed that the French knew of the invading force he was to abandon the plan "of surprising the town." Instead, he was to be particularly concerned with the successful amphibious landing of his force preferably at Flat Point Cove:

> If the situation of affairs be such, that intelligence or discovery influence you not to attempt the surprise; and you find the enemy alarmed; you will doubtless think it necessary, to prevent any accident before the troops are landed, to send out a proper number of scouts; who, if they discover any ambuscade, or preparation to receive you, must give you due notice thereof, either by signals or by not returning...and if there be no opposition in landing, it will be best, for order sake, to land the men, regiment by regiment; who may be formed and drawn up into order, at proper distances, as they land, till the whole is completed. But if you should meet with opposition, and the landing be disputed, or difficult, you must then make a false descent, in order to draw off the enemy from the spot, designed for landing, or at least to divide their force...some of the vessels...will cover the landing, both by the execution they may do on the enemy and the smoke of their powder.

With his troops on dry land, Pepperrell was to organize two commando-like assaults—one upon the Grand Battery and the other upon the Island Battery. Both were expected to fall without too much difficulty. Then the regular siege of the fortress would begin. Pepperrell was instructed to concentrate his artillery upon the western walls of the town, which were considered to be in poor repair by Shirley and his advisers. In addition, nearby hills commanded the western land approaches to Louisbourg. It was also effectively argued that since the glacis on the western side of the fortress was not undermined with bomb galleries, a land assault was possible there.[7]

Pepperrell was not to devote all of his attention to the siege of Louisbourg. He was to send raiding parties to all corners of the island to destroy French "fishing vessels, houses, stages, flakes, etc."[8]

Even if Louisbourg were not captured, at least the Cape Breton fishing industry could be devastated!

The reading of his instructions only made Pepperrell increasingly aware of his military inexperience and the tremendous load of responsibility that he now carried. He was therefore somewhat relieved to note that he was able to share his onerous load with his officers. He was informed:

> On all emergencies it will be necessary for you to convene a council of war; and most expedient to act agreeably to their advice; and this council is to consist of yourself (as President) and the other general officers the colonels of the several regiments, their lieutenant colonels, and the captain of the train of artillery...five of whom to make a quorum of said council.[9]

Pepperrell was therefore the first among equals; such an arrangement was the only one acceptable to the Piscataqua merchant and to his officers. Seeing the utter foolishness of being slavishly tied to any set of instructions, Pepperrell was delighted with the short postscript to his instructions from Shirley:

> Sir, Upon the whole, notwithstanding the instructions you have received from me; I must leave it to you, to act upon unforseen emergencies, according to your best discretion.[10]

While his fleet lay sheltered at the mouth of Kennebec River, Pepperrell found time to make inquiry into the state of affairs in the fleet and gave "orders for their better regulation."[11] On April 9, the weather clearing and the wind more favourable, Pepperrell ordered his fleet to make sail for the barren, inhospitable, rocky island of Canso.[12] The fleet of tiny fishing vessels made considerable progress until noon of the following day when a "Tarible North Eeast Storm"[13] struck. On each violently pitching ship, the troops were quickly herded into the foul-smelling holds where they were "Much Crouded, even So as to Lay, one an Another."[14] The volunteers from the interior of Massachusetts were especially alarmed as "the weather Grew, Thicker and more Stormy."[15] One observed:

> ...we Lay Rowling in ye Seas with our Sails Furl'd with Prodigious wave[s]...all y^t I Took To Eat or Drink vomit up again Sick Day & night So bad y^t I have not words To Set it Forth, nor Can I give any Body an Idea of it y^t hath not Felt ye Same or Some thinge like it.[16]

Another landlubber graphically asserted:

> The weather was exceeding bad for us; there arose a great storm, and the seas ran mountains high, and it did rain very hard, and the wind did blow very hard, so that we was fain to

let down our sails and let drive where the seas would carry us. And a terrible storm we had, so bad that I thought that every minute would be the last. And in the meanwhile our men was exceeding sick, and did vomit as if they would die. And in this troublesome time and in the mount of difficulty, I hope every man called upon his God for his deliver[ance].[17]

The "hurricaning"[18] storm, which did not abate until late on April 12, scattered the fleet in all directions and the ensuing thick fog kept most of the ships apart.[19] When on April 15 Pepperrell and a cluster of twenty ships limped into Canso,[20] he was greatly relieved to find several other vessels of his fleet safely anchored, as well as the ships that had sailed from Boston two days after the departure of his fleet and the New Hampshire contingent that had arrived on April 11.[21] By April 21 only three vessels were not accounted for, and these eventually reached Canso.[22]

To many of the troops the safe arrival of all the New England ships at Canso, in spite of the never-to-be-forgotten storm, was unmistakable evidence that their God had stamped the expedition with the imprimatur of success. The Almighty had made it abundantly clear that he was "willing to save and succour all them that put their trust in him."[23] How could the forces of anti-Christ in Louisbourg successfully resist such a challenge?

The day following his arrival at Canso, Pepperrell ordered the troops ashore to undergo basic military training.[24] From the beginning the training sessions took on a carnival atmosphere. The troops were encouraged in their dreary drills by drummers who furiously beat their drums, by "Fidlers" who energetically squealed away hopelessly off-key, and by iron-lunged "Trumpetters" who were more interested in making noise than in making music.[25] But the training sessions were all too infrequent because of the prevailing "rainy...very raw and cold"[26] weather. One disgusted Massachusetts officer complained bitterly after spending a few weeks at Canso:

This is the Strangest Country that I was ever in, in my life. We have not had two fair days together since we have been here.[27]

On his first Sabbath at Canso, April 18, Pepperrell solemnly "drew up and reviewed the Forces on Canso Hill."[28] He was visibly shaken on finding so many of his troops "very deficient in the necessary accoutrements" of war. He resolved not to permit any substantial number of them to "proceed [to Louisbourg] with such arms as (to say the best) are very mean and slightly."[29] Consequently he ordered his armourers to repair the faulty arms as quickly as possible and to replace those that were beyond repair.[30]

As he made his way up and down the wavering lines of his motley force, Pepperrell was undoubtedly impressed by the youthfulness of the men. A random survey of thirty-nine New Hampshire volunteers reveals that ten were teenagers, twenty were in their twenties, only three in their thirties, four in their forties, and two in their fifties.[31] It would be expected that most of the volunteers under the age of thirty had few family responsibilities and that their adventurous spirits and a strong desire for plunder had drawn them to the Louisbourg expedition.

On April 18 Pepperrell also issued the "full instructions for forming the several detachments proposed" in Shirley's instructions. He "ordered the commanding officer of each, to draw out his men together, and that they be furnished with everything necessary for prosecuting the part assigned them, respectively." Each of the four detachments was to leave Canso for Louisbourg "in a distinct squadron, and be landed accordingly."[32]

Pepperrell and the members of the council of war were eager to move against Louisbourg with the first favourable wind. But their hopes for an early assault were thwarted, since on April 18 the vessels carrying "ammunition, artillery, and the other most material stores"[33] had not yet arrived at Canso. These vessels were nestled instead in the commodious Country Harbour to the south of Canso.[34] Consequently, on April 18 the impatient council members were forced to agree that only when "the necessary ammunition and stores for the men were arrived" would the expedition "with all possible dispatch"[35] sail for Gabarus Bay.

It was not until April 22 that six of the seven transport vessels from Country Harbour finally anchored at Canso.[36] On April 24 the council of war decided that "if w[d] & weath[r] permit"[37] the fleet was to sail on the following day "Not waiting for Commodore Warren or Connetticut forces."[38] Moreover, believing that St. Peter's was no longer a threat, the council of war "unanimously agreed that ye attended att[ack] on St. P. shd be deffer'd & that those forces shd attend ye main body to Gabbarouse."[39] But the wind and weather refused to comply with the earnest wishes of the New Englanders. Finally on April 27, Pepperrell was informed by Captain Jonathan Snelling of the *Molineux* that there was "so much ice on the [Gabarus] coast, that there will not be any coming down with the fleet till it is clearer."[40] The easterlies that had been blowing strongly for weeks had piled up mountains of ice in Gabarus Bay, forming a barrier that only time could remove. Pepperrell had to be content with keeping "the men employed in such exercises, as might contribute to the benefit of the expedition in general, as well as keeping them in health and spirits."[41]

The delay worried Pepperrell. He feared that the St. Peter's inhabitants were bound to learn of the forces at Canso and would carry the intelligence to Louisbourg. To counter such a possible development, Pepperrell on May 2 sent some seventy men in two schooners with five whaleboats "to go there in the night, and if possible surprise the officer and men, burn the houses, etc. and bring off the vessels."[42] The enterprise was a miserable failure. The New England troops were afraid to land, thinking the French force to be "so considerable." In the ensuing wild retreat of the whaleboats three New Englanders were wounded.[43] If the suspicions of the inhabitants of St. Peter's had not been aroused before May 2, they certainly were after the abortive raid. Pepperrell's worries suddenly multiplied.

Apparently it was not until May 6 that news reached Canso that Gabarus Bay was at last free of ice.[44] It was therefore decided to sail with the first favourable early morning breeze, since Pepperrell and the council of war were intent upon surprising Louisbourg. If the fleet left Canso at dawn with a strong favourable wind, it could anchor in Gabarus Bay that same evening, in accordance with Shirley's instructions.

By May 6 Pepperrell was well pleased with the military and naval strength at his disposal and his troops confidently expected the "Campaign will be very short...the place will surrender without any bloodshed."[45] For on May 3 Captain Durell in the 40-gun *Eltham* had arrived at Canso, followed the next day by Warren with the *Superbe*, *Launceston*, and *Mermaid*.[46] Moreover, May 5 saw the arrival of the Connecticut contingent of volunteers.[47]

Without receiving instructions from Shirley, Pepperrell magnanimously and tactfully gave the command of all the colonial ships then endeavouring to blockade Louisbourg to his old acquaintance Warren, of whom he thought highly. Pepperrell described his attitude towards Warren thus:

> I shall on all occasions, be fond of the assistance and advice of
> a gentleman, whose generous attachment to the welfare of
> the colonies in general, and this expedition in special, added
> to his well known personal merit, in his active and successful
> service of our nation, entitles him to the highest esteem and
> regard from every well wisher to New-England.[48]

While his ship was off Canso, Warren also received news from Knowles at Antigua that the feared French fleet commanded by the Chevalier de Caylus was in Caribbean waters.[49] Warren was not even tempted to return to the West Indies, being assured that the Admiralty, aware of Caylus' movements, would send a sufficient naval force there to cope with the French threat.[50] In addition, Warren feared that without his warships the New England expedition would probably fail.[51] In fact, Warren was in such a hurry to join the New England blockading force off Louisbourg "to Intercept any Provisions, or Succours, being carried Into that Port"[52] that he did not even go ashore at Canso. After he received a copy of Shirley's instructions to Pepperrell, Warren directed the four men-of-war to sail for Louisbourg.

On May 10, between five and six in the morning, "with a Small Gail of Wind"[53] from the northeast by north, Pepperrell's fleet finally weighed anchor to sail for Gabarus Bay. A separate force of 270 New Hampshire men under the command of Colonel Jeremiah Moulton sailed at the same time for St. Peter's "with Orders (persuant to the...Plan of Operations) to take the Place, burn the Houses, and demolish the Fort."[54] Only two companies of men under the command of Ammi Cutter remained to defend Canso from possible French attack.

6

Louisbourg
(November 1744 –
April 1745)

THE ARRIVAL of the *Compagnie des Indes* fleet in September 1744 had been responsible for lulling the majority of Louisbourg inhabitants into a false sense of security. The fleet stayed until the last day of November,[1] but the complacency of Louisbourg was interrupted early in that month when the privateer Doloboratz returned from Boston. He brought intelligence regarding a proposed Anglo-American assault upon Louisbourg planned for the spring of the following year. This report was confirmed a short time later upon the return of Du Vivier,[2] who had received similar information while unsuccessfully besieging Annapolis Royal.

The acting governor of Cape Breton, Du Chambon, carefully considered both the details and the obvious implications of the astonishing report of Doloboratz. Du Chambon was inclined to discount it. He found it incredible that 6,000 New Englanders, or even a fraction of that number, would volunteer to take part in the proposed spring offensive against Louisbourg. But the report furnished Du Chambon with a means of convincing the Louisbourg inhabitants—both military and civil—of the necessity of full preparations for a real and immediate military threat. In addition, he felt the report would be useful in inducing the French Minister of Marine, Maurepas, to initiate immediate and drastic defence measures for the defence of Louisbourg.

Du Chambon, however, was not unalarmed. He anticipated some kind of British naval blockade in the spring "to stop any kind of help from reaching us.... Their intent is to starve the entire colony and by so doing to capture it." If the blockade failed to bring about the surrender of the fortress, he expected the British warships to attempt to force their way into Louisbourg harbour by having "some ships loaded with material producing a thick smoke that would envelop the Island Battery and by this method the ships would enter without being seen."[3]

To deal with what he considered to be a very real threat to Louisbourg and to all of Cape Breton, Du Chambon advocated both a defensive and an offensive policy. The general conceptual framework within which his policy was formed was, however, limited. Du Chambon, who was greatly influenced in his military thinking by the talented François Bigot, was certain that the British men-of-war would strike at Louisbourg's main strength, her harbour-oriented defence system. The thought that an enemy force might be landed at one of the many fine beaches along Gabarus Bay, march overland and commence a regular land siege, apparently never flashed through the governor's mind. Therefore, he considered the landward defences of the fortress to be of little importance as far as the immediate threat was concerned.

Du Chambon's defensive policy, like the man himself, lacked imagination. Furthermore, his attempt to impress upon the Louisbourg inhabitants the real danger of the British threat completely failed. By November 10 he had ordered Bigot to supply some 10,000 faggots of spruce and to have them ready to be loaded on all available fireships when the British fleet was sighted.[4] These giant floating torches were to be used in the event of a favourable wind to prevent the British warships from forcing their way past the Island Battery into Louisbourg harbour. Morpain, the Port Captain, who undoubtedly possessed the best military mind in Louisbourg, was chosen by the governor to direct all defensive operations once the fortress was attacked by sea.[5]

However, Du Chambon was reluctant to have his defence policy completely dependent upon what he considered to be the largely inadequate military resources available to him. Nor did he wish to rely solely upon purely defensive measures. In various letters written in November to Maurepas, Du Chambon painted the blackest possible picture of the state of military preparedness in Louisbourg.[6] In so doing he was following the example set by most of his predecessors, who were eager to obtain various concessions from the rather apathetic and indifferent French colonial authorities. But he possessed a much stronger bargaining lever than any of his predecessors—Doloboratz's report—and he was eager to press his advantage. He used the report and the threat that Louisbourg "cannot be defended with such a tiny garrison if it were besieged"[7] in an attempt to wring badly needed reinforcements and military supplies from the distraught Maurepas. Du Chambon used these arguments not because he was convinced of their validity but because he thought they could be used to win significant concessions from Maurepas.

There is strong evidence to suggest that Du Chambon and Bigot, at least in November and December 1744, were confident that the proposed British naval assault would fail. They probably felt this way because they had a great faith in the defensive strength, if not the invulnerablility, of the Island Battery and the Grand Battery and because they did not have too much fear about the consequences of a naval blockade. For in late November 1744 Louisbourg had sufficient food supplies to hold out until at least August 1745.[8] Surely by that date, it was argued, French naval assistance would be forthcoming. No French Minister of Marine, possessing as he did such an excellent intelligence system both in the British North American colonies and in Great Britain, would permit the free movement of any large number of British warships into French waters.

To ensure that Louisbourg would not even be threatened by a British naval force in the spring of 1745, Du Chambon and Bigot on November 14 advocated a large-scale French naval assault upon Annapolis Royal as well as upon the tiny British fort at Placentia in southeastern Newfoundland.[9] If the British could play at the offensive game, why could not the French? Like Shirley, Du Chambon and Bigot believed that Annapolis Royal had considerable strategic and symbolic importance. If it could be captured in the early spring, and they were certain it could be, any intended Anglo-American thrust against Louisbourg would unquestionably be deflected to recover Annapolis. Moreover, it was felt that with Annapolis Royal in French hands, the New Englanders would be immediately thrown on the defensive, fearing possible French-Acadian-Indian raids. Thus with one bold offensive stroke Louisbourg would be effectively shielded from possible attack, Nova Scotia would become French territory once again, and the New Englanders would find their northeastern frontiers threatened. If, as an added bonus, Placentia were captured, the French could drive the British from the valuable Newfoundland fishery and also remove a base for possible British naval raids against French settlements in North America and against French shipping to and from Cape Breton and New France.

In their detailed plan of operations sent to Maurepas, Du

Chambon and Bigot urged that at the beginning of March 1745, two men-of-war of 50 to 60 guns, two frigates of 40 guns and one large supply vessel should sail from France for Annapolis Royal. The ships were to be guided to their eventual destination by Du Vivier and three experienced pilots from Louisbourg. These men sailed for France with the *Indes* fleet on November 30. It was hoped that the French fleet would anchor in Annapolis Basin by at least April 15.[10] The French vessels were to carry at least 800[11] men for the land assault and it was hoped that they would be supported by 200 or 300 Micmacs[12] from Nova Scotia and "Fifty Canadians and Fifty Indians"[13] whom Beauharnois, the Governor of New France, promised to send to the Chignecto region early in 1745.

After the troops were landed "out of cannon-range, and the artillery that they will require was landed, they were to besiege the said fort."[14] It was expected that Mascarene's troops would put up little resistance when they were attacked both by land and by sea. Only 250 French troops were to be left to garrison the fort and they were to be assisted by an unspecified number of Micmacs and Acadians armed with French guns and supplied with French ammunition. Finally, "Once the expedition was over...the vessels were to be divided into two groups, the one was to make its way to New England waters and the other for Isle Royale."[15]

In all likelihood, even though it was never expressly spelled out, the ships destined for Cape Breton waters were the ones intended to carry out the attack against Placentia. Du Chambon and Bigot had been informed that Placentia was only defended by forty-five soldiers, three officers and thirteen small cannon "in a crumbling battery."[16] As a result the two Louisbourg officials were of the opinion that two ships, each carrying 150 fighting men in addition to their crews, would have no trouble whatsoever in capturing the strategically located British fort.[17]

When Maurepas examined the Du Chambon-Bigot plan either in late December 1744 or early January 1745, he came to the conclusion that the recapture of "*la Province de l'Acadie*"[18] and Placentia was unquestionably the most vital offensive move the French could make in North America. Believing that it was imperative "that the Nations active in maritime commerce should possess sufficient naval strength to sustain and to retain this commerce,"[19] he urged Louis XV to send the desired expedition. Maurepas estimated the proposed expedition would cost 741,550 livres—money he considered wisely spent if it ensured the retention of Cape Breton, the control of the Newfoundland fishery and the return of the Acadians to the French cause.[20] In addition, Maurepas wished to use the Cape Breton problem as an example to the Continent-obsessed Louis XV of the indispensable need of a powerful naval force "for the protection of commerce and the defense of a Maritime Nation."[21] From the moment he assumed the onerous responsibilities of his office, Maurepas had endeavoured to persuade the king of the wisdom of building up France's naval strength. But Louis XV had been singularly unimpressed with his Minister of Marine's arguments.[22]

Fully aware of his monarch's military prejudices, and fearing that he might laugh to scorn the Du Chambon-Bigot plan, Maurepas recommended that if the plan was unacceptable to the king perhaps three warships could be immediately sent to Cape Breton. These ships would be responsible "for the protection of the fishery...for the defence of Isle Royale and for the security of supply vessels which Louisbourg needs for its subsistence."[23] It was estimated that the total cost of sending these three vessels would be approximately one-half of the proposed expenses of the Du Chambon-Bigot expedition.[24] As Maurepas feared, Louis XV selected the less expensive plan of operation[25]—a plan both men hoped would at least be responsible for containing any British naval thrust against Louisbourg.

On February 7 the *Renommée,* a 32-gun frigate, sailed from France for Louisbourg.[26] The sailing of the *Renommée* at such an early date revealed the concern that Maurepas felt for the safety of Louisbourg. It also gave Maurepas an opportunity to inform Du Chambon and Bigot that their plan had been rejected by the king. Probably because his spies in Britain and the American colonies had been silent regarding any prospective large-scale British naval assault upon Louisbourg, Maurepas was satisfied to send only one vessel early in February. However, he planned to send another frigate, the *Mars,* sometime during the following month, and he expected the *Castor,* then being built at Quebec, to join the two other French warships at Louisbourg.[27]

Soon after leaving France on February 7, the *Renommée* was battered by a severe storm and was forced to return to Cadiz.[28] After necessary repairs were made, she sailed again on March 10.[29] A week later, Maurepas decided that since the *Mars* would not be ready to sail until April 25, the 64-gun *Vigilant* would sail instead.[30] Maurepas therefore had his three ships to carry out his alternate policy. But having set aside three ships to implement a policy was one thing; having them at Louisbourg in a position to implement the policy was an entirely different matter. The *Vigilant,* under the command of Alexandre Boisdescourt de la Maisonfort, did not leave Brest until April 26,[31] while the *Castor* was not even launched until May 16.[32]

After the *Indes* fleet sailed from Louisbourg on November 30, Du Chambon and Bigot were content to sit back to wait for Maurepas to make the next move. What else could they do? The long, raw Louisbourg winters were conducive to general inactivity and little else. But the Swiss mercenaries and many of the French "colonial regulars" had other ideas!

On the whole the Louisbourg troops were a motley lot, to say the least. In 1739 the perceptive governor Forant had observed:

> With the utmost sincerity I may say that I have never seen such bad troops. We would not keep one hundred soldiers [out of over 500], if we discharged all those who are below the regulation height. But without regard to stature and physique I believe that it is better to discharge invalids, who are pillars of the hospital and occasion much expense, and are of no use whatsover, as well as rascals who not only are incorrigible, but are even capable of leading others into vicious ways.... It is better to have fewer men than to have them of this character.[33]

By 1744 the general character and mood of the Louisbourg troops had been only slightly improved. The so-called "incorrigible rascals" were still assiduously at work and on December 27, 1744, were responsible for precipitating the most acute crisis Louisbourg had ever faced. For on December 27 the troops mutinied.[34] Thus the first blow struck against the fortress during the war with Britain was a blow from within.

Soon after the outbreak of hostilities with Britain, the garrison began to show unmistakeable signs of a pervasive and seething discontent. Led by the Swiss mercenaries, members of the Karrer regiment, the Louisbourg troops did not hesitate to disclose to the New England and Canso prisoners their "mutinous spirit." Accounts of the "Uneasiness of the Switzers,"[35] carried to Boston by the returning prisoners played a significant role in building up support in Massachusetts for the Louisbourg expedition.

There were two main reasons for the general "Uneasiness" prevalent among the Louisbourg troops during the summer and fall of 1744. First, the troops were understandably disgusted with their living conditions. They were forced to live in the vermin-infested, inadequately ventilated and badly heated barracks of the

Citadel.[36] Second, and probably more important, they were frequently cheated and badly treated by their officers. The critical "Habitant de Louisbourg," who was present during the whole episode, observed:

> The mutineers did not complain of the bread nor of any other provisions. (Some say that they complained also about beans:—but their greatest grievance was about the codfish, taken as booty at Canso, which M. du Quesnel had promised to them, and which the officers had appropriated to themselves, for a low price at long credit. Some of these knew how to enrich themselves by trade.... It is certain that the officers treated the soldiers badly, reckoning his pay fraudulently, and often making a profit out of his work. These soldiers worked upon the fortifications and ought to have been paid.)[37]

De Ulloa, the Spanish traveller and writer, who visited Louisbourg in 1745, maintained:

> ...that France every year sends a remittance to Louisbourg of money and provisions for the payment and subsistence of the garrison, together with other sums, for the repairs and improvement of the fortification; at which the soldiers themselves, when not on guard, very gladly work at being a comfortable addition to their pay. But through covetousness, one of the general vices of mankind, those who were commissioned with the payment of the soldiers, and even the very officers of the garrison, besides wronging them in what they earned by their work, curtailed them even in their subsistence money.[38]

Military discipline and the presence of the *Indes* fleet kept the prevailing discontent within reasonable bounds throughout the summer and autumn months. But with the departure of the *Indes* fleet and with an obviously weak governor temporarily at the helm of the colony, dissatisfaction was intensified by the insensitivity if not outright stupidity of the captains. Just managing to exist in the barracks during the long, dark and cold winters was arduous enough. But in December the captains appear to have been eager to make life as difficult as possible for their men. They suddenly refused to supply their men with the usual quantity of firewood, probably because the officers had decided to make some money on the side by selling the wood to Bigot for possible use in the fireships. In addition, the captains refused to supply the new recruits with badly needed clothing.[39] Finally, the captains were providing their men with "bad vegetables"[40] when everyone in Louisbourg knew that there were plenty of fresh vegetables in fine condition available.

In spite of the exacerbated sense of dissatisfaction among the troops in December, had it not been for the leadership provided by three Swiss mercenaries—"incorrigible rascals"—there would not have been a mutiny on December 27. Abraham Du Paquier was the ringleader and his two lieutenants were named Renard and So-ly.[41] While drinking brandy late in the evening of December 26, these three men became increasingly courageous and daring with every gulp of liquor.[42] There were too many injustices in Louisbourg, they agreed, and the only way to rectify the situation was for the soldiers to speak with "one voice"[43] to make a show of force. If this were not done, they were sure that conditions would further deteriourate.

Fortified with brandy, Du Paquier, Renard and Soly rushed from room to room in the Swiss section of the barracks and urged their amazed fellow soldiers to prepare for a show of force.[44] Rubbing sleep from their eyes, the Swiss troops, almost to a man, grabbed their muskets and bayonets and stumbled out to the parade ground outside of the Citadel, where they quickly fell into some semblance of order.[45] The speed and eagerness with which the Swiss troops responded to Du Paquier, Renard and Soly's call to arms was amazing, and certainly was convincing proof of their profound dissatisfaction with "the oppressions of the rapacious...officers."[46] But the three rebel leaders had failed to spur the French "colonial regulars" to revolt.[47]

The one Swiss officer who was on duty at dawn at the Citadel could hardly believe his eyes as he saw his troops forming up on the parade ground under the direction of the confident Du Paquier. After promising all that the leaders of the revolt wanted, the officer succeeded in persuading the troops to return to their beds and "to remain quiet in their rooms."[48] But instead of remaining quietly in their quarters, the Swiss troops, in all likelihood led by Du Paquier, Renard and Soly, dashed into the rooms housing the French troops and had little difficulty persuading almost every one of them to join the Swiss in a show of force. Over 400 men now marched out of the barracks and made their way to the parade ground. Then the drummers were ordered to beat the general alarm throughout the town, accompanied "by thirty fusiliers armed with guns with their bayonets ready."[49] Soldiers were selected to guard all the entrances to the Citadel, and when officers endeavoured to force their way in, the soldiers pushed them back by thrusting bayonets at them and by threatening them with muskets.[50]

De la Perelle, the town-major, attempted to stop the drummers from marching through the town, but he was unceremoniously pushed aside by the thirty soldiers accompanying the drummers. After the drummers had completed their march through the streets of Louisbourg, they returned to the Citadel and were followed in, probably at a safe distance, by De la Perelle. He discovered, much to his relief, that his officers had already restored order and that the troops were now willing to acknowledge him as their officer.[51] The latter was indeed a strange development. Had a democratic army suddenly come into being in Louisbourg?

Du Chambon was also on the scene, as was Bigot. Both men were eager to make concessions to the soldiers. On the one hand Du Chambon promised a general amnesty to all those men who took part in the uprising.[52] On the other, Bigot received from the soldiers their complaints that were "extremely critical of their officers, who, as they maintained, had kept a part of their pay, or of their clothing or of their food, and they now demanded that the officers give them all that was rightfully theirs."[53] He promised them that they would receive what was rightfully theirs. On the following day, December 28, according to one contemporary account:

> The rebels, taking advantage of the fear in which they were held, proceeded...to the commissary's door and under frivolous pretexts such as that their money had been previously kept back, caused themselves to be paid all that they wished and to be reimbursed even for their clothing.[54]

The troops had won a notable victory. Du Chambon and Bigot had been compelled to accede to their demand; the revolt had been supported by all the troops except for the French sergeants and a small company of French artillerymen. But the troops were not yet satisfied and were eager to take further advantage of the blatant weakness and vacillation shown by their superiors. The troops coveted further concessions and further victories to atone for the numerous injustices they had been forced to experience. Therefore, they next turned their attention to the Louisbourg merchants, many of whom had accumulated huge fortunes over the years, in part at least, at the expense of the soldiers. The soldiers made the frightened merchants sell them whatever they wanted at prices the soldiers were willing to pay.[55] This revolutionary commercial development was apparently shortlived. The coming of the new year witnessed a lessening of tension.[56] The troops had made their point;

they had their concessions and they were pleased with themselves.

On December 31, 1744, Du Chambon and Bigot surreptitiously placed on board a merchant vessel sailing for the French West Indies a letter describing the revolt, addressed to the Minister of Marine. They demanded that as soon as possible the Swiss mercenaries be replaced "by some companies of Marine which could be used to restrain the other troops."[57] Maurepas received the startling news concerning the revolt towards the end of April[58] and immediately ordered the 64-gun *Vigilant* to sail, which she did on April 26.[59]

From the beginning of the new year until the middle of March, Louisbourg largely reverted to its usual state of hibernation.[60] Then, on March 14, its somnolence was disturbed when a vessel was sighted three or four leagues from the harbour entrance. But a strong southwester soon blew it out of sight again. Five days later Du Chambon received intelligence that two foreign vessels had been spotted near "Menadou" [Main-à-Dieu]. Afraid that these vessels might be the harbingers of the naval assault Doloboratz had predicted, Du Chambon called together all the inhabitants from Louisbourg and surrounding areas. He organized those from the town into four militia companies and he ordered those men living in the nearby settlements "to make their way to the Royal Battery and to the Island Battery, on my giving them the signal."[61]

On April 9 four ships were noticed making their way through the drift ice in the general vicinity of White Point. One of the ships fired a number of cannon shot as a signal and her fire was returned by an enthusiastic gunner at the Island Battery. Du Chambon was sure that these "were French ships that were trying to break through the ice to come into the harbour."[62] However, some of his officers suspected that the ships were from New England, but they were uncertain.[63]

In order to be sure that these vessels were neither New England nor British in origin and in order to confirm a report from St. Peter's that "there were British ships at Canso,"[64] Du Chambon sent instructions to the commanding officer at St. Peter's to discover if, in fact, a naval assault upon Louisbourg was being organized at Canso. The commanding officer, Benoit, therefore ordered one of his soldiers, as well as an inhabitant of the settlement and a Micmac, to investigate the situation at Canso.[65] Unfortunately for the French cause in Cape Breton, the two Frenchmen were captured near Canso on May 2 by a party of New Englanders. The wily Micmac, however, "in the Scuffle got away;"[66] but he refused to make his way to Louisbourg with his valuable information.

On April 29, the *Renommée,* unable because of treacherous ice conditions to enter Louisbourg harbour, sailed towards Canso.[67] She was confronted off Canso by the *Massachusetts,* the *Caesar,* the *Prince of Orange,* the *Boston Packet,* the *Molineux,* the *Fame* and the *Shirley,* but had little difficulty in evading the badly outclassed New England vessels.[68] After striking fear into the Connecticut troop convoy off Canso on May 4, the *Renommée* sailed further south to seek shelter and to wait for the ice conditions to improve off Louisbourg. Because of contrary winds and the presence of the British blockading fleet, Captain Kersaint decided to return to France.[69]

By the last week of April, Du Chambon was still of the opinion that the ships sometimes to be seen off the harbour were not attempting to blockade Louisbourg. Rather they were French supply ships unable because of the ice conditions to enter Louisbourg harbour. The confident Du Chambon had gone so far as to send a considerable supply of guns and ammunition on April 23 to the invading force of some 100 Frenchmen and Indians from Quebec, then wintering in the Chignecto Isthmus region.[70] This force, under the command of Marin, was expected by the governor to combine with a naval force from France in a spring attack upon Annapolis Royal. The governor felt that Marin would make better use of the guns and ammunition than the troops at Louisbourg; Marin at least was intending to fight the British at Annapolis Royal. There was no guarantee that the Louisbourg troops and militia would be battling the British in 1745.

But not all of the Louisbourg inhabitants shared Du Chambon's sanguine viewpoint. To assuage what he considered to be their irrational fear, Du Chambon ordered supplies and firewood to be transported to the Grand and Island Batteries and had the fireships made ready, just in case.[71] Du Chambon had heard nothing about Pepperrell's force at Canso; he was ignorant of the *Renommée's* failure to enter the harbour. He was particularly concerned, at the end of April, with his and Bigot's plan to recapture Annapolis Royal. Even if the British blockaded Louisbourg, Du Chambon was not especially concerned. Furthermore, he almost seemed to welcome a naval assault since he was certain that the Louisbourg guns would devastate any British naval attacking force. That the British would attempt a land assault was beyond the governor's comprehension.[72] He was living in a fool's paradise, thanks to Louisbourg's isolation.

Map of Town and Fortifications of Louisbourg, 1745

Photographs by Ronald Caplan taken at
Fortress of Louisbourg National Historic Park

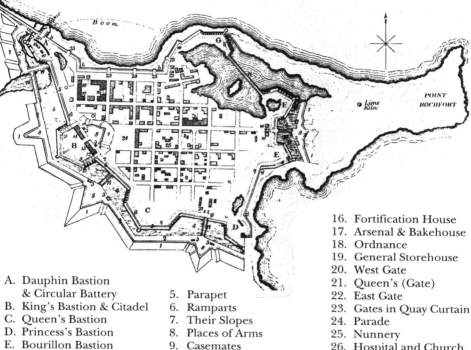

A. Dauphin Bastion
   & Circular Battery
B. King's Bastion & Citadel
C. Queen's Bastion
D. Princess's Bastion
E. Bourillon Bastion
F. Maurepas Bastion
G. Battery de la Greve
1. Glacis
2. Covered Way
3. Traverses
4. Ditch

5. Parapet
6. Ramparts
7. Their Slopes
8. Places of Arms
9. Casemates
10. Guard Houses
11. Wooden Bridges
12. Governor's Apartments
13. Chapel or Parish Church
14. Barracks for Garrison
15. Powder Magazine

16. Fortification House
17. Arsenal & Bakehouse
18. Ordnance
19. General Storehouse
20. West Gate
21. Queen's (Gate)
22. East Gate
23. Gates in Quay Curtain
24. Parade
25. Nunnery
26. Hospital and Church
27. Proposed Monument
    & Museum
a. Pallisading with rampart
   for small arms
c. Picquet raised during
   the siege of 1745

The de Gannes house

The de la Plagne house

The Lartigue house

The King's Bastion

The Dugas-la Tour house

Looking over the fence toward the Duhaget house

View towards the Frédéric Gate

7

The Gabarus Bay Landing

THE FIRST FEW DAYS OF MAY saw Du Chambon and many of the Louisbourg inhabitants still little concerned about the ships momentarily sighted through the thick and persistent spring fog. It was agreed that vessels from France were probably awaiting favourable conditions to enter the harbour. Du Chambon and his officers simply believed what they wanted to believe, thus dulling whatever perceptive and critical faculties they possessed. A vitally important requirement for men at war was therefore absent—a sharpened sense of pessimism with the courage to expect the worst. There was little room for baseless optimism in Louisbourg in May 1745.

Du Chambon was so complacent and optimistic that at the beginning of May he stopped the transportation of various necessary supplies to the Island and Grand Batteries.[1] It was not until May 7 that the governor's peace of mind was shattered. For on that date the 18-gun *St Jean du Luz* carefully picked its way through the offshore ice field and entered the commodious ice-free Louisbourg harbour. The captain of the French vessel, the Sieur Janson Dufoure, informed Du Chambon that he had had a running battle with three New England privateers, one a 24-gun frigate, the previous day and that a small New England fleet was blockading Louisbourg.[2]

Dufoure's intelligence precipitated a crisis in Louisbourg. Du Chambon now declared that a naval assault was imminent. Wood and supplies were once again transported to the Grand and Island Batteries. Almost overnight he became a prophet of doom, an extreme position diametrically opposed to his earlier mood of complacent optimism. At dawn the following day, May 8, the nervous Du Chambon feared that the New England ships were intending to force their way into Louisbourg.[3] He therefore ordered the prearranged signal to be given to warn the inhabitants of Louisbourg and the surrounding areas that the British naval assault was coming. The cannon barked their ominous warning; the frightened inhabitants of Louisbourg formed themselves into their four militia companies, while the troops marched to their defensive positions. Some of the inhabitants from the Lorambecs and Baleine streamed into the Grand Battery while others paddled to the Island Battery. All was made ready for a naval onslaught but nothing happened. Instead, the New England vessels chased and captured two tiny French ships carrying firewood from St. Peter's to Louisbourg and a "vessel coming from Isle Madame loaded with firewood."[4] Du Chambon had been wrong again.

Nevertheless, the governor remained undaunted. He may have been wrong about the imminent naval assault but what if he had been right? This kind of thinking apparently bolstered Du Chambon's sagging confidence in his own ability. To refurbish his tarnished prestige, Du Chambon on May 9 decided to prevent the New England blockading vessels from obtaining fresh water and other supplies in the Gabarus Bay region. The governor therefore prepared an ambush for the sloop that was sometimes sent ashore in Gabarus Bay for the purpose by the New England vessels.[5] A land detachment consisting of some twenty[6] regular troops was dispatched overland to Gabarus Bay, while a force of thirty-nine militiamen under the command of Sieur Daccarrette[7] sailed to Gabarus in a small vessel.[8] The two forces were expected to remain in the Gabarus Bay area for at least eight days.[9] There is absolutely no evidence to suggest that they were sent in order to prevent a large-scale British troop landing. Nothing could have been further from Du Chambon's strategic thinking.

Still expecting an imminent naval assault, Du Chambon, also on May 9, sent instructions to all the male inhabitants residing in the Lorambecs, Baleine, and Ninganiche [Ingonish] to hasten to Louisbourg and prepare for the defence of the fortress.[10] Women and children were not welcome and the governor expected them if necessary to flee temporarily to the safety of the woods. Furthermore, late in the evening of May 10, under cover of darkness and fog, the ship *La Société* slipped quietly out of Louisbourg harbour with intelligence for Maurepas that Louisbourg was blockaded.[11] The sending of *La Société* was not a desperate gamble to obtain assistance from France. Such assistance was almost hourly expected by the Louisbourg officials. Besides, it was felt that Louisbourg's guns would turn back almost any naval assault. *La Société* simply carried news of the blockade to Maurepas.

At the moment when *La Société* headed for the open sea late on May 10, Pepperrell's invading fleet of some 100 vessels was only a few miles away to the southwest. After leaving Canso at daybreak on May 10, Pepperrell's fleet of "fishing schooners, sloops [that]...rolled and pitched malevolently...and stank abominably of their former cargoes"[12] sailed in an east-northeast direction hugging the Cape Breton shore. Carefully following his instructions, Pepperrell had divided the transports into "Four Divisions"[13] in preparation for the planned four-pronged secret attack upon Louisbourg. In addition, again according to his instructions, he had placed the "Four Divisions" of troop and supply transports under convoy of one armed snow—the *Lord Montague* with only six or eight guns, and two armed sloops, the *Boston Packet*, twelve or sixteen guns, and the *Massachusetts*, eight or ten guns.[14]

As the vessels slowly moved along the Cape Breton coast the troops on board began peeling off the heavy clothing they had been forced to wear during their cold and damp sojourn at Canso. For May 10 was in Pepperrell's words "the most warm & pleasant day since our arrival."[15] One of the pious volunteers petitioned that "the Lord go forth with our armies & Give us Courage & Resolution that we may go forth in ye name of ye Lord of Hosts."[16] Another noted in his journal:

> ...wee Are now Set Sail for Cape Breton, We did Rejoice. But Considering what Our Design was, Might'nt it Justly be with trembling O! our Friends (Tho't I) Did you but know that this day wee were sailing forth to Encounter with Our Enemies how wou'd you pray for Us. I have Indeed Such Confidence in you That I Can Request nothing Greater Than to have you're Request's Granted.[17]

The unprecedented fine early morning weather undoubtedly had convinced many of the volunteers that the Almighty had indeed placed His special blessing upon the expedition. But by ten o'clock in the morning these same men were having serious doubts. For by that hour the fleet was becalmed on a placid sea under a warm May sun. It was not until late in the afternoon that a slight offshore breeze filled the sails of the fleet, and when the leading vessels encountered Warren's men-of-war it was discovered that Gabarus Bay was still at least six leagues to the northeast.[18] Seeing that it was now impossible to anchor in Gabarus Bay by "about nine of the o'clock in the evening,"[19] Pepperrell decided to "lay aside the thoughts of surprise,"[20] and to follow Shirley's alternate plan of an amphibious daylight landing. Raw, untrained New England militia were to carry out a manoeuvre that would have taxed the ingenuity of the best-trained British regulars. In fact, under the circumstances such an amphibious landing was probably beyond the capacity of British regulars accustomed only to the barrack square and the battlefields of Europe. Perhaps it was fortunate that New Englanders, ignorant of the accepted rules of war, adaptable and unorthodox in their approach to fighting, should undertake such a potentially difficult military assignment.

The landing was to be made at Flat Point Cove, as Shirley had suggested, where Landing Cove Brook flows into Gabarus Bay. Here there was an excellent small beach that provided not only a sheltered landing area but also ready access to the rocky and marshy ridge of land that thrusts itself into Gabarus Bay. The whaleboats carrying Pepperrell's shock-troops were to be covered by the fire of the *Lord Montague*, the *Boston Packet*, and the *Massachusetts*. Furthermore, on May 10, on meeting Pepperrell's fleet, Warren decided that "it will favour the Generals landing, with the Troops, to make a feint with the Squadron, as if wee Intended to go into the Harbour of Lewisbourg."[21] Once the shock-troops had gained a firm foothold at Flat Point Cove, the remainder of the troops were to be landed. Then a force of 500 men under Colonel John Bradstreet was to move against the isolated Grand Battery.

At least one officer who was to serve with Bradstreet, Captain Thomas Westbrook Waldron of the New Hampshire Regiment, had serious reservations concerning the plan to capture the Grand Battery. He regarded the plan as a *"Mad Headlong Ignorant Scheem"* which would have Entirely ruin'd [the] army."[22] As the New England fleet slowly moved toward Gabarus Bay late on May 10 and during the early hours of the following day, Waldron probably became increasingly critical and depressed regarding his written instructions:

> From [Flat Point Cove, Bradstreet's force] are to march well arm'd (Carrying what Scaling Ladders may be order'd, with half a Dozzen at least good Cutting axes, and as many Iron Crows) till they Come to ye...back of said Battrey, and then they are to march to it, as fast as may be, and Scale at ye East End, which is a Low Wall unfinished if they can't all enter fast Enough there, a Party may go round under the Cannon of ye

front and Enter at ye Embrazures, many of which are Empty
of Guns, or by help of Some Longer Ladder carried for that
purpose, a Party may Enter at ye back, which is a Dead wall,
being ye Back of ye Barracks, and Either slip down the Roof,
into the Parrade ye Inward part of ye Roof not being above
Eight feet high at most or by help of ye Crows git a breach
through the back of the wall and in Case our Men enter at ye
End or front and ye Enemy take to Close Quarters, by ye axes
ye Roof may be Cut open, to throw in Grenades.[23]

Undoubtedly other officers shared Waldron's bitter criticism of
these totally unrealistic instructions—instructions probably drafted
by Bradstreet. Moreover, many New England volunteers resented
being led into battle by the egocentric and brash Bradstreet—a
man who was not a New Englander.[24]

Soon after daybreak on May 11, some sharp-eyed Louisbourg
lookout first sighted from the fortress ramparts the leading vessels
of Pepperrell's fleet.[25] The fine sunny morning provided excellent
visibility for the lookouts, and the gentle breeze blowing from the
southwest greatly facilitated the movement of the fleet.[26] By eight
o'clock in the morning most of Pepperrell's fleet was "off the
Mouth"[27] of Gabarus Bay. It was a sight that the Louisbourg inhabitants would never forget. They began to count the number of vessels—twenty, thirty, fifty, sixty, eighty, and even more;[28] they also
carefully noted the presence of the British warships—the *Superbe,*
Launceston, Mermaid, and the *Eltham.*[29] On observing the host of
white sails at the entrance of Gabarus Bay, the French officials "immediately fired some Cannon, and rang their Bells in the Town, to
alarm and call in their People living in the Suburbs."[30] Amid the
ominous cacophony of booming cannon and pealing church bells
Pepperrell's fleet endeavoured to find suitable anchorage near Flat
Point Cove. The troops lining the decks of the transports gazed
with awe at Louisbourg's "Steeples, etc"[31] and with growing apprehension at the rocky Gabarus shore where the landing was to be
made. After over an hour of difficult manoeuvring Pepperrell's
fleet finally anchored "at the Distance of about Two Miles from the
Flat-Point Cove."[32] The long anticipated New England landing was
at last imminent.

Pepperrell had certainly been blessed with good luck. Between
nine and ten o'clock on the morning of May 11, he found himself a
few miles from his predetermined landing place—with the vast majority of his troops at his disposal. These troops had had an easy
passage from Canso and were in first-rate physical condition for an

assault. They also enjoyed the physical and moral support of Warren's squadron. In addition, and this was of great consequence, the weather during the morning of May 11 could not have been better. If it had been foggy and windy and wet, a landing would have been out of the question. It is not surprising then that the Reverend Joseph Sewell detected the hand of Providence:

> And indeed if we observe the Footsteps of God's Providence plainly appearing in this great Affair, we shall be constrain'd to say, This is the Lord's Doing, it is marvellous in our Eyes. Give me leave then just to mention some remarkable Providences by which God formed this important Enterprize and crown'd it with Success.... In sending so seasonably to our Help a Number of his Majesty's Ships of War needful to prevent Succours going to the Enemy, and to defend us by Sea. In ordering the Weather so favourable for the Landing our Forces on the Enemy's Shore.[33]

It was abundantly clear by eight o'clock in the morning of May 11 that a large-scale New England land assault would shortly be attempted either at Flat Point Cove or at Kennington Cove [Anse de la Coromandière], about two miles to the west of Flat Point Cove. Du Chambon had plenty of time to send a considerable detachment of soldiers and militia to the area to support the handful of troops that had been sent to Gabarus Bay two days earlier. But the governor procrastinated. Apparently immobilized by fear,[34] dazed with the realization the the New Englanders had quickly moved against Louisbourg's weakest point, the governor was incapable of making intelligent and quick decisions. He was urged to act in a bold and forthright manner by at least two veterans—Morpain, and Poupet De La Boularderie, the retired officer of the Regiment de Richelieu. Morpain pleaded with Du Chambon for three or four hundred men "in order to confront the enemy and prevent them from landing"[35] as he had done at Port Royal in 1707. But the governor turned a cold shoulder to Morpain's request, arguing "that he had no men to sacrifice."[36]

De La Boularderie also asked Du Chambon for "a Detachment of troops that would ambush the invaders in the woods...near where they would land." The veteran of the Richelieu Regiment, who considered himself to be the most enlightened military tactician in Louisbourg, further argued:

> that he was embarrassed for not attacking these invaders as they desembarked, that it was necessary to use one half of the garrison for this purpose...all the advantages were on our

side, there is always confusion during an assault landing, in addition it was cold and these men were poorly dressed, and very wet, most of all they were badly armed and were frightened.[37]

Taking everything into consideration, De La Boularderie's plan was probably the right one to adopt at that moment. A considerable number of troops could have marched from Louisbourg at approximately nine o'clock and they could have been in position at both possible landing places—Kennington Cove and Flat Point Cove—by ten, for it was only a three-mile march from the ramparts of Louisbourg to Kennington Cove. It is difficult to see how the untrained New Englanders could have successfully established a beachhead on Gabarus Bay if confronted by persistent and stubborn resistance on the part of the French. If, however, the New Englanders had been able to land in force, the French troops could then have been withdrawn to the safety of the fortress walls.

But Du Chambon refused to send any troops to Gabarus Bay until after the New Englanders had begun to land. When energetic leadership was absolutely essential, Du Chambon displayed unpardonable procrastination.[38] He had never been in battle before, and evidently did not really know what to do when confronted by the New England threat.

He was badly confused, for the New Englanders were determined to do something that he had imagined was impossible. Du Chambon's military thinking had been carried on within a very limited conceptual framework. He had thought that if Louisbourg were attacked, it would be by warships attempting to force their way into Louisbourg harbour. However, his refusal to send a sizeable detachment of troops to Gabarus Bay before the landing also owed something to his lack of faith in the loyalty of his troops. Had they not mutinied only a few months earlier? There was therefore a very good chance, as far as the governor was concerned, that the "colonial regulars":

>...being once without the walls, would go over to the enemy, either from a dread of the punishment which they were conscious their disobedience deserved, and would on some favorable opportunity be inflicted on them, or to be revenged for the oppressions they had undergone.[39]

Thus Du Chambon's belief that some of his troops might desert to the banner of the invaders if given an opportunity, his general lack of military sense, his very real fear, and his lack of leadership qualities all combined to prevent him from implementing Morpain's or

De La Boularderie's plan. It is inconceivable that Du Chambon was of the opinion the small force of soldiers and civilians that he had sent to Gabarus on May 9 was sufficient to turn back the invaders.

Immediately on anchoring, Pepperrell ordered the launching of the whaleboats that were to carry his shock-troops. Then the rope-ladders were flung down and the troops clambered into the bobbing whaleboats. Gabarus Bay was no longer placid—"by 11 o'clock the Surffs Ran high which Made it Dificult Landing etc."[40] Colonel John Gorham, who had played such an important role in the successful defence of Annapolis Royal during the previous year, was in charge of the assault landing. After leaving Annapolis in January 1745, Gorham had taken it upon himself to raise a company of Indian Rangers for the Louisbourg expedition. In the late morning of May 11 these Rangers under Gorham led the first assault on Flat Point Cove.[41]

It was a simple offensive thrust. The whaleboats were rowed through the choppy Gabarus waters "but coming near to ye shore found it impracticable"[42] to land. They found it "impracticable" because of the unexpected presence of French troops in the Flat Point Cove region—the twenty troops that had been sent there on foot by Du Chambon two days earlier. Daccarrette's naval force, on seeing the New England fleet moving into Gabarus Bay, had fled to Fourchu Bay, to the southwest, where they abandoned their vessel and began to trek back overland to Louisbourg.[43]

One anonymous New England volunteer was certain that had the force "Landed where they Expected, and where wee at first made an Attempt wee Should Almost Certainly Susstain'd the Loss of A great Many men."[44] Seeing that his troops had been unable to land at Flat Point Cove, Pepperrell decided to use the unsuccessful assault as a feint and instead land his men at Kennington Cove.[45] Such an improvisation would give the impression at least that he had conscientiously endeavoured to follow Shirley's instructions—the chronology of events was of little consequence. Shirley had written to Pepperrell:

> But if you should meet with opposition, and the landing be disputed, or difficult, you must then make a false descent, in order to draw off the enemy from the spot, designed for landing, or at least to divide their force.[46]

The whaleboats were rowed back to the anchored ships and "joined another Party of Boats"[47] and under cover of the cannon-fire of the *Lord Montague, Boston Packet* and the *Massachusetts*, the flotilla of whaleboats moved in the direction of Kennington Cove.[48] It was a race between the whaleboats and the Frenchmen on shore for the gently sloping beach that extended for almost a third of a mile, the long stretch of sand "being broken only in the middle by a promontory of tumbled rock."[49] The New Englanders easily won the race. One of them described the course of events thus:

> [the feint] diverted the Enemy from proceeding further till they saw the Boats put back and row up the Bay, and by this Means some of the Troops landed and drew up on the Beach before the Enemy got to the place of their Landing—When about 100 of our men were on Shoar, part of them marchd towards the Enemy, and Scouts were ordered to to [sic] search the neighbouring Thicketts—lest a large Body of the Enemy might have Sallied, and concealed themselves, in order to draw on our men too hastily—in the mean time the men continued landing with all the Dispatch possible.[50]

Circumstantial evidence suggests that the Frenchmen who had turned back the assault upon Flat Point Cove, on seeing the New Englanders firmly in control of Kennington Cove retreated precipitately into the neighbouring woods. They returned to Louisbourg late in the evening of May 11.[51]

While the New Englanders were beginning to wade ashore at Kennington Cove, Du Chambon, after some two hours of heated debate with Morpain and De La Boularderie, finally decided to send a small detachment of troops to Gabarus Bay.[52] Of course Du Chambon was not aware of the fact that the New Englanders had already established a beachhead at Kennington Cove. If he had known this, it is highly unlikely that he would have sent any men to the general region of Gabarus Bay.

As might be expected the governor selected the popular Morpain to lead the expedition. He was to be assisted by De La Boularderie and the governor's youngest son, Mesillac.[53] Some eighty men,[54] including only twenty-four "colonial regulars,"[55] joined Morpain. Du Chambon stubbornly refused to send any more soldiers—perhaps he could only trust twenty-four—and he severely limited the number of civilian volunteers who wished to accompany their hero Morpain.[56]

After coming within sight of Kennington Cove, De La Boularderie realized that a considerable number of New Englanders were already ashore; he estimated that at least 1,500 men had landed. Consequently the veteran of the Richelieu Regiment urged Morpain to return immediately to Louisbourg. De La Boularderie argued "that it was useless to attack such a superior force, that they had missed their opportunity, and that they could not stop the English from laying siege to Louisbourg." Morpain curtly replied: "It does not matter, let us march on."[57] On seeing Morpain's force "advancing along the Shoar,"[58] the captains of the *Lord Montague*, *Boston Packet*, and the *Massachusetts* "Play'd with Great Guns"[59] at the onrushing French. It was estimated by the New Englanders that there were at least 200 men in Morpain's detachment.[60]

To counter the bombardment from the New England vessels, the unorthodox Morpain ordered his men into single-file at "fifteen paces apart to evade enemy fire." While the New England ships fired at the oncoming French, the exasperated De La Boularderie thundered at Morpain! "Order the troops to halt in order to reorganize; you know nothing about land warfare as I know nothing about naval tactics." De La Boularderie demanded that Morpain order a retreat in the classic drill-book style. The New Englanders were almost within gunshot and De La Boularderie was certain that unless there was "an honourable retreat"[61] the French force would be annihilated. But Morpain refused to listen to his distraught second-in-command and instead led his men into the midst of the invaders.

"Though under the Advantage of being covered with their Woods,"[62] Morpain's force, once it came within range of New England muskets, received "a violent fire."[63] Seeing some of his men writhing in pain, Morpain ordered his force to flee to the woods. It was every man for himself. But De La Boularderie refused to obey the command. Instead, while New Englanders "kept popping"[64] at the remaining French, De La Boularderie shouted at Morpain:

> Morpain, you made a stupid blunder, it is useless to retreat in
> complete disorder, it is dishonourable; this place where we
> stand is our grave.

Morpain showed his disdain for De La Boularderie by shouting "Everyman for himself!" While Morpain ran into the woods, protected by two of his faithful Negro slaves, De La Boularderie stood his ground "with my twelve brave Soldiers." Some of these men were killed, while others even though wounded were able to return to Louisbourg. Realizing the futility of battling against such tremendous odds, "without one hope of being rescued," De La Boularderie arrogantly threw "the sword into the midst of the enemy."[65] He became a prisoner-of-war.

The New Englanders had expected much tougher opposition. One observed in his journal: "we had But a Small Schurmidg To what we Expected."[66] Another laconically noted: "immediately at-

tacking them after the first fire they flee precipitantly away."[67] The
New Englanders had won an easy victory. Not one had been killed
or seriously wounded or captured in the brief exchange, while "six
or seven"[68] Frenchmen had been killed, six or seven taken prisoner,
and a large number wounded. It is not surprising therefore that
many New Englanders on the evening of May 11 fell on their knees
to thank their God for the "contemptible Opposition"[69] of the
French. This first taste of warfare had a great sobering impact on
many of the New England volunteers. Lieutenant Daniel Giddings
of Ipswich, Massachusetts, wrote in his journal on May 11:

> ...as the Lord ordered it, We mett them Beat them Back
> Killed Some Capituated others of them; & but one or two of
> our men Slitely wounded: as I passed by a Dead man Tho an
> Enemy it Shewed me my frailty.[70]

Theophilus Woodbridge of Connecticut observed in a letter:

> ...you would Think [it] is an awful thing to See men wounded
> and wollowing in their one blud and breething oute their
> Last breths which I was present my Self in the Action I
> thought att first that it was Very Awfull.[71]

While some New Englanders eagerly pursued the fleeing
French "as dogs hunt foxes in ye woods,"[72] others began to look for
plunder. There was absolutely no discipline in the New England
ranks and the volunteers were free to roam wherever they pleased.[73]
Pepperrell was apparently content to see his troops dashing off in
all directions, since he refused to exert his authority on land but instead remained on one of the transports in Gabarus Bay. He was accompanied by most of his senior officers.

By the early afternoon a large contingent of New Englanders
was within one mile and a quarter of the western ramparts of the
fortress.[74] Here they were sighted by the French gunners who immediately began to fire upon the invaders. One of the New Englanders reported the incident in his journal:

> wee had a fair View of it [Louisbourg]. The french Shot att
> Us Several times, one of the Balls wee took Up while it was a
> roalling (wee Judg'd it to be a A 24 Pounder).[75]

The New Englanders observed that the French were strengthening
the weak and exposed eastern extremity of the wall by planting a
row of pickets and at least one volunteer maintained that they also
had placed "a great Number of Swivel Guns upon the Wall next to
the Harbour."[76] The French hoped that these guns would effectively protect the southeastern corner of the fortress from a possible
land assault. In addition, the New Englanders saw the French put

to the torch some of the houses located between the Dauphin or West Gate—the western extremity of the fortress—and the salt pond called the *Barachois*.[77] Some potential cover for the attackers was thus removed. Moreover, in order to clear the harbour some French ships were sunk at their moorings.[78]

With the New England invaders within cannon-shot, Du Chambon at four o'clock ordered all the gates leading into the fortress closed.[79] All the French inhabitants unlucky enough not to be within the walls by that hour were expected by the governor to find safety and shelter in the Grand Battery. Next, Du Chambon ordered all able-bodied civilians to take their places in order to assist the regulars in the defence of Louisbourg.[80] The governor did not know what to expect from the New England invaders.

He had little to fear in the late afternoon and evening of May 11. Most of the New Englanders had encamped "Within Cannon Shot of ye Syty."[81] But they were not interested in carrying out a night attack upon the French fortress. They were far more concerned with roasting huge chunks of beef from the French cattle they had killed[82] and in reminiscing about their first whiff of warfare. The beef was washed down with liquor and by nightfall "There was Singing and Great Rejoicing."[83] The sounds of celebration were clearly heard by the frightened and morose Louisbourg inhabitants. Eventually the New Englanders went to sleep:

> ...wee Lay this Night in the open air—But wee Cut a few boughs to keep Us from the ground. Vastly the most Comfortable Nights Lodging This! Since I left Boston...wee should be Carefull to Rejoice in the Lord which has Done all for Us. It was a Very pleasent Evening it was the first time [we] heard any froggs Peep or Birds Sing for there was none at Canso.[84]

There was a great deal for which the New Englanders could be thankful. By the evening of May 11 some 2,000 of them were ashore within cannon-shot of Louisbourg. Not one New Englander had been killed or seriously wounded in the assault landing. Success bred confidence. One New England balladier expressed this confidence thus:

> St. Georges Colours we did hoist upon the land so high,
> Which caused the French Foes to look upon us very Shy,
> They being so much in Surprize and in such a dismal Fright,
> That they never dar'd to Sally out to give us a Field Fight.[85]

8

The Taking of
the Grand Battery

DURING THE EARLY HOURS of May 11, while many of the New England troops were boisterously celebrating within cannon-shot of Louisbourg, Du Chambon received a brief note from the commanding officer of the Grand Battery, Chassin de Thierry. It was blunt and to the point. De Thierry informed the governor that since it was virtually impossible to defend the Grand Battery from any concerted land assault, the Battery should be blown up after the cannon had been properly spiked and the 200 soldiers and civilians responsible for the Battery's defence had been evacuated.[1]

De Thierry's decision was easily arrived at, dictated by what he considered to be simple common sense. How could 200 men successfully resist a land assault when the land defences of the Grand Battery seemed totally inadequate? The outer defences—the crescent of the palisades and the covered way—had been permitted to crumble into uselessness.[2] The inner defence works, a loopholed wall of masonry flanked by two towers, were also crumbling and badly in need of refacing.[3] Even so, the masonry wall would have withstood considerable bombardment and even without the protection of the outer defences the swivel guns in the towers would have played havoc with any invading land force. The virtual non-existence of the outer defences and the general decay of the inner masonry wall were therefore insufficient reasons in themselves for de Thierry's urgent plea for the immediate destruction of the Grand Battery. What especially concerned de Thierry was that at the eastern landward extremity of the Battery "there were two breaches which had never been repaired."[4] Du Quesnel had been responsible for these breaches in the inner wall, since he had rear-ranged the cannon in that area of the Battery.[5] When he died in 1744 the walls were still down.

The British and New England prisoners who had been sent from Louisbourg to Boston in the latter part of 1744 were there-fore quite accurate in their description of the "low part of the wall [of the Grand Battery] that is unfinished at the east end."[6] In actual fact, John Bradstreet was so confident the Battery was indefensible from any large-scale land attack that he had persuaded Shirley to order the casting of "a number of 42 pound Shott."[7] This shot was far too large for the expedition's heaviest siege cannon, a 22-pounder. But it would fit perfectly the "Twenty-Eight Cannon of Forty-two Pound Shot"[8] to be found in the Grand Battery. These French 42-pounders, together with two 18-pounders also to be found in the Grand Battery, would of course strengthen considera-bly the largely inadequate siege ordnance of the expedition.[9]

It should be emphasized that Pepperrell had only eight 22-pounders, ten 18-pounders, twelve 9-pounders and four small mor-tars at his disposal.[10] Most of these "(the 10 guns of 18 lb. shot...from New-York excepted) were bad, old, and honey-combed."[11] Bradstreet's audacity, aptly criticized by one contempo-rary New Englander as "too manifest a disposal of the skin before the bear was caught,"[12] was therefore solidly based upon practical strategic considerations.

Du Quesnel's successor, Du Chambon, was not particularly concerned about the gaping holes in the masonry wall or about the sad state of the outer defence crescent. Until the unexpected land-ing of the New England troops he had refused to believe that Louisbourg and the Grand Battery would ever be attacked from the land side. De Thierry's request came as no surprise to Du Chambon, who was fully aware of the Battery's weak landward de-fences. But the governor was unable to consider de Thierry's rec-ommendation in a dispassionate manner. Du Chambon, like de Thierry and the majority of inhabitants in Louisbourg, was terri-fied. He saw New Englanders taking "possession of the surround-ing country;"[13] he saw a powerful blockading fleet at the mouth of the harbour. And then he examined his own military resources. He had 590 soldiers and some 900 civilians to defend the fortress of Louisbourg, the Island Battery, and the Grand Battery.[14] How many of the soldiers would remain loyal he could not say; Du Chambon could not forget the December mutiny.

Gripped by a kind of "panic fear,"[15] Du Chambon called a council of war to discuss the contents of de Thierry's letter.[16] The ensuing debate was described as being "tumultuous."[17] Apparently all of the officers present, except for the engineer Verrier, advocated the swift implementation of de Thierry's recommendation.[18] The advocates of the destruction of the Grand Battery were led by Du Chambon and Bigot. But Verrier refused to be intimidated and he refused to accept de Thierry's plan. He vehemently argued that there was a good chance the siege would be lifted. If the Grand Battery were demolished, it would have to be reconstructed by the French, since all agreed that it was indispensable for the successful naval defence of Louisbourg.[19] He agreed with the others present that the New Englanders, estimated to number 6,000, would easily capture the Grand Battery at the first opportunity.[20] It was therefore essential for the 200 soldiers and civilians in the Grand Battery to reinforce the relatively tiny French force in Louisbourg and the Island Battery. It would be foolish to sacrifice 200 French lives in a hopeless cause. Verrier therefore appealed to the council to accept a compromise. The men from the Battery were to be withdrawn as soon as the cannon were properly spiked. Verrier's compromise was quickly accepted by all those present.[21]

Sometime before midnight on May 11, de Thierry received a note from Du Chambon. Du Chambon was far more brief than de Thierry had been in his note to the governor. Du Chambon wrote:

> Mr. Thiery, Commander of the Royal Battery, is ordered to abandon the said Battery after having spiked the cannon and after having removed as much food and military supplies as possible to Louisbourg.[22]

On receiving Du Chambon's letter, de Thierry ordered that the cannon be immediately spiked. His frightened troops, anticipating an imminent attack, rushed about in the darkness hammering steel rods into the touch holes. Most of the trunnions were left untouched and nothing was done to destroy the carriages.[23] The spiking of the cannon took very little time, for at about midnight de Thierry and his troops arrived at Louisbourg with only a small portion "of food and military supplies."[24] The civilians who remained in the Grand Battery were expected to collect and to transport to Louisbourg as quickly as possible the remaining ammunition, powder and food supplies. But the precipitate flight of de Thierry and his troops was no inspiration to the remaining civilians, who were just as eager to escape to Louisbourg. They considered their lives to be far more important than gunpowder, shells or cannon balls.

Not everyone in Louisbourg was pleased with Du Chambon's

decision to abandon the Grand Battery. The "Habitant de Louis-bourg" caustically observed:

> From this moment [late on May 11] the talk was of abandon-ing the splendid battery, which would have been our chief defence had we known how to make use of it. Several tumul-tuous councils were held to consider the situation. Unless it was from a panic fear which never left us again during the whole siege, it would be difficult to give any reason for such an extraordinary action. Not a single musket had yet been fired against this battery, which the enemy could not take ex-cept by making approaches in the same manner as to the town and besieging it, so to speak, in the regular way.... The alleged reason for such a criminal withdrawal is that there were two breaches which had never been repaired. If this is true the crime is all the greater, for we had had even more time than was necessary to put everything in order.
>
> However this may be, the resolution was taken to aban-don this powerful bulwark, in spite of the protestations of some wiser heads, who lamented to see such a stupid mistake made. They could get no hearers. In vain did they urge that we should thus proclaim our weakness to the enemy, who would not fail to profit by such huge recklessness, and would turn this very battery against us; that, to show a bold face and not reinforce the courage of the enemy by giving him from the first day such good hope of success, it was necessary to do all that we could to hold this important post; that it was quite clear that we could hold it for more than fifteen days, and that this delay could be utilized by removing all the cannon to the town.[25]

In many respects the "Habitant" was undoubtedly right. The breaches in the wall could at least have been temporarily plugged; and a rear-guard action could have been fought from the Grand Battery until it was absolutely imperative to abandon it. By that time the cannon could have been either carried off by boat to Louisbourg or else properly spiked, the trunnions removed, and the carriages destroyed. Moreover, and of considerable impor-tance, the Grand Battery could have been used as the centre for sallies against the besieging New Englanders.[26] But unfortunately for the "wiser heads" they lacked a leader; he was hiding in the woods with his two Negro slaves. Morpain was unquestionably the only man capable of persuading the council of war to reject de Thierry's recommendation.[27] Morpain stood head and shoulders above the inexperienced Louisbourg officers. He was the only man with any real military experience, and he appeared to be the only Frenchman in the Louisbourg area able and willing to take the offensive initiative against the invaders. Without Morpain to badger and to inspire them, the frightened Louisbourg officers eagerly took what they considered to be the easy way out of their dilemma.

Soon after it was light on the following morning, May 12, Pepperrell ordered the landing of the rest of his men and their supplies and he accompanied the troops ashore.[28] However, "the Surff running very high on the Beach almost contenually"[29] made landing very difficult. The troops were therefore forced:

> ...to wade into the Water, to their Middles and often higher, for almost every thing they got on Shoar which would other wise have been spoild with the Salt water.—and were obliged when their Labour was over to lay on the Cold Ground in their Wet Cloaths under no better covering than some Boughs laid together.[30]

In spite of these adverse conditions, the landing troops, in one volunteer's words, showed "no Signs of Discouragement or Complaint" but rather "seemed resolved to surmount all Difficulties."[31] Another New Englander noted:

> Our Men seemed spirited with a flaming Zeal for the Reduction of the Place, and can hardly be kept from running into the very Mouth of their Cannon.[32]

On landing, Pepperrell was either unwilling or unable to enforce any discipline upon his troops. The marauding and looting of the previous day had only whetted the appetites of his men. One anonymous New Englander wrote in his journal on May 13.

> Many of the Army Went Up towards the Grand Battery to Plunder (and Indeed! we fill'd the Country for as Yet, wee had no Particular Orders,—But Everyone Did what was Right in his own Eyes) Among which I was one.[33]

Another anonymous volunteer observed in his journal on May 13:

> This We Kild Several Cows and Took Several More—Som horses Sheeps and other Sutable things for our Casses rum Wine Mollasses Sider But these Thing Was son Scejrse Again.[34]

On the same day Benjamin Cleaves' marauding group "Took about 12 men & 2 horses and 5 Cows,"[35] while on May 12 and 13 Benjamin Stearns' friends captured "several cows and horses and some plunder, viz., some pots, some kettles, some gridirons—some one thing and some another, and burnt several houses."[36]

However, not all of Pepperrell's troops were plundering, burning French homes and killing innocent French inhabitants. A few, but apparently only a few, spent the day at "the sea side" where they were "drawn up & Exercised."[37] Late in the day, Pepperrell ordered the indomitable William Vaughan to lead "A detachment of 4 or 500 men"[38] to the northeastern part of Louisbourg harbour "to seize upon all Vessels, Men or Cattle that could be found beyond the Grand Battery."[39] It was to be a night assault.

While Pepperrell was finding his land legs and while many of his troops were rushing off in search of plunder and excitement, the French continued to transport their supplies from the Grand Battery to Louisbourg.[40] Special emphasis was placed upon the moving of food supplies and of gunpowder. Some careless individual was responsible for the explosion of a large barrel of gunpowder, an explosion that "nearly blew up several persons, and burnt the robe of a Récollet friar."[41] While the supplies were being moved, the French cannon in Louisbourg thundered at various curious New Englanders who had carelessly wandered within range of the fortress walls.[42]

By sunset, the French had withdrawn all of their food supplies and most of their gunpowder, but only a few of their cannon balls and shells from the Grand Battery. They had also burned a number of vessels in the harbour "in order to prevent the enemy from using them."[43] Du Chambon apparently had decided to collect the shells and balls early the following morning. Furthermore, by sunset Du Chambon's ears were ringing with the bitter criticism of Morpain who had returned to the fortress sometime during the day. Morpain could not understand how any responsible military leader could have ordered the abandonment of the Grand Battery.[44] But it was too late to rectify the situation.

About midnight on May 12 Vaughan's force arrived at the settlement about one mile west of the Grand Battery.[45] By this time Vaughan had completely lost control of his men. They set ablaze sixteen homes and then put to the torch "Store-houses fill'd with Sails Cables and other Ship, Tackling, Many that were there Suppos'd what was Burnt was worth li 100,000."[46] Most of the men returned to the camp east of Flat Point Cove, carrying with them "some hund[d] quint[ls] of fish."[47] They arrived at about two in the morning, causing "A great tumult and Noise all this Night."[48] But Vaughan with twelve men spent the night within 400 yards of the Grand Battery to "discover the most commodious Place for erecting a counter Battery."[49]

With the coming of the dawn Vaughan and his party prepared

to retreat towards Gabarus Bay, having lost the protection of darkness. But just before withdrawing Vaughan observed that "the chimnies of the barrack were without smoke, and the staff without a flag."[50] Suspecting a French ruse, Vaughan offered one of his men, a Cape Cod or Connecticut Indian,[51] a bottle a brandy if he would crawl up to one of the embrasures and see whether the Battery was "deserted by the Enemy."[52] The Indian carefully crawled up to the masonry wall, hoisted himself through one of the breaches and waved frantically to Vaughan. The Grand Battery was indeed deserted!

New England Indians had played a significant role thus far in the Louisbourg expedition. They had acted as shock-troops in the Gabarus Bay landing and now one of them had singlehandedly captured the Grand Battery. However, after performing their services, the Indians were unceremoniously thrust aside by the New Englanders who assiduously sought the limelight of military glory.

After marching into the Grand Battery, Vaughan discovered that the French had left behind 350 "Shells of Thirteen Inches, and Thirty Shells of Ten Inches, with a large Quantity of Shot."[53] Seeing that there was no flag waving from the flagpole, William Tufts, an eighteen-year-old volunteer from Medford, Massachusetts, shinnied up the pole with his red coat clutched in his teeth. When he reached the top he triumphantly nailed his coat to the pole.[54] No British flag had ever looked better to the jubilant New Englanders. Vaughan promptly sent a messenger to Pepperrell with the following note:

> May it please your Honour, to be informed y^t with ye grace of God and ye courage of about thirteen men I entred place about nine a clock and am waiting here for a reinforcemt and flag.[55]

Before Pepperrell was able to respond to Vaughan's message, the latter sighted "seven large Boats full of Men coming from the City."[56] Pepperrell, who at this time was on "the West Hill near the town," also saw the French rowing off to the Grand Battery, but he noticed only "4 shalloways full of French."[57] Vaughan immediately took the offensive. With eight of his men (he left four behind to defend the Grand Battery) he set off westward along the shore to the nearest beach to oppose the landing of the French.[58] While hurrying to the possible landing area Vaughan's small force was joined by four New Englanders who had been out marauding and looting before breakfast. After a brief skirmish, the boats returned to Louisbourg "notwithstanding that the Cannon of the City (within point blank Shot) played incessantly on [Vaughan] & his small party."[59] While returning to the Grand Battery Vaughan found in one of the houses nearby "two English Ships Ensigns, which on his Return he hoisted on the said Grand Battery."[60] Young William Tufts reclaimed his coat.

Pepperrell was convinced that the French in the boats intended to recapture the Grand Battery.[61] He was wrong. They had been sent by Du Chambon to obtain the shells and cannon balls that remained. Furthermore, there is some evidence to suggest that they were also under orders to burn the buildings in the Battery.[62] Not only did Du Chambon send a considerable number of men to the Grand Battery on May 13, he also ordered:

> all the militia members with their axes and instruments to demolish the houses that stretched from the West Gate to the Barachois to obtain fuel for the garrison which had none of it, and to burn all those houses that they were unable to demolish in order to prevent the enemy from living in them.[63]

To protect the militia from possible attack, the governor dispatched eighty troops.[64]

Before this large force left the West Gate, Pepperrell had ordered Bradstreet to lead what remained of the disorganized First Massachusetts Regiment to reinforce Vaughan's handful of men.[65] At noon Bradstreet's troops marched off in the direction of Louisbourg.[66] A short time after they had departed from Flat Point Cove, Pepperrell received word that a large French force had left Louisbourg and was making its way overland towards the Grand Battery. Pepperrell therefore ordered Samuel Waldo and his Second Massachusetts Regiment "to march and reinforce Col Bradstreet and get the Enemy between two Fires or intercept them in their Retreat."[67] On discovering the vanguard of the New England troops the French immediately retreated. A few shots were exchanged, but only at long range, much to the disgust of Waldo.[68]

When Bradstreet entered the Grand Battery he was relieved to see the cannon still in their embrazures, even though they were spiked. His gamble had paid off. Not only had he persuaded Shirley to send 42-pound cannon balls to fit the Grand Battery cannon, but he had also persuaded the governor to provide "proper Workmen and Tools for Drilling them out."[69] Bradstreet informed Pepperrell:

> I find the Grand Batery in but a bad condition, but not withstanding we can soon repair it as well as ever. I beg you'l send the smiths & armerores as soon as possible to drill open the

vents of the cannon. We shall want hanspicks, ramers &
spunges & a quantity of powder; ball we have a great quantity,
& shells of all sorts.... We may have four 42 pounders ready to
play on the town by to-morrow by 12 o'clock, if the above
things are sent express hast.[70]

Pepperrell duly sent the gunsmiths and supplies "express hast" to
Bradstreet. There were "above twenty smiths"[71] and they were
placed under the direct command of the experienced gunsmith
Seth Pomeroy. By ten o'clock of the following morning one 42-
pounder had been drilled and had already fired its first ball against
Louisbourg.[72] The "Habitant de Louisbourg" sadly noted: "From
the fourteenth the enemy greeted us with our own cannon, and
kept up a tremendous fire against us."[73]

It is not surprising, after the unexpected capture of the Grand
Battery, to find a New England volunteer rejoicing that "Providence seems to smile on us in every Shape."[74] The New Englanders
were convinced that the burning of the storehouses west of the
Grand Battery, causing "such a thick smoak, that the garrison were
unable to discover an enemy,"[75] was responsible for the precipitate
evacuation of the Battery. It was taken as an unmistakable sign that
the Almighty was continuing to lead the New Englanders against
"Babylon the Great."[76] Unquestionably, therefore, the easy capture
of the Grand Battery "proved a mighty Encouragement and Advantage"[77] to the inexperienced invaders. If instead of simply handing
the formidable Battery with its cannon, shot and shell to the enemy, Du Chambon had used the Battery to launch offensive thrusts
against the undisciplined New Englanders, the New England offensive against Louisbourg would have been delayed.[78] It is clear that
any large-scale assault against the New Englanders which resulted
in heavy New England casualties would have severely undermined
the morale of the invaders. But by refusing to confront the New
Englanders at the beginning of the siege, Du Chambon was responsible for building up their confidence. It can be argued that Du
Chambon's arms were tied because he could not trust his troops after the mutiny of the previous December. But it is interesting to
note that he felt safe in sending out over eighty soldiers on May 13,
many of whom were Swiss. If they were keen on deserting, surely
they would have deserted while their fellows were hastily retreating
to Louisbourg. But they showed no disposition to join the invaders.

It was unfortunate for the French cause in North America that
at a moment of very real crisis Cape Breton had an incompetent
governor. Du Chambon lacked all the necessary qualities of a suc-

cessful military leader. He was inexperienced, frightened, and unable and unwilling to inspire his men. He had the unhappy knack of doing the wrong thing in the wrong way at the wrong time. There was no reasonable justification for his encouraging such a precipitate abandonment of the Grand Battery.

9

Siege Preliminaries
(May 14-20, 1745)

IT WAS A COMMON SAYING in military circles in western Europe that *"Ville assiegée par Vauban, ville prise; ville fortifiée par Vauban, Ville imprenable."*[1] Although the fortifications of Louisbourg had not been planned by the famous French military engineer Vauban himself, but by some of his faithful disciples, in most respects Louisbourg was a *"ville fortifiée par Vauban"* according to his first system. It was unfortunate for the French in Louisbourg that Pepperell's troops were ignorant of Vauban's European reputation. Had they known, it is highly unlikely that they would have volunteered to join the expedition.

Many of the New Englanders thoroughly enjoyed their ignorance, carrying out the siege, especially the siege preliminaries, "in a tumultuary random manner, [that] resembled a Cambridge commencement."[2] Jeremy Belknap described the unusual carnival atmosphere thus:

> Those who were on the spot, have frequently in my hearing, laughed at the recital of their own irregularities, and expressed their admiration when they reflected on the almost

miraculous preservation of the army from destruction. They indeed presented a formidable front to the enemy; but the rear was a scene of confusion and frolic. While some were on duty...others were racing, wrestling, pitching quoits, firing at marks or at birds, or running after shot from the enemy's guns, for which they received a bounty.[3]

It appears that the firing of the first drilled-out 42-pounder from the Grand Battery on May 14 only added to the carnival air. It was a display of fireworks that most of the invaders and the besieged would never forget. The New Englanders fired forty shot towards Louisbourg, receiving in return from the French in the town and in the Island Battery 146 shot and fifty shells.[4] Fortunately for the New Englanders in the Grand Battery, the French cannon-balls did little significant damage while most of the French shells did not even explode. "They have either gott upon a vein of Parson Pain's hollow ware or their powder is badd,"[5] Brigadier-General Samuel Waldo, the commanding officer of the Grand Battery, explained to Pepperell.

The following day, May 15, Seth Pomeroy and his team of gunsmiths drilled out two more 42-pounders and these were also fired against the French in Louisbourg.[6] Only four of the guns in the Grand Battery had their embrazures facing in the general direction of Louisbourg; the others commanded the harbour mouth and the northeast section of the harbour.[7] With their three cannon, the New Englanders, like a group of schoolboys with a new toy, enthusiastically fired 115 shot towards Louisbourg.[8] But because of poor marksmanship "Many [balls] Struck on the water 40 rods from the Citty."[9] The cannon were not aimed at the walls of the fortress or at any special target; they were merely aimed in the general direction of Louisbourg, and if the shot fell within the town the gunners were almost ecstatic and the many New England spectators jubilant.[10] The spirit of the New Englanders was admirably captured in the following verse:

> The wide mouth'd Cannon, with their heavy Balls,
> And strength of Power, scale the City Walls,
> Like thunders roaring & the lightning bright,
> Do Execution, both by Day and Night.[11]

In spite of the fact that it has been argued that some twenty of the New England volunteers "were or had been members of the Ancient and Honorable Artillery Company of Boston,"[12] experienced gunners were almost as scarce as experienced siege officers. Undoubtedly, most of the twenty members of the Ancient and

Honorable Company had either learned nothing about artillery or had forgotten what they had once been taught.

While the Grand Battery cannon were bombarding Lousbourg on May 14 and 15 and being bombarded in turn by the French, Pepperrell was in the vicinity of Landing Cove Brook, endeavouring to deal with at least four major problems. Three of these problems were discussed in some detail in Shirley's instructions, but the fourth was not even alluded to. It is interesting to note that Pepperrell attempted to deal with only those problems referred to in his instructions. The problem not referred to in his instructions concerned what Waldo called "our Morrodery." Waldo was convinced that:

> ...what they pillage is not of so much Consequence as their being so disorderly, and having now gotten a taste for private Plunder it may be fatall, should we have the opportunity to enter the City.[13]

Pepperrell agreed with Waldo's observations when he wrote to Warren on May 15 that "The unaccountable irregular behaviour of these fellows & of some maroders is the greatest fatigue I meet with."[14] Pepperrell hoped that he would be able "to reduce them to a better discipline soon."[15] Pepperrell may have hoped hard, but he refused to take the initiative and enforce discipline upon his troops. He apparently feared that such a policy would alienate a large number of his troops, whom Warren perceptively described as having:

> ...the highest notions of the Rights, and Liberties of Englismen, and indeed are almost Levellers, they must...be treated in a manner that few Military Bred Gentlemen would condecend to.[16]

Because Pepperrell preferred to give his troops considerable freedom, in spite of the evil consequences, Waldo discovered on May 14 that "Three fourths of the forces [at the Grand Battery]...are partly employed in speculation on the neighbouring hills & partly in ravaging the country."[17] Since he had only some 100 troops to defend the Grand Battery, Waldo was of the opinion that a force of 200 Frenchmen could easily have captured the Battery on the 14th or 15th.[18] But in spite of Waldo's cries of alarm, Pepperrell was content to assure Waldo that something would be done eventually. In fact nothing was done during the period of the siege preliminaries or even later. Pepperrell sent what he hoped would be sufficient quantities of rum and powder to Waldo and expected these supplies to assuage his colleague's fears.[19]

Of the remaining three problems the carrying out of a regular siege was by far the most important. Nevertheless, Pepperrell was compelled to do something about Shirley's instructions to destroy all the French fishing settlements to the north of Louisbourg and also to "secure a proper spot to encamp them [the troops] on; which must be as nigh as possible to some convenient brook, or watering place."[20]

After being tactfully prodded by Warren early on May 15 to agree to the sending of some of the New England vessels "to look out to the northward, and to have destroy'd all the fishing houses,"[21] Pepperrell gave his consent.[22] Consequently, at six in the afternoon the *Massachusetts*, the *Fame*, the *Prince of Orange* and a schooner, were ordered to join the 40-gun *Eltham* "on a Cruize...round Cape Breton on the East End."[23] The chaplain of the Connecticut fleet, the Reverend Adonijah Bidwell, took part in the expedition and described in some detail the systematic destruction of the French fishing villages:

> May [17] In ye morning we anchored at ye south end of this large bay,...St. Anns Bay. In ye afternoon we sailed several miles up the bay to a narrow Strait there were several houses on the east side.... We anchored and several men went on shore.
>
> May [18] This day ye men ransacked ye town & woods, burnt ye town of about 20 houses & about ye same number of shallops, took 12 or 15 Feather Beds, 3 or 4 cases with bottles, Chests with Cloths, Iron Pots, Brass Kittles, Candlesticks, Frying Pans, Pewter Plates & Spoons etc. took one prisoner....
>
> May [20] Two boyes went on shore up Angonish Bay & burnt a Town of about 80 houses which stood up that bay, about noon stear'd for Louisbourg.[24]

As he had been instructed by Shirley, Pepperrell had devastated the French cod fishery "without running too great risk."[25] This policy had no bearing upon Pepperrell's siege preparations. However, it would satisfy many of the New England fishing magnates if the siege of Louisbourg should fail.

By May 14 those troops who were not at the Grand Battery or marauding in the interior were encamped on both sides of the Landing Cove Brook. Here provisions, cannon and ammunition were landed in "the Extraordinary Surf of the Sea Common to this Shoor."[26] The New Englanders were not regularly encamped, "but stretch'd [them]selves about a mile in Length, and built little Hutts to shelter [them]selves from the weather."[27] These "Hutts" were made of either turf and branches or of sailcloth, since proper tents were unavailable.[28] Being faithful to his instructions and afraid of a night assault by the enemy, Pepperrell ordered his troops to encamp regularly on both sides of the Landing Cove Brook.[29] This site was also destined to be the location for Amherst's camp during the siege of 1758. Pepperrell did not feel it was necessary at first to put up proper lines about his camp. He was content to depend upon his "Scouts and Guards"[30] to protect the camp from a French night assault. Pepperrell thus had a camp with an abundant fresh water supply at a safe distance from the French cannon and excellently located for supplies. However, most of his troops were over two miles away from the West Gate which Shirley considered to be the most vulnerable section of Louisbourg's fortifications. "The wall there is weak, and a breach may be made,"[31] Shirley had informed Pepperrell on March 30. Taking everything into consideration, the advantages of encamping on both sides of the Landing Cove Brook outweighed the disadvantages. Pepperrell deserves some credit for making this not insignificant decision.

Without question the most urgent and challenging problem confronting Pepperrell on May 14 and 15 was that of carrying out actual siege operations against Louisbourg. His instructions from Shirley were surprisingly specific and probably clearly reflected Bradstreet's strategic thinking. Pepperrell was instructed to launch a three-pronged siege offensive once the Grand Battery was captured and his troops were in a position to implement his commands. First, the Island Battery was to be attacked at night by 300 men in whaleboats, who were to land "in a little well-known beachy Cove at the southeasterly point, just within the breaking point of the rocks." Although not spelled out in the instructions, such a move was intended not only to keep out any French supply ship or warships but also to enable New England and British vessels to enter the harbour. Second, on "a rocky hill...a large half-mile" southwest from the King's Bastion, Pepperrell was to build a battery that would be "continually employed endeavouring principally to demolish their magazine, citadel, walls, etc.," as well as covering the movement of the New England troops to and from the Grand Battery and other possible batteries. Finally, a small battery was to be built immediately to the west of the West Gate of the fortress.[32]

On May 14, Pepperrell's council of war had met for the first time on the island of Cape Breton. There were eleven officers present—Major General Roger Wolcott, Colonel Joseph Dwight and Lieutenant Richard Gridley of the Train of Artillery, Lieutenant-Colonel John Storer of the First Massachusetts Regiment, Colonel Samuel Willard, Lieutenant-Colonel Thomas Chandler of the Fourth Massachusetts Regiment, Colonel Robert Hall of the Fifth Massachusetts Regiment, Lieutenant-Colonel John Gorham of the Seventh Massachusetts Regiment, Colonel Andrew Burr and Lieutenant-Colonel Simon Lathrop of the Connecticut Regiment, and Colonel Sylvester Richmond of the Sixth Massachusetts Regiment.[33] Bradstreet, Waldo and Vaughan, the most influential officers, were not present; they were too busy at the Grand Battery. There was no question of not carrying out Shirley's three-pronged siege offensive, but Pepperrell asked the council to give serious consideration as to "whether there should be sent to the commanding officer at Louisbourg a summons to surrender up that place."[34] Pepperrell wanted the summons to be sent immediately. Three was only the slightest possibility, of course, that it would be accepted by Du Chambon. But as long as there was at least a slight possibility, Pepperrell was eager to take the easy way out. And who was to blame him? Why sacrifice needless lives and considerable energy, when the French might be easily persuaded to surrender? But the council refused to act upon Pepperrell's proposal until after Waldo and Bradstreet had an opportunity to comment upon it. Until then, the council was apparently content to see a battery constructed upon the Green Hill—Shirley's "rocky hill."

When late in the afternoon of May 14 Waldo and Bradstreet heard of Pepperrell's proposal, they were furious with indignation. Waldo immediately wrote Pepperrell:

> ...the Gov' of Louisbourg would give a very ready answer to a sumons for surrender by hanging up the messenger thereof, unless we had made a more formidable gen¹ appearance than we have been yet able to make.[35]

He urged his commanding officer to build the Green Hill Battery and other batteries before organizing any attack upon the Island Battery and before sending any summons to Du Chambon.[36] After receiving Waldo's letter late on May 14, Pepperrell found himself on the horns of a dilemma. Waldo and Bradstreet were not only against sending a summons to Du Chambon, they were also advocating the indefinite postponement of the Island Battery assault. On the other hand, Pepperrell was being pressed by Warren[37] to strike against the Island Battery without a moment's hesitation, and by some of his own officers to demand the immediate surrender of Louisbourg. Since he believed that he could not arbitrarily disre-

gard the opinions of Warren as well as those of Waldo and Bradstreet, Pepperrell put forward a compromise plan. The surrender
of Louisbourg would not be demanded until after at least one new
battery could play upon the fortress. In addition, Warren was appeased with the promise that the Island Battery would be attacked
at "the first favourable opportunity after the battering cannon and
mortars are ready to play on the town."[38]

By early on May 15, one 13-inch mortar and one 9-inch mortar
had been dragged for almost two miles through the heavy under-
brush and over jagged rocks to be put into position on the Green
Hill.[39] At a council of war held on the same day it was decided "that
the two nine pounders cannon and two of ye galloping pieces (fal-
conets)" be landed from the ships and transported to the Green
Hill Battery to support the mortars.[40] The Battery was indeed "a
large half mile" from the Citadel—it was at least 1,550 yards away.[41]
The mortars were carefully anchored and then the first shells "Like
blazing Comets in the open Skie"[42] arched towards the fortress. But
in spite of the laborious efforts of the gunners and the cheers of
some of the 500 troops set aside "to sustain this battery,"[43] the "Blazing Comets" fell far short of the fortress walls.[44] These small mortars
were totally inadequate as siege weapons at 1,550 yards.

Sunday, May 16, was no day of rest for either the New England
or the French forces. It was certainly a day of bustling activity for
the chaplains accompanying the New England troops. The Reverend John Newman, the Chaplain of Waldo's Regiment, preached
the first Protestant sermon in the Grand Battery. He selected for
his text Psalm 100, verses 4 and 5:

> Enter into his gates with thanksgiving,
>> and into his courts with praise;
> be thankful unto him, and bless his name.
> For the Lord is good: his mercy is everlasting;
>> and his truth endureth to all generations.[45]

Pepperrell's chaplain, the Reverend Elisha Williams, also preached
from the book of Psalms, chapter 108, verse 8: "It is better to trust
in the Lord y^n to put confidence in Princes."[46]

After the service at the Grand Battery some of those who had
listened to Newman's sermon began to doubt whether God's mer-
cy was everlasting, for a 42-pound cannon had burst and wounded
five men.[47] The cannon had been given a double charge by the inexperienced gunners in the hope that the shot would carry farther
and with greater velocity.[48]

This loss of one of the 42-pounders was the least of Pepperrell's worries on May 16. He had received a disconcerting letter from Warren in which the commodore proposed an elaborate "Plan, of Operation, for the Speedy Reduction of the Town."[49] Warren was annoyed by Pepperrell's procrastination with regard to the attack upon the Island Battery. He therefore proposed "to attack the Island Battery, as soon as possible, with all the Whale Boats and the Boats belonging to his Majesty's Ships, and the Private Ships of war, man'd, and arm'd." The attacking force was to consist of 500 of Pepperrell's troops and 200 or 300 men from Warren's vessels and those from New England. A New Englander appointed by Pepperrell was to be commander of the assault. Moreover, Warren urged Pepperrell:

> ...about an hour, or two before the attack, of the Island Battery, a feint was to be made, by the Troops, on shore,...as if they Intended, to storm the town, in Several places, it wou'd greatly take off the attention of the Enemy, from the Island Battery, and probably be the means of their drawing off some of their Troops from thence.

Warren promised Pepperrell that once the Island Battery was captured, his fleet would sail into Louisbourg harbour:

> When I propose to go in, I wou'd hoist a Red Flagg, at the Foretop Gallant Masthead, about an hour before that, all our Troops from the Royal Battery, except a proper number, to manage the Guns there, against the Enemy, shou'd march to joyn the General, and Army, who shou'd when I hoist the Red Flagg, attack the town, in such places as not to be annoy'd by the Shott, which our Ships shou'd fire, at the Enemys Batterys in the town.

The impatient naval officer emphasized that it was absolutely essential to "take some Vigorous measures, for the Sudden Reduction of Lewisbourg."[50]

Pepperrell's council of war met twice on Sunday to consider Warren's proposal. Finally, after much debate "The determination of Com[re] Warren's plan of operation was deferred till another opportunity."[51]

Why was the council unwilling to accept Warren's proposal? There are probably two main reasons for its decision. First, there is some evidence to suggest that a number of the officers resented being told what to do by a British naval officer. There was a certain amount of friction throughout the siege between the British seamen and Marines and the New England volunteers.[52] Second, and of the greater importance, a growing number of officers believed that the siege should be conducted at long range. They looked with scepticism upon any frontal attack scheme. And their enthusiasm for Pepperrell's original plan of demanding the immediate surrender of Louisbourg was revived by Warren's audacious proposal.

But Bradstreet and Waldo, who attended the council meetings on May 16, were able to keep this enthusiasm temporarily in check. The council decided to move the mortars from the Green Hill, since they "would not reach the city." They were to be moved to the "Rabasse height near the Barachois,"[53] some 600 yards nearer the west wall and within mortar shot of the King's Bastion. They would be supported by a number of 22-pound cannon. Furthermore, it was resolved "that a battery be thrown up near the West Gate as soon as May be."[54] Because of the extraordinary difficulties encountered in moving the mortars and cannon from the Flat Point landing place into the interior,[55] the council proposed that two 18-pounders and two 42-pounders from the Grand Battery be transported to the new battery. It was also felt that the *Lord Montague*, which carried the New York siege train, should try to sneak into Louisbourg harbour and land her precious cargo in the general vicinity of the proposed West Gate battery.[56]

When the council met on the following day, May 17, Warren was present. Colonel Jeremiah Moulton was also there for the first time, having returned the previous day with his detachment of troops after successfully carrying out his assault upon St. Peter's.[57] From the available evidence it is impossible to ascertain exactly what was said at the meeting. Nevertheless, Warren unquestionably exerted considerable influence upon those present. He was a very persuasive man and knew how to use charm and toughness to get what he wanted.[58] It was agreed to send a summons to Du Chambon to surrender the fortress, and that "in case the terms thereof shall not be comply'd with the town be attack'd by storm as soon as possible."[59] The summons was a strange document, the naive product of an unmilitary mind. Warren could only stare with disbelief at its text. The summons began:

> Whereas there is now encamped upon the island of Cape Breton near the city of Louisbourg a number of his Brittanic Majesty's troops under the command of the Hon[ble] Lieut-General Pepperrell, and also a squadron of his said Majesty's ships of war under the command of the Hon[ble] Peter Warren, Esq[r], is now lying before the harbour of said City, for the reduction thereof to the obedience of the Crown of Great Brittain, we the said William Pepperrell and Peter Warren, to prevent the

Siege Preliminaries

effusion of Christian blood, do in the name of our Sovereign Lord, George the Second, of Great Brittain, France, and Ireland, King, etc., summons you to surrender to his obedience the said city, fortresses, and territories, together with the artillery, arms and stores of war thereunto belonging. In consequence of which surrender, we the said William Pepperrell and Peter Warren in the name of our said Sovereign do assure you, that all the subjects of the French King now in said city and territories shall be treated with the utmost humanity, have their personal estates secured to them, and have leave to transport themselves and said effects to any part of the French King's dominions in Europe. Your answer hereto is demanded at or before five o'the clock this afternoon.[60]

Nevertheless, Warren was willing to swallow his military pride and sign the summons, since he was sure that it would be curtly rejected by Du Chambon. It was an indirect way of getting the New Englanders to accept his plan of striking against the Island Battery. It was decided to send the summons at eleven the following morning; it was to be carried by a Mr. Agnue, Warren's aide-de-camp.

While the decision was being made to send the summons, more cannon were being drilled out at the Grand Battery,[61] and Captain James Gibson with a force of almost 100 men was setting out from the same battery for a plundering expedition to "the North-East Harbour."[62] Of greater consequence, Lieutenant-Colonel Nathaniel Meserve, a ship-carpenter from New Hampshire, experienced in "masting and logging,"[63] discovered a means of transporting the cannon over the swampy and rocky land to the west of Louisbourg. He constructed sledges "of about Sixteen Feet in Length, and Five Feet in Wedth, and Twelve Inches thick."[64] On these sledges the cannon and mortars were placed and dragged by teams of hundreds of men, often under cover of darkness. The ropes used to pull the sledges burned into the hands of the New Englanders as they hauled their heavy loads "over rocky Hills—or thro low marshy Grounds where the Cannon were oftentimes almost buried and the Men that hawl'd them, up to their knees in Mire."[65]

At eleven in the morning of May 18, the Grand Battery cannon suddenly stopped their barrage, as did the coehorns, small portable mortars, that had been playing upon the town from the new Rabasse Battery.[66] The ominous silence was broken by the monotonous beating of the drums at the Landing Cove Brook camp signalling a general muster.[67] After shuffling into position, the New England troops saw Captain Agnue, with the summons clutched in his hand and accompanied by a drummer and a sergeant carrying a flag of truce, set out for the West Gate of Louisbourg.[68] At noon the troops were dismissed for a period of over two hours, and then the drums called them to muster once again to await Du Chambon's reply.[69]

When Agnue reached the West Gate, he was met by Morpain, who ceremoniously blindfolded him.[70] Morpain then led Agnue to Du Chambon and Bigot. Once the envoy was in the presence of the governor, the blindfold was removed and Agnue handed Du Chambon the summons. The governor considered the contents carefully before penning his reply. He was not impressed with the way in which the New Englanders were conducting the siege. The fortifications within Louisbourg were still intact, and only the most flimsily constructed buildings had been demolished by the Grand Battery cannon. The Green Hill mortars and those from the Rabasse heights had done little real damage.[71] The women and children were relatively safe in the casemates of the King's Bastion, while the troops and militia manned the fortifications.

Moreover, Du Chambon was convinced that French reinforcements would soon lift the siege. He not only expected a large naval squadron from France, but also Marin's force of seasoned French bushfighters and Indians, which was at that moment, unknown to Du Chambon, marching to Annapolis Royal.[72] Completely reversing his policy of the previous month, Du Chambon had sent Marin a letter on May 16 urging him to come to Louisbourg "as quickly as possible...with the Canadien and Indian force that you command."[73] The password for Marin to enter Louisbourg was to be "St. Remy et Lion."[74] But Du Chambon's messenger did not reach Marin and his force of 600 to 700 Micmacs, Malecites and Frenchmen[75] until probably June 3.[76] Had Du Chambon in April asked Marin to come to Louisbourg rather than directing him to Annapolis Royal, the French position in Louisbourg in May might have been radically different.[77]

Du Chambon's reply to Pepperrell and Warren's summons reflected the governor's disdain for the New England siege preliminaries. He wrote:

> On receiving the summons made this day, May 7, old style, from his honourable Lieutenant General Pepperrell...and...Peter Warren...demanding the surrender of the said city, with its dependencies, artillery, arms and munitions of war to the dominion of the King their master.
>
> The King of France, our King, has given us the responsibility of defending this city, we cannot except after the most

vigorous attack, consider a similar proposition; and the only reply we make to this demand is from the mouths of our canon.[78]

In an attempt to save some face, Agnue "proposed that the ladies should be sent out with the guarantee that they should not be insulted, and that they should be protected in the few houses that were still standing."[79] Du Chambon rejected Agnue's proposal, since he felt that the Louisbourg women were quite safe in the shelter afforded them in the fortress.

It seemed a much longer walk back to the camp for Agnue and his drummer and sergeant. They arrived at the camp at five o'clock in the afternoon.[80] Du Chambon's reply in translation was immediately read to the expectant troops, who answered it with three thunderous huzzas.[81] For that split second many of the excited troops desperately wanted to answer Du Chambon's reply with the mouths of their own muskets. Quickly Pepperrell and the council decided to channel this unusual aggressiveness into an assault upon the Island Battery that very evening.[82] Besides Pepperrell had promised Warren that such an assault would take place if Du Chambon rejected the summons. Warren's strategy had worked. While volunteers for the Battery raid were stepping forward, the New England cannon and mortars recommenced firing against Louisbourg and the Island Battery.[83]

Warren was not satisfied to leave the assault entirely in the hands of the New Englanders and consequently he ordered 150 of his men, mostly Marines,[84] to take part in the expedition. It is impossible to be definite concerning the number of New Englanders who volunteered. Pepperrell was of the opinion that there were at least 650 volunteers,[85] while Theophilus Woodbridge, who was one of them, maintained that there were only 150.[86] However, it is possible to be more definite regarding the motives of the volunteers. Waldo believed that some of the New Englanders were eager for "an opportunity to play the Hero."[87] Others were interested in the plunder that had been promised them if they captured the Battery and in a share of the £500 reward offered to them by the generous Warren.[88]

Lieutenant-Colonel John Gorham was given command of the expedition.[89] He and his Indian Rangers had led the successful assault-landing at Gabarus Bay and they were expected to play the same role at the Island Battery. The flotilla of whaleboats set out from the Landing Cove Brook area late in the evening. Theophilus Woodbridge observed:

...(being a fine Night wee went aboute half way up their) we

heard No Nois nor See No Light which we Supos'd that their
was but few if aney french in the fort which Grately Incur-
aged us but we was Sun Comanded to Retreet backe again
our men hering of that was Redy to tair the hair of their
heads for Suppos^d that wee Could have Taken it without the
Lose of one man.[90]

Gorham ordered the retreat for two main reasons: he felt that a
Landing would be impossible since "surff was large,"[91] and he estimated that before a landing could even be attempted it would be
daylight and there would be no element of surprise.[92] Gorham may
have been entirely right in his assessment of the situation. Nevertheless, because of Gorham's decision which they considered to be
both unnecessary and stupid, many of the volunteers and their
friends lost faith in their officers. Morale, which had reached its
peak at the camp after the reading of Du Chambon's reply, began
to decline noticeably.

Plans were made throughout the following day, May 19, for another amphibious night attack upon the Island Battery.[93] In addition, the council of war decided that "in the mean time preparation be made for a vigorous attack of the town as soon as
possible."[94] After sunset, those volunteers who were still interested
in the Island Battery raid crowded on the beach near the camp
waiting for the whaleboats to be launched. They sullenly waited
"on the Beach all Night Until Day brake;"[95] but there was no raid.
Perhaps the officers considered the sea to be too rough or perhaps
they were disconcerted by reports of a French sally from Louisbourg.[96] These excuses did not impress the volunteers and other
New Englanders; morale dipped even lower.[97]

Early in the morning of May 20 the council of war held an
emergency session. Warren vociferously argued that since an amphibious assault upon Island Battery was apparently not feasible
from the seaward side, Louisbourg should be attacked from the
landward side by the New England troops that night.[98] Four days
earlier, on May 16, the majority of council members had expressed
strong opposition to such a plan. But by the morning of May 20 the
majority had become a minority and Warren was clearly in the as-
cendancy. After listening to Warren's convincing arguments that it
was possible to mount a successful frontal attack upon Louisboug
before making any breaches in the walls, the minority decided to
accept the majority's will. It was unanimously resolved "that the
town of Louisbourg be attack'd by storm this night with all the
force and vigour possible."[99] At ten in the morning the troops in

the camp received "Orders to Prepare [them]selves to Scallade the walls this Night."[100]

There was little enthusiasm among the rank and file for the frontal attack, even though Warren promised to send 100 of his Marines to add backbone to the assault[161] and offered £500 prize money to the New England troops if Louisbourg were captured.[102] Most of the New Englanders ordered to take part in the assault were "Sorry to hear there was Such A Determination. Before We had Used our Cannons and Mortars longer."[103] The ordinary volunteer was expressing the point of view held by his officers a few days earlier.

Approximately an hour after sunset all the New England volunteers, except those defending the Grand Battery or marauding in the interior, were formed into their respective companies in preparation for the frontal attack. As Warren "Walk'd Back and forth in the front of the army," he sensed "a Great Uneasiness...Thro out the army." The troops made it quite clear to him that they felt it was the height of folly to undertake such an assault. The worried Warren turned to a group of officers and asked them "Gentlemen; what is your Communication?" An officer quickly answered "I suppose your Honor's Aquainted with our Design Against the Town this Night and I Always tho't Actions of this Nature Should Be Done with the Greater Vigour and Resolution." "To be Sure," replied Warren "But Seeing Such a General Uneasiness, —Makes me fear what the Consequences of This Night Will Be." He then walked over to Pepperrell and suggested that all the captains be interviewed to discover the general consensus of the rank and file. All the captains told Pepperrell and Warren the same thing. The enlisted men and the subalterns were strongly opposed to the planned frontal attack.[104] Late that evening the council of war:

> Advized, that inasmuch as there appears a great dissatisfaction in many of the officers & soldiers at the design'd attack of the town by storm this night, and as it may be attended with very ill consequences if it should not be executed with the utmost vigour whenever attempted, the said attack of the town be deferr'd for the present.[105]

The council of war had no alternative but to abandon the assault. The New Englanders were volunteers and they could not be forced to do something they did not want to do. They were—to use Warren's description—"almost Levellers, they must...be treated in a manner that few military bred Gentlemen would condecend to."[106] But because they were free and willing to criticize their officers' bold plan, the New England invading force undoubtedly avoided being severely decimated. For the French in Louisbourg were awaiting just such a frontal attack and were prepared for it. Pepperrell had no other choice but to conduct the siege in the traditional manner, using his cannon and mortars to batter down the walls. Once a breach was made the Island Battery could be assaulted. Pepperrell refused to abandon his plan to capture the Island Battery regardless of proven difficulties.[107]

10

Siege and Blockade (May 21 - June 7, 1745)

THE DRAMATIC REFUSAL of his troops on May 20 to obey his orders to attack Louisbourg had a considerable impact upon Pepperrell. This serious rebuff was convincing proof to him, as well as to many of his officers, that he had been unduly and unwisely influenced by the impetuous Warren, who desperately wanted to see Louisbourg "attempted by storm...speedily & vigourously."[1] It seemed to some New Englanders that Pepperrell had become a puppet in Warren's hands and that as a result Warren had assumed effective control over the New England land operations. In order to counter such charges and also in order to reassert his authority over his men and to win back some of their confidence, Pepperrell was forced to inform Warren that he and not Warren was "the chief officer...on shoar."[2] Warren, who at times gave the impression to the New Englanders that he believed in the effortless superiority of British naval officers, was to be content with directing the naval blockade of Louisbourg. The New Englanders did not want to see the control over *their* expedition appropriated by a British officer.

But informing Warren that he should concentrate all of his attention upon the naval blockade was not in itself enough to reassert Pepperrell's authority. Pepperrell therefore decided to abandon any frontal attack scheme and turned a deaf ear to Warren's persistent pleas for such an attack.[3] Instead Pepperrell decided to return to the policies he and the members of the council of war had agreed upon before they had fallen under Warren's spell. Pepperrell thus returned to the strategy of Shirley's instructions.[4]

By May 21 it was clear to the New England volunteers as well as to Warren what Pepperrell's immediate objectives would be. First, he urged the capture of the Island Battery; it was almost an obsession with him. Second, by using the Green and Rabasse Batteries as giant stepping stones, he wished to facilitate the construction of fascine batteries which could beat down the vulnerable West Gate. Third, he continued to encourage marauding expeditions into the interior. These would serve at least two main purposes. They would keep the Indians and the French inhabitants in the interior on the defensive and discourage them from making guerrilla forays against the besieging New Englanders. Moreover, these marauding expeditions would act as escape-valves for frustrated New Englanders and provide them with the much-coveted plunder. Fourth, Pepperrell wanted some of his troops in "proper guard boats to cruize in the night under the point of the light house, to prevent the introduction of succours into the garrison by boats, shallops, or any other small vessels from any part of this island."[5] The man who had ordered Warren to devote his entire attention to the blockade had now decided to take an active part in the blockade himself. Pepperrell was reasserting his authority with a vengeance.

As far as Pepperrell was concerned, the pleasant period of siege preliminaries came to an abrupt end early on May 21. Such a development appeared to him to be the natural concomitant of his breaking away from the yoke of Warren's influence. Inspired by their commander, most of the New Englanders were eager to carry out his commands. Since he believed that it was impossible to organize a successful assault upon the Island Battery from Gabarus Bay, Pepperrell ordered his men to carry the whaleboats overland to the Grand Battery.[6] He planned yet another attack on the Island Battery that evening—the fourth proposed assault in almost as many days. As those carrying the whaleboats stumbled over the sharp rocks and tramped through the sticky morass on their way to the

Grand Battery, they passed teams of their friends laboriously pulling sledges upon which were to be seen the 22-pound cannon intended for the Rabasse fascine battery. By the late afternoon four 22-pounders were in position behind the rude fascine wall ready to bombard the west flank of the King's Bastion which they commanded.[7] The whaleboats were also in position to be launched against the Island Battery. But the day that had started with so much promise and enthusiasm ended on a note of profound disenchantment.

There were two reasons for the disillusionment that settled like a cloud upon the besieging New Englanders late on May 21. And the successful planting of four 22-pounders at the Rabasse Battery did not even begin to offset this sense of disillusionment. News reached Pepperrell's camp, probably late in the afternoon, that some twenty New Englanders "stragling toward North East Harbour" had been "inhumanly butchered"[8] by a scouting party of Micmacs and Frenchmen. Crazed by their hatred of Englishmen, the Micmacs "Scalped and Chopt and Stab'd & Prodigiously mangled"[9] their enemy. The savages were encouraged by their French allies who wanted to see the invaders punished for the terrorist tactics they had used against many unsuspecting French inhabitants in the interior.[10] On hearing the intelligence one anonymous diarist sadly observed: "this is the Most Unfortunate Day that has hapned to our Sid yet."[11] But this was not all that was to make May 21 such an "Unfortunate Day" for the New Englanders.

After sunset the volunteers for the Island Battery expedition, along with almost 200 of Warren's men, crowded on a beach near the Grand Battery.[12] The whaleboats were ready, the harbour calm and the volunteers eager to get their fingers on the rumoured wealth in the Island Battery. A few of the men apparently jumped into some of the whaleboats, but they did not get very far. For orders were given, apparently by John Bradstreet, for the force to disperse. The excuse given to the volunteers for the abandonment of the assault was the absence of a commanding officer to lead them.[13] This excuse satisfied few of them. Rumours were rife that there was a traitor in the ranks of the New Englanders. He was no ordinary volunteer—he was believed to be one of the more influential officers. A scapegoat was needed by the rank and file to account for the failure of four Island Battery expeditions. One disgusted volunteer exclaimed:

> ...wee Cant but think that it is nothing but a heep of Trechersey and wee have found oute that they have Had News in the

Sittey from time to time. Our mens Harts begin to faint with in them on the Acc^u of the Divelish trecheresey that their is Ammong us and fering they are maid a pray to our Enemies.[14]

By the early morning hours of the following day, May 22, a scapegoat had been found.[15] There was a widespread rumour that John Bradstreet was the traitor. It was said that he "had been seen going into and coming out of the City."[16] It was possible, it was argued, that he was the man responsible for the abandonment of at least three attempts to attack the Island Battery. It was known that he had friends in Louisbourg, having been a prisoner in the town the previous year as well as a trader there before the outbreak of war. It was easy for many of the New Englanders to think the worst and expect the worst of Bradstreet since he was detested by many because of his arrogance. There were some New Englanders, no doubt, who were willing to go so far as to blame Bradstreet for the slaughter of the twenty marauders by the Micmacs. As a traitor Bradstreet provided an easy answer to the perplexing problem of accounting for embarrassing failure and shocking defeat.

The rumour proved so persistent that Pepperrell was forced to discuss it with his council of war on the afternoon of the following day, May 22. He was particularly concerned because one member of the council, Lieutenant-Colonel Thomas Chandler of the Fourth Massachusetts Regiment, "had been guilty of great imprudence in entertain^g and reporting such surmizes without the least reasonable foundation."[17] Moreover, Pepperrell was urged by Warren:

> For God's sake, Sir, put a stop to that disagreeable and ill-grounded suspicion that some unthinking people have pretended (for I can think it no other) to conceive of Collonel Broadstreet, it may otherwise be of fatal consequence to the expedition.[18]

There was an atmosphere of tension at the council meeting. Chandler was there and so was Bradstreet. The tactful Pepperrell asked those present if there were any grounds for the rumour that had caught the imagination of so many of the New England volunteers. After a protracted and careful examination of the evidence, all of the council members agreed:

> ...to testifie their approbation of Col. Bradstreet's behavior in the army, and that his zeal for the success of the expedition was undoubtedly manifest by his active and prudent behaviour on all occasions.[19]

Seeing no other alternative, Chandler acknowledged that he had been foolish to accept, embellish and pass on the rumour, and asked Bradstreet to pardon him. Bradstreet did so.

The Bradstreet incident and the failure of the Island Battery expedition only served to aggravate the strained relationship between Pepperrell and Warren. Disgusted with what he considered to be Pepperrell's procrastination, Warren ordered his 200 men to return to their ships.[20] He was, to use Captain George Curwen's understatement, "not a little dissatisfied."[21] On the other hand, Pepperrell had been annoyed by the drunkenness prevalent among Warren's men and "the many disorders they committed when ashore."[22] Warren blamed the New Englanders, since they had sold rum to his men and then stolen their guns. The Old World was at conflict with the New, and at times there was as much animus shown by the New Englanders towards the British as was shown by the New Englanders towards the French in Louisbourg.[23]

In spite of the council's declaration of faith in Bradstreet and in spite of the fact that the four 22-pounders at the Rabasse Battery had begun to bombard Louisbourg, morale dipped to a new low on May 22.[24] Captain George Curwen noted in a letter:

> I must honestly tell you, y^t if I was at home I would not come again in this capacity, for wee meet with a great deal of trouble.[25]

Captain Thomas Waldron wrote to his father:

> I am sorry to find our New England Troops...Say that they want to go home, home, is all ye Cry and if I was well at home, I'l ingage? they should never find me such a fool again this is the Language of those who are as well Us'd as can be.[26]

Morale continued on its downward trend on Sunday May 23. Most of the ministers used the slaughter of the twenty New Englanders on May 21 as the basis of their sermons. One preached from the text "for itt is a Pinted for Man once to Die,"[27] another from John 3:16, "For God so loved the world that He gave His only begotten Son that whosoever believeth in Him should not perish but have everlasting life,"[28] and another from "thou art weigh'd in ye Ballances & found wanting."[29] The morbid sense of introspection emphasized by the ministers only helped to undermine morale even further. The troops began to be aware of the proximity of death as never before. Some demanded to be returned to New England as "the smell of gun-Powder made [them] sick."[30] Others were somewhat relieved when they discovered they had dysentery and were therefore able to remain hospitalized in the camp.[31] Others turned to rum in an attempt to flee from reality.[32]

There was little bombarding from either side on the Sabbath. The French in Louisbourg, however, took advantage of the lull to continue work on an eight-foot-high palisade they were building from the Maurepas to the Princess Bastion.[33] Du Chambon suspected that the New Englanders might try to land at this exposed section of the fortifications, and wanted to be ready for them. Pepperrell was aware of the activity in Louisbourg, but he had other more important things to worry about. He carefully considered two letters that he had recently received from the Grand Battery, one from Vaughan and the other from Waldo. Both concerned the Island Battery. Vaughan felt confident that he could lead a successful assault:

> I am fully persuaded y^t I can take ye Island Batery from this place with ye boats y^t are here, if you think it proper to give ye taking of y^t place to myselfe. I dare to engage with ye blessing of God to send you ye flag within forty-eight hours from this time, if you think proper to give me ord^r to conduct ye affair intirly by my own judgmt; with ye concurrance of ye party to go with me, I doubt not of successe. I think I perfectly know ye rocks we have already split on, and can avoid them or any other for ye future. If my offer be accepted ye sooner I have ye ord^{rs} ye better, being persuaded I can find men enough y^t will willingly go with me.[34]

On the other hand, Waldo wanted the glory of having his men capture the Island Battery. He certainly did not want Vaughan, whom he hated, to lead the assault. Waldo therefore "offered [his] Regiment Soley to undertake the [attack] wch will prevent the usual Confusion by Mixture and Detachments of Voluntiers."[35] Rather than alienating either man, Pepperrell chose to procrastinate. It was an easy way out of a ticklish situation. He decided to delay the Island Battery assault indefinitely. This was rightly regarded as a rebuff by Vaughan,[36] but it satisfied Waldo, who was really not very interested in the Island Battery scheme anyway.

Pepperrell was especially concerned about the poor morale of his troops. He hoped that once the Rabasse Battery 22-pounders began to bombard the fortress in earnest, the morale would improve. He therefore ordered a heavy barrage from the 22-pounders for the following day, May 24.

Soon after the 22-pounders began their fire against the King's Bastion, two of them split, wounding seriously four or five gunners.[37] One of these men, who lost a leg in the explosion, was from Warren's ship.[38] Experienced gunners were now scarcer than ever, and Pepperrell was therefore forced to ask Warren for assistance.

Warren replied that he could spare only two gunners, expressing the hope that these men would be treated better by the New Englanders than the two he had previously sent.[39] The splitting of the cannon was another shattering blow to the New England morale, as was the arrival of a 10-gun French supply vessel "close under the walls of the town."[40]

The vessel, estimated by Waldo to be "of about 150 tons," had threaded its way through the blockading fleet, aided immeasurably by the fog, and then by hugging the Lighthouse shore had sneaked into the harbour. As soon as the French saw the ship, they began a heavy fire, some 52 discharges in less than a half hour, upon the Grand Battery. "The smartness of the enemy's fire beat off our people from the guns," Waldo informed Pepperrell. But Waldo also reported that if he had some "good gunners that have a disposition to be sober in the daytime,"[41] the vessel might have been distroyed.

Even after the vessel had been grounded "close under the walls of the town," Vaughan refused to give up hope of destroying it. He and Captain James Noble of Waldo's regiment prepared two fireships and sent them against the French vessel. But the fireships did not even come close to their goal, largely because of "carelessness and want of proper sails."[42] Understandably frightened because of the fireship threat, the French quickly unloaded the supply vessel and stripped her of her cannon, which were placed in the empty embrazures along the fortress wall.[43]

Seemingly undaunted by the twin disasters of the day, Pepperrell ordered four more 22-pounders to be dragged to the Rabasse Battery, together with two 9-pounders and a 13-inch mortar from the Green Hill.[44] These guns were ready to be fired on May 25.[45] Pepperrell described the range of their fire in this manner:

> From this Battery the City was bombarded. And as the Shot
> from the said Battery ranged through the Centre of the City,
> it damaged not only the West Flank of the King's Bastion,
> which it flanked, but also the Citadel, and the greatest Part of
> the Houses in the Town, and even Porte Maurepas, in the
> Easternmost Part of the City.[46]

To counter this effective fire from the Rabasse Battery, Du Chambon had two 18-pounders placed on the cavalier of the King's Bastion and also new embrazures for two 24-pounders cut into the parapet of the western face of the Bastion.[47]

Bad luck continued to plague the Rabasse Battery, for on May 26 another 22-pounder split while "the enemy's canon ball broke another."[48] The splitting of the three 22-pounders came as no surprise to the experienced artillerymen. Most of the cannon from Massachusetts were in bad condition, and furthermore some of the gunners were prone to overcharge their badly "honeycombed" cannon.[49]

While the noisy cannon duel was taking place between the King's Bastion and the Rabasse Battery, preparations were being made by the New Englanders for the construction of two new fascine batteries nearer the West Gate or the Dauphin Bastion. On May 27 a number of coehorns, and the 9-inch and 11-inch mortars from the Green Hill Battery were mounted on "a Hill within 440 Yards of the West Gate."[50] They began to play upon the Dauphin Bastion the same day.[51] During the following evening an 18-pounder from the Grand Battery was mounted on a platform "in the shelter of a knoll"[52] only some 220 yards from the West Gate. It began to bombard the West Gate the following morning and was joined on the evening of May 29 by two 42-pounders and another 18-pounder.[53] All of these cannon had been "brought from the Grand Battery, upwards of two Miles, as the Road goes, over a very rough, rocky, hilly Way."[54]

The new mortar battery was not the only thing that gave Pepperrell satisfaction on May 27. He also received the startling intelligence that John Gorham had discovered a huge cache of about thirty cannon on the eastern side of the harbour, under water, near the Careening Wharf.[55] They had apparently been left there ten years earlier by the French and then promptly forgotten.[56] Pepperrell hoped that he would be able to raise these cannon and drag them to Lighthouse Point for use against the Island Battery. When Du Chambon learned that afternoon of Gorham's discovery, he immediately resolved to send a force of 100 men under cover of darkness to ensure that the cannon could not be used by the New Englanders.[57] In addition to Gorham's discovery, Pepperrell was gratified to learn of the arrival in Gabarus Bay late on May 27 of seven transports under convoy of Captain Rouse of the 24-gun *Shirley*.[58] These vessels carried an estimated "four Months Provision"[59] for the troops, but no badly needed gunpowder.[60]

Pepperrell's satisfaction with developments on May 27 was significantly tempered, however, on his receiving a sharply worded letter from Warren.[61] Warren emphasized that he was totally dissatisfied with having to be content with the mundane responsibilities of carrying out a naval blockade. He therefore urged Pepperrell to reconsider an immediate frontal attack on Louisbourg. He not only urged Pepperrell to adopt "more vigorous measures," but he also

presented him with an elaborate plan which called for a simultaneous amphibious and land assault upon Louisbourg:

> I wou'd have the seamen and whale boat men, appointed to
> make the attack in the boats from the Grand Battery, the gra-
> nadiers, marines, and the most regular of the land troops, to
> a proper number...in three different places....
>
> I woul'd have the attack begun by a signal, so as to be in
> the town a quarter of an hour before day.
>
> I woul'd have a sustaining party of two hundred men and
> good officers march in the rear of the main body within ran-
> dum musquet shott of the wall to cover a retreat if necessary,
> and to prevent any men from leaving their posts.

Warren was concerned about the poor discipline of the New Englanders and was blunt about this fact:

> I wou'd have every officer know his command and every Cap-
> tain muster his company, and the whole shou'd be told that if
> they presum'd to shrink, or put back, or utter any words to
> induce others so to do, shou'd be punish'd with death, and
> they shou'd know that a rear guard was appointed to take up
> as cowards all those that should be found without the walls af-
> ter the main body was got over and in the town, and that any
> retreating from the town without the main body shou'd be
> look'd upon in the same light, and shou'd for such crime suf-
> fer death.

Finally, he suggested that only those "who are actually upon the attack, or posted otherwise by particular orders, [are] to have any
share in the plunder or riches of the town."[62] Such a stipulation, he
was certain, would assure a large New England participation in the
assault.

The attitude of Pepperrell and the members of the council of
war to Warren's proposal was a foregone conclusion. They understood the mood of their men and resented Warren's proposed
harsh disciplinary measures. The council unanimously decided
"that the circumstances of the army not allowing of an immediate
determination thereon, the consideration of it be defer'd to a further opportunity."[63]

Late in the evening of May 27 Du Chambon's force of 100
"young local men, and some others from the militia and some fili-
busters,"[64] under the command of the retired officer Beaubassin,
climbed into three "chaloupes" and began to paddle towards the Careening Wharf across the harbour. Each man carried over thirty
balls for his musket and a large horn of powder, together with suffi-

cient food supplies to last ten days.[65] Their objective was to prevent
the New Englanders from using the recently discovered cannon to
bombard the Island Battery. Du Chambon never explained his willingness to send such an expedition to the Careening Wharf. He
had been unwilling to send out any sallies to prevent the New Englanders from building their batteries so near to the West Gate.
Surely he must have realized that cannon immersed in seawater for
a decade could not be readily utilized for siege purposes. If he saw
fit to order Beaubassin's sortie, there is no excuse for his refusal to
send any significant expeditions against the New Englanders on
the fortress side of the harbour. He argued that he did not have
the men to spare for such offensive thrusts.[66] But if he had enough
men for the strategically questionable Beaubassin raid, he certainly
had enough men for other more important sorties. Furthermore,
he undoubtedly must have come to the conclusion by May 27 that
it was just a matter of time before the New Englanders would drag
some of their cannon to Lighthouse Point. It can be argued therefore that Du Chambon was finally making the right move, but at
the wrong time and the wrong place.

The following afternoon "ab^t one P.M.,"[67] one of Gorham's
scouts spotted Beaubassin's force near the Careening Wharf and
sounded the alarm. Forty New Englanders, most of them Gorham's
Indian Rangers, silently crept through the dense forest cover until
they were almost within musket-shot of the French.[68] At that moment the New Englanders were sighted and there was a brief thunderous exchange of gunfire. Then the French turned and ran away
from the New Englanders into the woods. The French left five dead
behind, and another was captured. Only one New Englander, an
Indian, was killed.[69] The French had been ignominiously routed by
a much smaller force, largely because they were young and inexperienced and because the New Englanders had taken advantage of
the element of surprise.

A New Hampshireman, Captain Joseph Sherburne, was singled
out by Pepperrell to command the Advanced Battery, located some
220 yards west from the West Gate.[70] Sherburne was able to induce
six men to serve as gunners. He found recruiting very difficult,
since most of the New Englanders were afraid of being injured by
bursting cannon or by the nearby French guns. Sherburne wrote in
his diary on May 29:

> Satterday morning, I went to the Advance Battery...we had
> One 18 pounder Mounted but very poor Intrenchments for
> the most Shelter we had from the french fire (which was very

hott) was Some hhds [hogsheads] filled with earth. I had no Cartaridges but was forsed to Load with Loose Powder which was much to our Disadvantage the Fish flakes Lay [b]e tween us and the west Gate was forst to Beat them away with our Shott to have a fair Sight at the Gate as wee ware Loading the 5th time William Coomes [a gunner] was Killed with a Muskett Ball, we Discharged our Guns 56 times that Day which was as often as the[y] would bare—(Soldiers killed) Capt. [Joshua] Pearce by a Cannon Shott Joseph Merell Do: one Bickford and Jackson by musket Balles. Thomas Ash by a Bomb Some other Carried of[f] wounded.[71]

Another New Hampshireman posted at the Advanced Battery on the first day of its operation was Captain Thomas Waldron. He graphically described the terror experienced by those defending the Battery:

We lay much Expos'd and ye french kept a firing small armes and great guns the greatest part of ye Day we had Kild and wounded sundry men...it was such a day as new England men never see that is very few of them. The bullets flew in whole Showers as did bombs Cohorns and Cannon as well from us as from our Enemies. May I have a proper sense of gods covering me in that day Engagement when whole showers of Death flew all around me and my company.... The sky being Darkned with Sulpher and Smoak.... When night came on ye Enemy Let us alone for they had a breach to mend which we had made in their gate...and we Let them alone allso, we mounted two 42 lb and one more 18 lb which we had hall'd ye night before.[72]

The Advanced Battery had been "assolted...Very furiously"[73] by the French, especially by the cannon from the west face of the King's Bastion. Fortunately for Sherburne the Dauphin Bastion had little firepower.[74] If there had been a number of cannon facing landward from the Dauphin Bastion, the Advanced Battery would probably have been demolished without any great difficulty. Instead, French cannon from the Grand Battery were mounted at the Advanced Battery and used to shatter the West Gate and transform it into a useless mountain of rubble.

During the evening of May 29 and the early morning May 30 the two 42-pounders and the other 18-pounders were mounted at the Advanced Battery behind what Sherburne described as a "pritty Good Intrenchment."[75] William Vaughan directed the digging operations, "continually encouraging the Army to keep up their Spirits wh. were almost cast down through their extraordinary Fatigue & Slavery."[76] The effort of this night provided inspiration for a New England bard:

> Some with the Pick-ax, penetrate the Soil,
>> Others with Spades and Shovels sweat & toil.
> Some Fascines place, others each Instrument,
>> Improve, assign'd them, for this grand Intent,...
> What adds a Lustre, to this Work so great,
>> Is, in one Night, 'twas rendred near compleat,
> The *Gallics* are secure, nor ever dreamt,
>> Of such a Bold, Couragious Atttempt,
> Till darksom Shades disperse, & Morning Light
>> Present, these mighty Labours to their Sight
> Beholding which, surpriz'd , amazed cry,
>> Who may, or dare, with English Men to Vie?
> Whose Counsels, Aids, and Politicks, do prove
>> Agents, if not from H-ll, are from Above.[77]

Vaughan's crew of trench-diggers continued their laborious work until an impressive network was constructed connecting all the New England batteries to the west of the West Gate.[78] In addition, where the trench cut some twenty yards to the east of the Advanced Battery, one 18-pounder and two 9-pounders were mounted by the last day of May.[79] They were played "at the Citydall Guns with Such truth that [the New England gunners] Soon beat the Enemy from theirs."[80] The trenches served a number of purposes. They facilitated the movement of men and supplies from one battery to another, and they also provided excellent protection from French fire for those men covering the gunners as they loaded their cannon.

On Sunday, May 30, the New Englanders in the batteries had little time to worship, since in Daniel Giddings' words "This Lords Day is a Day of fighting the Cannons Roaring."[81] But the cannon could not roar without gunpower. At noon Sherburne at the Advanced Battery decided "to Seasce our foire for want of Powder they Guns then being very warm."[82] While he and his gunners were searching for powder Vaughan arrived with a supply of his own.[83] Undaunted by the fact that he knew nothing about cannon, he promptly packed over fifteen pounds of powder into the mouth of a 42-pounder, inserted the shot and then ignited the powder. The cannon burst, killing "two on ye spot and wounded 2 or three more...Dismantled one of the 18-pounders,"[84] and "blowed up 1 1/2 bbs powder."[85]

During and after Vaughan's unplanned fireworks display, there was a crucial naval engagement taking place just off Louisbourg harbour.[86] The previous day Warren had been informed by Captain Daniel Fones of the *Tartar* that the Rhode Island vessel had captured a small French brigantine. Fones had discovered from the French captain "that four sail of men of warr, one of seventy-two guns, the other three of fifty-six, and three Company ships of thirty guns each, may be daily expected."[87] As a result of Fones' intelligence, Warren had put his ships on special alert. In the afternoon of May 30 the *Mermaid*, commanded by Captain James Douglas, sighted a large French warship, the 64-gun *Vigilant*. Douglas immediately changed course and drew the *Vigilant* towards the British fleet. Before the captain of the *Vigilant*, the Marquis de la Maisonfort, realized that a trap had been sprung, the *Mermaid*, the *Superbe*, the *Launceston*, the *Eltham*, and the two New England vessels, the *Shirley* and the *Massachusetts*, were upon him. After receiving numerous broadsides, de la Maisonfort surrendered at nine in the evening.[88] It was estimated that the French "had about 35 killed and 26 wounded" and the British and New Englanders only six.[89] Because of a heavy fog the *Vigilant* was not boarded by its captors until the following morning. They discovered that the French vessel had been manned by over 500 men and had 1,000 barrels of powder and forty cannon for Louisbourg as well as food supplies.[90]

The capture of the *Vigilant* was certainly one of the turning points in the siege of Louisbourg. J. S. McLennan has argued that it was probably *the* turning point:

> Had the *Vigilant* successfully entered the harbour the effect on the siege must have been great. Its crew would have about doubled the number of the defenders of the town. The stores she carried would have most opportunely supplemented those of the defence, which were so low that the powder was sparingly used. The rashness of De la Maisonfort would have animated the defence with the spirit needed. The courage and tenacity with which he and his crew fought on the *Vigilant* until she was completely disabled, we must believe, would have proved too much for the few and unskilled gunners of the Grand Battery. Had they silenced these guns, then, from some such position as the *Arethuse* occupied in 1758, the siege batteries would have been laid open to the devastating broadsides of the *Vigilant*. The fortunes of France suffered grievously from the rashness of her commander.[91]

But it is fruitless to pursue the elusive "ifs" of history. From the available evidence, it appears that the capture of the *Vigilant*[92] was no more important as a turning point in the siege than the hasty abandonment of the Grand Battery by the French.

When the New Englanders heard of the capture of the *Vigilant*, there was a spontaneous outburst of relief and joy.[93] The opposite was the case with the inhabitants of Louisbourg, who did not receive the shattering intelligence until June 19. "L'Habitant de Louisbourg" indignantly declared:

> It is right to say to the credit of M. de la Maisonfort that he showed great courage in the struggle, but the interests of the King demanded that he should have proceeded to his destination. The Minister did not send him to give chase to any vessel; his ship was loaded with ammunition and provisions, and his one business was to re-victual our wretched town, which would never have been taken could we have received so great a help; but we were victims devoted to the wrath of Heaven, which willed to use even our own forces against us.[94]

The capture of the *Vigilant* noticeably lifted the morale of the New England troops. But even before this intelligence was received, their spirits were reviving. The defeat of Beaubassin's force, and the considerable damage being done by the Rabasse and Advanced Batteries to the Dauphin and King's Bastions had instilled some badly needed confidence and enthusiasm into the New Englanders. The completion on May 31 of Titcomb's Battery, with two 42-pounders, across the Barachois from the Rabasse Battery, added to the growing morale.[95] Titcomb's Battery was located 800 yards from the West Gate; it commanded the spur of the Dauphin Bastion which in turn commanded the entrance to the harbour. Thus by the last day of May the New Englanders had four batteries within 900 yards of the West Gate and their largely inexperienced gunners had forced the French gunners in the King's and Dauphin Bastions into an awkward defensive position. Consequently the cannon in the Advanced Battery were relatively free to carry out their breaching operation. Du Chambon's attempt to silence the New England batteries by cutting new embrazures in both the King's and Dauphin Bastions[96] had failed to achieve its essential purpose. Delay was no substitute for destruction. What was needed was a sally in force to spike the cannon, break the carriages and drive away the New Englanders. But Du Chambon chose not to send out any sallies against the New England batteries.

Pepperrell shared the newly found enthusiasm and sense of purpose of many of his men, and was determined to take full advantage of the new mood. His men now had an abundance of food supplies; they were no longer dependent upon salt pork, stale bread and what they might discover in scavenging raids. Moreover, the serious shortage of gunpower had come to a sudden end with the capture of the *Vigilant* and the arrival on June 1 of supplies from Boston.[97] Once again Pepperrell's attention turned to the Island Battery and he was further encouraged in this direction by Warren. By the closing days of May, Warren was no longer pressing for a simultaneous amphibious and land assault on Louisbourg. He was now content to help Pepperrell capture the Island Battery.[98] However, at least one New Englander, the Reverend Nathaniel Walter, Chaplain of the Sixth Massachusetts Regiment, disagreed with both Pepperrell and Warren. He was of the opinion that the siege would come immediately to an end if Pepperrell sent a simple ultimatum to Du Chambon:

> That unless you forthwith deliver up Louisbourg with its Batteries, Forts etc to us, We will place the Captives we have [over 900] in the Front of our Army, push them forward in Shackles, over the Breaches made in your Walls, and enter Sword in Hand, sparing neither Man, Woman nor Child; while the whole of our Naval Force are attacking you by Sea.[99]

Pepperrell disregarded Walter's inhumane plan which ran counter to the accepted rules of warfare.

Pepperrell selected Samuel Waldo to organize the assault upon the Island Battery.[100] Vaughan had fallen into disfavour largely because of the explosion in the Advanced Battery on May 30. Thus Waldo's offer of May 23 to undertake the attack was given preference over the offer made by Vaughan. On June 2 Waldo was reasonably successful in his efforts to "Beat up for men to go to the Island Battery."[101] That evening, on hearing of Waldo's intention, Warren promised that he would send 200 men from his warships "to Meet the whale Boats (who I presume will have all the Ladders) at the time and place that you shall appoint."[102] Once again the volunteers crowded on the beach, but as had happened four times before, the assault was called off. Waldo found many reasons for postponing the raid. He wrote to Pepperrell:

> The night oweing to the moon & the northern lights was not so agreeable as may happen the ensuing one, and the appearance of small detachments of men without officers was much less pleasing, many of which only under the conduct (not influence) of a sarjeant & many others only centinells without any officer of any kind, & not a few of them noisy & in liquor.[103]

Waldo's decision "gave a great uneasiness"[104] to the volunteers, but under the circumstances he had no other choice. He had learned one important lesson—that without respected officers to lead the volunteers, the planned assault would never succeed.[105]

He therefore persuaded Colonel Arthur Noble of his own regiment and John Gorham to lead the assault on the following evening, June 3.[106] Waldo discovered that mustering volunteers was more difficult this time, since some of the New Englanders were "discouraged from an apprehension that the enemy are apprised of the design & prepared for them."[107] Nevertheless, by midnight a force estimated by one participant to be "about Eight hundred"[108] in number milled about the beach near the Grand Battery. Before they were ordered into their whaleboats, they were informed that the password was "King George" and the reply "For ever."[109] Each boat was checked to see that it had a sufficient number of oars, paddles and ladders. Then the men were commanded to jump into their respective boats and row for the Island Battery. It was a calm, foggy evening. As the whaleboats neared the Island Battery the volunteers expected Noble and Gorham to take the initiative and lead the assault upon the Battery. But Noble and Gorham were not to be seen and "For want of an offercer ye Soldiers Return'd."[110]

When they got back to the Grand Battery in the early morning hours of June 4, the volunteers heaped abuse upon their officers, Noble and Gorham. Noble was called "a Couard."[111] Rumours about traitors were heard once again. The situation was so serious that Pepperrell was forced to call a special council of war:

> Upon examination made, and a number of the officers and others who were order'd on that attack being heard, the Council were of opinion that it did not appear that Col. Noble or Col. Gorham were chargeable with misbehaviour in the affair.[112]

Furthermore, the council decided "That if a number of men to the amount of three or four hundred appear as voluntiers for the attack of the Island Battery they be allowed to choose their own officers and be entitled to the plunder found there."[113] To all intents and purposes the council was giving the rank and file the freedom to determine when and how the Island Battery should be assaulted. Moreover, the Council had given its imprimatur to the creation of a democratic force.

The failure of the Island Battery expedition on June 3 may have disheartened Pepperrell, but it encouraged Warren to attempt to take the strategic initiative once again. On June 4 and 5 Warren felt

supremely confident in his grasp of military tactics and in the naval
strength at his disposal. His fleet had been considerably strengthened with the capture of the *Vigilant* and the arrival of the 60-gun
Princess Mary on June 2 and the 40-gun *Hector* on June 3.[114] The arrival of the two additional ships provided Warren with convincing
proof that the British government had resolved to use all available
means to ensure the capture of Louisbourg. It is noteworthy that
Captain Joshua Loring, who had brought word to the Duke of Newcastle at the beginning of March of the planned Louisbourg expedition, "stay'd but twelve Hours in London, before he was ordered
to go on board the princess Mary."[115]

Warren's plan of operations was dated on June 4 and considered by Pepperrell and the council of war the following day. Warren proposed:

> ...to go into Lewisbourg harbour in order to attack the town
> with all his Majesty's ships of warr and Collony cruizers, if the
> General will put sixteen hundred men on board, six hundred
> of them for the Vigilant, the rest to be distributed among his
> Majesty's ships, and that all transports, schooners and other
> vessells in the pay of the government of New England go into
> the N.E.[t] Harbour at the same time.... All the ships of warr
> and Collony cruizers to have on third of their number of
> men ready to land, properly arm'd, when I shall order boats
> for them.[116]

Rubbing more salt into the open sores of friction between the naval and land forces, Warren suggested that Captain James Macdonald, one of his Marines, should "command the first attack on
shore, not doubting of his being effectually sustained"[117] by the
New Englanders. Even to the least perceptive observer, Warren's
motives were easy to grasp. He wanted his men to capture Louisbourg, so that he and not Pepperrell would receive all of the glory.

The council of war quickly rejected Warren's proposal and
drew up a new plan of operations of its own. The council maintained that it was impractical to send 1,600 New Englanders aboard
Warren's ship when there were over 1,000 sick and hundreds marauding in the interior. Who would remain to man the batteries
and defend them from possible Indian attacks? The council's own
plan of operations contained six proposals:

> That five hundred men be taken out of the cruizers and
> transports, and distributed in the ships of war, in order to fa-
> cilitate the manning the *Vigilant*.
>   That the ships and other vessels proceed into the har-

bour at the time agreed upon in such manner as Com[re] Warren shall direct.

That five hundred land men and what men can be spared from the cruizers be in readiness at the Grand Battery to put off in boats upon a signal, and to land and scalade the wall on the front of the town, under the fire of the ship's cannon. The marines and what seamen Com[re] Warren thinks proper to attack at the same time and place.

That five hundred men, or more if to be had, scalade the wall at the southeast part of the town at the same time.

That five hundred men make an attack at the breach at the West Gate, and endeavour to possess themselves of the Circular Battery.

That five hundred men be posted at a suitable place to sustain the party attacking at the West Gate.[118]

The council's plan was almost the antithesis of Warren's proposal and it was intended to be such. The New Englanders were becoming increasingly suspicious of Warren's real motives, and they resented his attempts to usurp their power and authority.

Before Warren had an opportunity to comment upon both the council's rejection of his proposal and its own counter-proposal, the Island Battery was attacked by the New Englanders. Late on Sunday, June 6, some 400 volunteers who had chosen as their commanding officer a Captain Brooks, began making preparations for the assault.[119] Waldo did everything in his power to see that they were properly supplied with arms, ammunition and ladders and that the whaleboats were in seaworthy condition. He went so far as to write to Gorham at Lighthouse Point, asking him to send between 100 and 150 of his men "to sustain ye attack."[120] Brooks' flotilla of whaleboats pushed off from the beach near the Grand Battery just before midnight. Louisbourg harbour was surprisingly calm and visibility was adequate. Sherburne in the Advanced Battery "gave them what Diversion [he] could with Round and Grape Shott."[121] The projected landing place was the beach at the northwest corner of the island.[122] As the leading boats ground to a stop on the beach, the volunteers jumped into the water with their ladders. A few who had consumed too much rum immediately bellowed out three hurrahs.[123] The cheers aroused the French in the battery but not before twelve ladders had been put up against the ten-foot-high wall.[124] The Island Battery contained thirty or thirty-one 28 pounders, seven swivels, and two 10-inch brass mortars and was defended by approximately 180 men.[125] While the first New

Englanders were landing, the commanding officer of the battery, Captain D'Aillebout, was nervously pacing the platform of the battery. Until the shouts, he was apparently unaware of the assault.[126] "With all the Valour and the 'sang froid' possible,"[127] D'Aillebout and his second-in-command, Du Chambon's son, sounded the alarm. Almost simultaneously, "the battery was in a blaze from their cannon, swivells and small arms, their langrell cutting boats and men to pieces as they were landing."[128] Dudley Bradstreet described the fierce fight thus:

> The Enemy played with Cannon upon the Boates which Distroyd Several Boates and Left the men floating on the water. Several Boates Landed their men But ye Enemy being Prepard Slew them at a Strange Rate Some of our Men after they fir'd all their Cartridges Retreated got into their Boates and made their Escape but Some were killd after they had got into y^r. Boates. Some Boates Stove against ye Rocks Some run a Drift. Some of our men fought manfully Till about Sunrise.[129]

Seth Pomeroy noted in his journal:

> Providence Seemed Remarkable To Frown upon ye affair: our People ware Discovered by Those at ye Island Battre; Before they got on Shore: & ye Franch being Prepared with there Cannon Pointed Down To Strike ye Boats Just befor they Came on Shore Loaded with Chain and Pattridge Shot: & a grate number of men with Small arms. as Soon as our People Came in Sight: with all ye Fury & Resolution Posable they Fired upon y^m & Cut of whole boat Loads of y^m: but in Spite of all there Fire 4 or 5 boat Loads got on ye Island & Injaged y^m for near an houre by Firing grate numbers of Small arms upon y^m not above 3 or 4 Rods apart & by ye Light of their Fire Saw well To Shut...other boats grate numbers of them behind not haveing a Pilat ware not able to git on Shore. Tried For a Long Time & in ye very heat of there Fire they Found y^t they ware not able To Land Returned those of y^m y^t ware able as Fast as they Could To Land again—Those y^t had got on ye Island as many of y^m as Cou'd git boats made ye best of there way of but many Left behind y^t there was no boats for; So ware obliged To Fall into ye hands of there Enimies many Taken many kill'd & many Drowned.[130]

In fact, sixty were killed and 116 taken prisoner.[131]

On the whole, the New Englanders who landed fought gallantly, but many of the others "never intended to land." Those who did battled against tremendous odds. They did not have the element of surprise; they were confronted by a wall ten feet high and shattered by a well-aimed heavy crossfire of langrel, cannon-shot and musket balls. Moreover, there was no effective military leadership.

June 7 was a day of soul-searching for many of the despondent New Englanders. Some were certain that the Island Battery defeat was a clear indication that the Almighty was angry with them and they called for a new spirit of repentance.[132] Others were just as certain that the defeat was meant to show them that Louisbourg was in fact impregnable. These men wanted to return home as quickly as possible. Morale had plunged to a new low, and even Pepperrell was forced to admit that "Now things look'd something dark."[133]

11

Pepperrell, Warren and the Fall of Louisbourg

DURING THE WEEK following the ill-fated Island Battery expedition, the New Englanders remained "prodigiously discouraged."[1] The "Thick Foggy weather"[2] that was prevalent from June 7 to June 13 provided a suitable atmosphere for the prevailing mood of sullen despondency.[3] In sharp contrast, the French in Louisbourg were in buoyant spirit for the first time since the beginning of the siege. The successful defence of the Island Battery had dispelled some of the gloom in Louisbourg and had given the beleaguered inhabitants some badly needed confidence. Foggy weather and the serious shortage of powder and ammunition in the New England batteries[4] meant that there was little cannonading during the week. The French took advantage of the respite on June 11 to build a boom of logs that stretched from the spur of the Dauphin Bastion to the Batterie de la Grave.[5] Du Chambon hoped that the boom would prevent any amphibious assault upon the largely exposed northwestern portion of the fortress. During the evening of June 11 the French also mounted nine new cannon on the walls near the West Gate.[6] Morever, Morpain, who feared an imminent New England assault upon the battered West Gate, directed the construction of a fascine battery near the Gate. Morpain's amazing energy was an inspiration to all of the inhabitants of Louisbourg.[7] He seemed to be everywhere encouraging the defenders, and he seemed to thrive on lack of sleep.[8] He was not only in command of all the militia companies but he was also a key figure in planning the artillery defence of the fortress.

By the second week of June, Morpain, Du Chambon and Bigot had drawn up a definite schedule for their daily activities. Morpain visited each of his militia companies at a specific time and in all probability was responsible for making huge fires along the walls in order to make more difficult an enemy night assault.[9] Du Chambon began a tour of inspection along the walls of Louisbourg at ten o'clock each evening.[10] He seldom slept at night, since he anticipated that the New Englanders would launch their assault under cover of darkness. Bigot, on the other hand, was extremely active during the daylight hours. He visited the hospital twice daily, distributed rations to all of the inhabitants and did everything in his power to satisfy their material wants.[11]

Furthermore, Bigot and Du Chambon encouraged the inhabitants to attend daily mass in the hospital, since they both realized the importance of spiritual sustenance.[12] Inside the walls of Louisbourg the French priests were entreating their God to annihilate the New Englanders, while outside the New England ministers were urging their God to silence "the Popes Artillery, Whereby he holds his Vassals in Idolatry."[13] Each side saw the conflict as one between the forces of light and the forces of darkness.

In all likelihood during the period from June 7 to June 13 Pepperrell was as disillusioned as the most despondent New Englander. On June 7 he had received a bitter letter from Warren in which the naval officer declared: "For God's sake let us do something, and not waste our time in indolence."[14] Warren's letter had been written before the Island Battery assault, but as far as Pepperrell was concerned that did not matter; he considered Warren's severe criticism of the New England siege effort to include the unsuccessful assault. Pepperrell was furious at Warren's effrontery. To make matters even worse, while Pepperrell was already seething with rage, he was openly criticized on shore by Captain Macdonald, the commanding officer of the Marines on board the *Princess Mary*. Macdonald, a protégé of the Duke of Newcastle,[15] found "fault that [the] encampment was not regulr, or y^t the soldrs did not march as hansome as old regulr troops, their toes were not turn^d enough out, etc."[16]

When Macdonald returned to his ship on June 9, Pepperrell wrote "we were glad to get rid of him."[17] And Pepperrell clearly meant what he said.

Early on June 8 Pepperrell felt compelled to answer what he considered to be Warren's unfair criticism. Pepperrell did not want to precipitate a crisis in their relations[18] but also did not want to give Warren the impression that he could be criticized at the latter's pleasure. After a brief listing of the accomplishments of the New England force since the beginning of the siege, Pepperrell informed Warren:

> ...the army is very much fatigued, and sickness prevails among us, to that degree that we now have about 2100 effective men, six hundred of which are gone in quest of two bodies of French and Indians we are informed are gathering one to the eastward, and the other to the westward....another attempt upon the island battery, by boats,...is impracticable. We shall still prosecute the best endeavours in our power for the effectual and speedy accomplishment of our designs against the enemy: in which desire, doubt not of your assistance. As soon as opportunity will admit, I propose to myself the pleasure to come on board your ship with some of my council to confer and determine on the most suitable measures therefor.[19]

The tone of Pepperrell's letter was conciliatiory but firm. He had made it clear to Warren that he had not retreated from his position of June 5, when he and his council had turned down Warren's proposal for a naval assault and instead had urged a joint naval-land assault upon the fortress. Pepperrell was content to maintain the siege and blockade and to continue to send out scouts to prevent the Indians and the French under Beaubassin from surprising the New Englanders in the besieging batteries. Furthermore, and Pepperrell emphasized this point, he was willing to discuss strategy with Warren, but only as an equal.

Pepperrell's scouts in the interior accomplished their purpose. By June 11 Beaubassin's force had been decimated and his Indian allies routed.[20] Only a handful of Beaubassin's original force ever returned to Louisbourg.[21] But because of the lack of ammunition and gunpowder and the foggy weather Pepperrell was not as successful in his effort to blast a breach in the Dauphin Bastion. Some of his gunners in the Advanced Battery at times used the lull in the siege operations to talk with the French defending the Dauphin Bastion:

> to the *French* they'd call,
> *Come out;* Jack Frenchman, come to us,
> And drink a Bowl of Punch.
> Jack Frenchman *cries*, you *English Dogs*,
> *Come, here's a pretty Wench.*[22]

Both sides enjoyed this kind of diversion and usually looked forward to the next battle of words.[23]

Before receiving Pepperrell's letter of June 8, Warren, who was still not aware of the abortive attempt to capture the Island Battery, wrote another sharply-worded letter to Pepperrell.[24] Heavy fog had been responsibile for the break-down of communication between them and jealousy in turn bred misunderstanding. In his letter of June 9 Warren lashed out at what he considered to be Pepperrell's most serious mistakes. Warren exclaimed:

> I am very sorry no one plan of mine, though approved of by
> all my Captains, has been so fortunate as to meet your appro-
> bation, or have any weight with you. I flattered myself, from
> the little knowledge I have endeavoured to acquire in mili-
> tary affairs, my advice singly would have had some influence
> on the conducting of the present expedition, and I believe
> Governor Shirley thinks so too.

Warren then went on to point out that in Shirley's letter asking him to take part in the proposed Louisbourg expedition the governor had offered him *"the command of the expedition."* Warren, however, maintained that he did not want to command the land forces as well as the naval force, he only wanted his suggestions to carry "some weight and force" with Pepperrell. Warren criticized Pepperrell for using too much gunpowder, for not moving the camp "near the grand or advanced batteries," for not guarding the trenches properly, for not firing "as many guns as you can at a time which is the only method to make a breach." In addition, Warren argued that a naval assault of Louisbourg was possible even before the Island Battery was captured and the battery located at the spur of the Dauphin Bastion was reduced. Such "a bold attempt where there is no retreat" was considered by Warren to be "worthy of Englishmen." Finally, Warren endeavoured to remove some of the sting from his criticism by explaining to Pepperrell:

> I beg nothing in this may be construed by you, otherwise than
> it is meant by me, which is only to forward the present
> scheme, without giving you the least offence, for I wish you
> well, and shall be much obliged to you, if you will point out
> any thing that may occur to you, that can conduce to the suc-
> cess of this expedition.[25]

During the two following days, June 10 and 11, Warren wrote
two more letters[26] to Pepperrell but both of these letters were radically different in tone from the one written on June 9. For Warren
had been finally informed by Captain Macdonald late in the evening of the 9th of the unsuccessful Island Battery assault. The news
significantly tempered Warrren's criticism of Pepperrell's conduct
of the siege. Warren now urged Pepperrell to meet with him immediately to discuss further strategy, to build a battery at Lighthouse
Point to neutralize the Island Battery, and to man the *Vigilant* with
New Englanders in preparation for a combined land-sea assault on
Louisbourg. Warren was willing to compromise in the hope that
compromise would spur the New Englanders to action.

Pepperrell called a council of war meeting on June 13 to consider Warren's letters. In spite of Warren's blistering criticism, Pepperrell urged the council that because of "the Sickness in the
Camp and our Exposedness in our Enemys Country"[27] it was essential to mount an assault upon Louisbourg as soon as possible. The
council therefore agreed:

> ...that the Vigilant be mann'd for his Maj. service in the pro-
> posed attack on Louisbourg out of the N.E. forces, viz., from
> the army and transports...six hundd.... That five hundred
> men be sent on board the ships the morning they propose to
> go into the harbour, in order to land with Com^re Warren's
> men.[28]

It was understood by the council of war that the 500 New Englanders would be replaced on shore by Macdonald and his Marines.
However, Pepperrell and the council had certain reservations regarding Warren's plea for the construction of a battery at Lighthouse Point. Gorham had already begun to build such a battery,
but since the New Englanders lacked 18-pound shot for the New
York siege train 18-pounders which were proposed to be installed
there, Pepperrell felt such a battery "must be Entirely Useless."[29]
Pepperrell feared that Warren's enthusiasm for a combined naval-
land assault upon Louisbourg might once again wane. He therefore decided to seek additional help not only from Shirley but also
from Annapolis Royal, just in case the siege dragged on to the au-

tumn. While waiting for the fog to lift on June 13, so that he could meet with Warren, Pepperrell wrote letters to Shirley and to various officials at Annapolis Royal.

In his letter to Shirley, Pepperrell expressed his profound sense of disillusionment. The New Englanders had run out of gunpowder and they were "also in want of shott of all sorts." The large mortar had burst and the smaller mortars had proved to be almost totally ineffective. Pepperrell therefore demanded adequate supplies of powder, shot, shells and another large mortar. Furthermore with "1500 sick & wounded men" in his besieging force Pepperrell was of the opinion "that a reinforcement of near 3,000 men [was] necessary."[30] He still hoped that Louisbourg would fall before the arrival of the reinforcements, but he intimated that he feared that Louisbourg could not be captured without the reinforcements and the military supplies. Pepperrell had learnt that it was far more realistic to be a pessimist rather than an optimist while commanding a military force. He could not forget his friend George Whitefield's warning "that the means proposed to take Louisbourg, in the eye of human reason, were no more adequate to the end, than the sounding of rams' horns to blow down Jericho."[31]

But Pepperrell wanted mortars and not "rams' horns"; he wanted trained engineers knowledgeable in siege warfare. Consequently he asked Mascarene at Annapolis Royal for "the loan of a thirteen inch mortar & a 7 inch brass mortar, with a number of shells for each"[32] and also for an experienced military engineer. Pepperrell realized that some of Warren's criticism, regarding the inadequate New England siege operations, was entirely justified and he was eager to do something about it.

Within only four days after writing to Shirley and to Mascarene, Pepperrell was dumbfounded to discover that most of his requests had been anticipated by the two men. For late on June 13 the *Resolution* arrived from Boston with a large mortar, shells and fifty barrels of powder.[33] This unexpected development "put new life and Spirits into all of [the New Englanders]."[34] Then on June 17 John Henry Bastide, the military engineer from Annapolis Royal, arrived in Gabarus Bay with "a good serjeant of artillery, two gunners, and four artificers."[35] To add further to Pepperrell's "great joy,"[36] between June 13 and June 17 four French supply vessels were captured by the blockading fleet.[37] Pepperrell was now certain that his God had not forsaken him. This conviction displaced his previous serious doubts and anxieties, and he now was eager to be used as an instrument in

God's hands to bring about the immediate capture of Louisbourg.

When the fog finally lifted on June 14, Pepperrell, Waldo, Dwight, Moore, Bradstreet, and Burr were rowed out to one of the New England transports and then carried to Warren's flagship, the *Superbe*.[38] Here they met with Warren, Captain Richard Tiddeman of the *Superbe*, Captain James Douglas of the *Vigilant*, Captain W. Montague of the *Mermaid* and Captain J. Calmady of the *Launceston*.

Since a general agreement had already been reached between Pepperrell and Warren concerning the advisability of organizing a combined land-sea assault, the council of war concentrated its attention upon the ticklish problem of French prisoners-of-war. There were approximately 1,000 French prisoners in transport vessels.[39] While these ships were in Gabarus Bay the prisoners had to be fed from the limited food supplies of the New Englanders and they had to be guarded by men who could be used more profitably elsewhere. Moreover, there was always a chance that a large number might escape to shore and make life miserable for the besiegers.[40] The council therefore agreed to send the prisoners to Boston in a fleet of transports. The fleet of over twenty transports under the convoy of the 30-gun *Bien Aime*, the *Molineux* and the *Caesar* sailed from Gabarus Bay on June 21.[41] The council also decided that at least eighty New England volunteers should be sent to man the *Vigilant*. These men climbed on board the *Vigilant* the following day, June 15.[42]

Riding the crest of his recently discovered confidence, Pepperrell on June 15 ordered the cannon at Titcomb's Battery to fire red-hot shot at Louisbourg.[43] He hoped the shot would set ablaze the many frame buildings in Louisbourg and terrorize Du Chambon into surrendering. Apparently Pepperrell was now willing to use any measure to achieve his desired purpose. Benjamin Stearns supported Pepperrell's policy, reflecting the general consensus:

> ...our men shot red-hot bullets into their houses and amongst them in the streets; and when they saw them role along the streets they went to take them up burnt their hands, they not knowing they was hot. So, by shooting the red-hot ball, it [g]ot many of their houses on fire, but they by their craftiness put them out again.[44]

However, there was a small vociferous minority led by Captain Thomas Waldron that strongly opposed the firing of red-hot cannonballs and considered it to be morally and militarily wrong, "for 'tis folly to shew teeth if you cant bite." He caustically referred to Pepperrell's plan as "this Piece of humane malice."[45] Warren was not the only one who was critical of Pepperrell's military strategy or lack of it.

Pepperrell's new-found confidence was suddenly jarred on June 16 when he was informed that Marin's force of "800 french and Indians"[46] was on its way to lift the siege of Louisbourg. There was feverish activity in the New England camp. The troops were "order'd to Move [their] Tents and Pitch 'em Clost together" on both sides of Landing Cove Brook near Gabarus Bay. Trenches were dug along the landward sides of the camp and carefully patrolled by troops and "Several Field Pieces"[47] installed. The arrival in the New England camp on the same day of the first French deserter from Louisbourg with the information that at least 100 troops were eager to desert did little to counter the impact of the news concerning Marin's force. Besides, many New Englanders suspected that the deserter was lying and was a key figure in some dastardly French plot.[48]

The news about Marin influenced in at least three ways the immediate siege strategy. First, on June 17, Pepperrell ordered part of the New York siege train landed "to the Eastward of the Light-House."[49] Realizing that Warren would not send in his fleet until the Island Battery was either captured or most of its cannon discounted by New England fire, Pepperrell wanted to prepare the way for Warren before the arrival of Marin.[50] Hence ten cannon were landed in whaleboats, then probably lifted by means of a series of pulleys "up the Bank of the Shore (which was a steep craggy Rock)." Then they were hauled on sleds "a Mile and a quarter, over an incredible bad Way, of Hills, Rocks, and Morasses,"[51] to Gorham's battery. However, they were not in a position to fire upon the Island Battery until June 21.[52] The second way in which the news about Marin influenced immediate siege strategy was in the determination of Pepperrell to use his batteries to make a breach in the West Gate. All available powder and shot were used on June 17, 18 and 19 by the New England gunners, dislodging many of the French guns but producing no breach.[53] But they refused to give up hope and only the shortage of shot and powder prevented them from firing most of the day and even part of the evening at the West Gate.

Finally, even Warren's strategic thinking was somewhat influenced by the information about Marin's force. As early as June 12 Warren had begun to toy with the idea that if Du Chambon were informed of the capture of the *Vigilant,* he might decide to surrender the fortress. Warren had written to Pepperrell on June 12:

> *When they know of the Vigilant being taken, and the reinforcement*

*we have lately had, and seeing a battery carrying on at the light
house, if they are in any great distress, they may surrender* upon the
articles of your first summons, though it should not be mentioned by us to them.[54]

Warren, who had looked down with scorn on the summons sent by
Pepperrell to Du Chambon less than a month before, was now proposing to do approximately the same thing in a rather indirect
manner. An easy solution to a perplexing problem had a great deal
of appeal. Nothing more was said about Warren's proposal until after the information arrived regarding Marin. On receiving it, Warren decided that the time was ripe for implementing his plan. If he
continued to delay, Du Chambon might receive information about
Marin, and this would mean that he would not consider surrendering under the circumstances. Therefore late on June 18 Warren
sent Captain Macdonald ashore with a letter addressed to Du
Chambon from de la Maisonfort, the captain of the *Vigilant*.[55] At
eleven o'clock the following morning the "very furious...fire between the batteries and town"[56] suddenly came to a stop as Macdonald, under cover of a flag of truce, began his short walk from the
Advanced Battery to the West Gate. Pepperrell and the New Englanders were pleased to get rid of Macdonald and they probably
hoped that Du Chambon would not permit him to leave Louisbourg. For they were sure that he would do less damage to the New
England cause within the walls than outside them.

Macdonald was ceremoniously led to Du Chambon, to whom
he presented de la Maisonfort's letter.[57] On reading of the capture
of the *Vigilant* Du Chambon became "Exceeding Sorrowful,"[58] but
he refused to consider surrendering the fortress even though prodded by the tactless Macdonald.[59] The New Englanders may have
been dismayed when they sighted Macdonald leaving the fortress
but they were even more dismayed when he pompously informed
them that French morale was excellent and that "there is no Such
thing as Scaleing ye walls."[60] Warren's easy solution had failed. It appeared that the siege and blockade would have to continue indefinitely, more New England lives would have to be lost and there was
also now the Marin threat to worry about.

However, as had happened so often before, the following day,
June 20, witnessed a drastic change in the general situation confronting the besieging and blockading forces. Two events were responsible for this sudden and dramatic change. First, early in the
morning of June 20 two Swiss deserters sprinted the two hundred
yards from the West Gate to the Advanced Battery.[61] They informed

the incredulous Pepperrell that the French had only 150 barrels of powder remaining and that many troops "would be Glad To Come Out and Deliver themselves"[62] to the New Englanders. They asserted that one of their friends who had been planning to desert had been found with a letter from one of the New England prisoners in his possession and had immediately been hanged.[63] What the two Swiss soldiers said only seemed to confirm what the other French deserter had declared a few days earlier. As far as Pepperrell was concerned, the end was now clearly in sight. He gave his gunners orders to "Fire Smartly att ye Citty"[64] until their cannon "ware So hott they could not fire any more."[65] He hoped that the heavy fire would force the French to use up what remained of their small powder supply .

The second significant event occurring on June 20 was the unexpected arrival of the 50-gun *Chester* with the news that two sister ships, the 60-gun *Sunderland* and the 60-gun *Canterbury*, could be expected at any moment.[66] The three British warships had sailed from Britain on May 5 with orders to prevent a French squadron of six warships under the command of des Herbiers de l'Etanduère from lifting the siege and blockade of Louisbourg.[67] The French squadron had broken through Admiral Martin's blockade of Brest sometime in the middle of April and the Admiralty officials were convinced that it was on its way to Louisbourg.[68] The Admiralty was wrong; de l'Etanduère's squadron was bound for the West Indies. In the middle of April Maurepas was not aware of the existence of the New England expedition to Louisbourg, and it was too late to change de l'Etanduère's orders when he did find out. It was not until July 16 that another squadron of five warships under the command of Perier de Salvert sailed for Louisbourg,[69] and after reaching the Grand Banks de Salvert decided to return to France. It is noteworthy that in one of the British vessels captured by this French squadron off Newfoundland was discovered Lieutenant-Governor Clarke of New York.[70] In 1741 and again in 1743 Clarke had urged the British authorities to organize an expedition against Louisbourg.

The arrival of the *Chester* led Warren to decide to sail immediately into Louisbourg harbour. He wrote to Pepperrell on June 21:

> As our two missing ships may be hourly expected I am now
> forming the plan for our going into the harbour with all the
> ships of warr and such a number of the Collony cruizers & ves-
> sells as shall be sufficient to go into the N.E.ᴵ Harbour with us,
> on the off side of our ships, with all the men of war's boats, ex-
> cept one to a ship, and all the other boats that can be musterd

everywhere, who shou'd, with the whale boats, shallops, etc, in Lewisbourg harbour already, be got ready with the ladders in them, to come on board our ships, upon my signal for that purpose, in order to assist in manning them from our ships and landing upon the town if thought necessary. So I propose to attempt this, God willing, the first fair opportunity of wind and weather after the ships joyn us, I think it will be necessary for you to form your disposition for attacking the town by land when wee do by our ships, and that you may know when I am determined to go in, and the wind is fair, and I expect to get in the same day, I will hoist a Dutch flagg under my pendant at the main top gall' masthead, and wish you cou'd then show me that you were ready with your troops by making three smoaks. I wou'd if I cou'd get in before noon.... Your people shou'd march when I hoist the Dutch flagg, and when they see most of our sails furl'd they shou'd approach near the town, drums beating and colours flying, and when I hoist a red flagg...you may then be assur'd I shall be in and begin the attack in a quarter or half an hour at farthest after.

Finally in a rare outburst of optimism and conviviality Warren suggested to Pepperrell that they should "keep a good house" in Louisbourg " and give the ladys...a gallant ball." [71]

Warren's plan of operations was accepted without any reservations by Pepperrell. It is interesting to note that Warren's plan was remarkably similar to the one proposed by Pepperrell's council of war on June 5 and curtly rejected by Warren. The fleet was to force its way into Louisbourg harbour and when anchored was to be joined by New Englanders with whaleboats from the Grand Battery. Then an amphibious assault by the New Englanders and the Marines under cover of Warren's guns would take place. Meanwhile, there would be a frontal attack from the landward side by what remained of Pepperrell's force. Such a plan, of course, in order to succeed, required careful timing and coordination. Neither Pepperrell nor Warren, however, could guarantee these prerequisites.

On June 21 and June 22 many eyes were glued to the southwest horizon in search of the British warships whose arrival would mark the beginning of the final push against Louisbourg. There was a newfound confidence in both the New England camp and in Warren's fleet. For the moment at least, relishing the sudden change in their fortunes, the New Englanders forgot about the tattered state of their clothes infested with lice, their ripped shoes and the ever-present threat of dysentery. [72] The end of the siege appeared at last to be in sight and the expected riches of Louisbourg once again assumed a position of paramount importance in the thinking of the New Englanders.

June 22 was a day of prolonged celebration in the New England camp. Ostensibly at least, the reason for the festivities was the anniversary of the coronation of George II.[73] But the anniversary was just an excuse for the New Englanders to hearten themselves with merrymaking before what many thought would be a bloody assault upon Louisbourg.

At noon all the New Englanders, except those in the batteries, gathered near Pepperrell's tent on the west side of Landing Cove Brook near Gabarus Bay. After being "Rally'd by ye Drums and Exercised,"[74] a number of barrels of rum were punched open and the troops sat around listening to "Violin flut & Vocal Musick."[75] While these New Englanders were thus boisterously engaged near Pepperrell's tent, Pepperrell and "the general officers went on board the commodore, were generously entertained and assured by [Warren] that he would come into the harbour with the ships."[76] However, the New Englanders in the batteries had little opportunity to drink rum and to listen to music. They were ordered by Pepperrell to keep up "an incessant Fire"[77] against the fortress and the Island Battery. Captain Sherburne noted in his journal:

> This morning had no fire on either Side—Received orders
> from The Generall In Honour to his Majesty at 12 O'Clock to
> fire a Salute from our Battery and Capt. Brooks to take up the
> Salute and then the Grand Battery; our Guns being well Shot-
> ted and pointed we payed the Complyment all Round which
> I followed all the Day and am Certain to the Discomfort of
> our Enemys.[78]

While on board the *Superbe* Pepperrell and Warren discussed the final details of the proposed assault. Warren was particularly concerned about the lack of discipline among the New Englanders and urged Pepperrell to give "directions against plundering, till leave given, upon pain of death."[79] Furthermore, Pepperrell was persuaded:

> to notifie all the Masters of Transports, at their Peril carefully
> to observe and obey all orders wch they shall receive from
> Comm. Warren and let them know that upon their Refusal or
> neglect, they will be severely punished according to the rules
> of the Navy.[80]

It was also agreed that if Du Chambon, on seeing Warren's fleet attempting to enter Louisbourg harbour, decided to discuss capitulation terms, Pepperrell was "to give directions that the Troops do not enter the town, till the terms shall be agreed to, by the General and Commander-in-chief at Sea."[81]

When Pepperrell returned to shore in the early evening, he received a warm reception from his troops and joined them in proceeding "by ye Beat of ye Drums To Prayers."[82] The New Englanders were well aware of what was in store for them. As soon as Warren's naval reinforcement arrived and there was a favourable wind, some 500 New Englanders would be sent aboard Warren's fleet and the others would be ordered to march on Louisbourg on seeing Warren hoist his Dutch flag. Most of them dreaded seeing the red flag flying on the *Superbe*, for this would mean the launching of the frontal assault.

June 23 dawned clear and bright. At ten in the morning a lookout on the *Superbe* sighted five vessels cruising to the southwest.[83] Warren immediately ordered a pursuit, and he soon discovered that the ships he was chasing were the *Sunderland*, the *Canterbury*, a 26-gun French prize, the 40-gun *Lark*, and the ordnance storeship for Annapolis Royal, the *Blacket and Fenwick*.[84] The latter two vessels had been sailing for Annapolis Royal when they met the *Sunderland* and *Canterbury* and the French prize.

Warren now had a powerful fleet of eleven warships, the 60-gun *Superbe*, the 40-gun *Eltham*, the 40-gun *Mermaid*, the 40-gun *Launceston*, the 60-gun *Princess Mary*, the 60-gun *Sunderland*, the 60-gun *Canterbury*, the 50-gun *Chester*, the 40-gun *Hector*, the 40-gun *Lark*, and the 64-gun *Vigilant*. These ships were manned by almost 4,000 men and carried a total of 554 cannon. In addition there were also the lightly armed New England vessels. The 14-gun *Tartar*, the 12-gun *Resolution* and the 6-gun *Bonetta* were cruising in the Gut of Canso looking for Marin's force, but the 24-gun *Shirley*, the 20-gun *Massachusetts*, the 16-gun *Defence*, the 10-gun *Abigail*, and others were in the general vicinity of Louisbourg.[85] Warren had more men at his disposal than either Pepperrell or Du Chambon, and probably possessed greater fire-power as well. It is not surprising, then, that he was now willing to sail into Louisbourg harbour, especially when it is also kept in mind that the Lighthouse Battery was now playing havoc with the Island Battery.

On being joined by the *Sunderland, Canterbury,* and *Lark,* Warren appealed to Pepperrell: "For God sake hurry off the men, and I will go in the moment the wind will allow."[86] Warren promised to send Pepperrell fifty barrels of powder, and in return desired "a schooner load or two of moss" in order to "barrocade [his] ships well against the enemy's small shott."[87] To exchange a few tons of moss for fifty barrels of powder was regarded by the shrewd Pepperrell as a remarkable business transaction. He ordered some of his men to collect moss and in a short time "a grat Quantity"[88] was found. Furthermore, in preparation for the combined assault, Pepperrell ordered two additional 42-pounders to be moved to Titcomb's Battery and the large mortar to be transported to the Lighthouse Battery.[89] But for some undetermined reason he procrastinated concerning the sending of the 400 or 500 New Englanders to Warren's fleet.

On June 24 on shore, "the Guns and Bombs played well on boath sides";[90] another 42-pounder was moved to Titcomb's Battery,[91] and on board Warren's vessels the seamen were "Employ'd Barracodeing the Ship and prepairing Matters for goeing into the Harbour of Louisbourg."[92] Pepperrell informed Warren on June 24 that he now had a sufficient number of volunteers to send to Warren's ships and would dispatch them "when you think it best." Furthermore, Pepperrell asserted that the whaleboats and other proposed landing craft in Louisbourg harbour were being fitted with oars and ladders and would be placed under the command of Waldo and Lieutenant-Colonel Richard Gridley, the commanding officer at the Lighthouse battery.[93]

On the following day "Most of the land men who were to go on board the ships embarked"[94] and Warren declared that he would sail into Louisbourg harbour on the following morning, June 26.[95] Moss and oakum were spread about his ships and the cannon made ready for the expected bombardment. On shore, ladders were carried to the Advanced Battery and also packed into the whaleboats and "Shalloways" near the Grand Battery.[96] Some New Englanders were busily engaged in collecting firewood and brush, which they piled into three mounds "on three Hills near the Town for a Becon for...Warren."[97]

Seeing the frenzied preparations being made by the New Englanders, especially at the Advanced Battery, the French began to expect an immediate frontal assault. In an attempt to counter such a move, they began that evening a heavy fire on the Battery:

> ...they Began to heave their Shells from all their mortars and
> hove them so fast that the Elements war almost on flame the
> Shells fell very thick.... The[y] Hove 47. Shells that night.[98]

Many factors combined to persuade Du Chambon on the night of June 24 that he should consider capitulating to the besiegers: the frontal assault preparations being made by the New Englanders, the arrival of four additional warships to reinforce Warren's already formidable squadron, the scarcity of gunpowder, the battered condition of the Dauphin Bastion and King's Bastion, the news about the capture of the *Vigilant,* the widespread damage throughout the town caused by over 6,000 New England cannon-balls and shells, the lack of any information about Marin, and the bad mauling the Island Battery was receiving from the Lighthouse Battery.[99]

The merchants and influential citizens of Louisbourg were also applying considerable pressure upon Du Chambon to capitulate. They had a great deal to lose if Louisbourg were taken by storm. Some had built up huge fortunes which they did not wish to surrender to the New Englanders. Possibly late on June 25 or early on the following day they presented a petition to Du Chambon. Fearing "a general pillage" they pleaded with the governor "that in order to avoid the total destruction...of the little that remained"[100] of their fortunes it was necessary to obtain the best terms possible from the invaders. This petition was just the excuse Du Chambon was desperately seeking. He did not want to bear the sole responsibility for making the decision to capitulate. He had blundered so often during the siege that he was almost delighted to be urged to do something he believed was unavoidable in any case. He asked the chief engineer Verrier and the artillery captain Ste. Marie to report on the state of the fortifications and the guns and ammunition.[101] Of course, Du Chambon knew exactly what these two officers would tell him. But he needed their reports to justify his actions to Maurepas.

Verrier declared on June 26 that the Dauphon Bastion and the right flank of the King's Bastion were entirely demolished and that their embrazures of wood, put up to replace those of stone, were useless. The breach in the West Gate was not large enough to permit the New Englanders to enter without ladders, but Verrier was certain that only a little more battering by the cannon of the Advanced Battery would be necessary to make the breach large enough so that the enemy would not have to use ladders. Furthermore, it was Verrier's opinion that the Island Battery had been neutralized by the Lighthouse Battery.[102] As far as Verrier was concerned that was no alternative to immediate capitulation.

Ste. Marie also arrived at the same conclusion. Most of the cannon in the Dauphin Bastion and those in the west flank of the King's Bastion had been knocked out of their embrazures by the persistent and effective New England fire. Moreover, Ste. Marie estimated that only forty-seven barrels of powder remained out of the

670 barrels that had been in Louisbourg at the start of the siege. To make matters worse, the French gunners had run out of fuses for their cannon.[103]

Even before Verrier and Ste. Marie had begun to prepare their reports, Warren had decided to postpone his assault until June 27. The wind was unfavourable, blowing gustily from the southwest.[104] Warren came ashore to discuss his change of plans with Pepperrell and also to speak to the New England troops who had been assembled new Pepperrell's camp. An anonymous New Englander described the scene in the following manner:

> The whole army was Called together to whom the Commodore made an Excellent Speech Well worth writing down but too Large to Reed He Says hes now Ready to go in with his Shiping into the Harbour and waits for nothing but a Fair wind and saies that if nothing Short of his Going at the head of the army (into the Town) Will do. He'll Chearfully Do it. for He'd Rather Leave his Body at Louisbourg, than not take the Citty.[105]

In forceful language Warren emphasized that the New England volunteers "Could not Take ye Citty with ye Land forces neither Could he wth ye Sea forces without ye assistance of each Other."[106] After "exhorting [the New Englanders] to enter bravely, like Englishmen...which would be the honour of their country, themselves and their latest posterity," the commodore was answered "with three cheerful Huzzas."[107] Once again the New Englanders had been carried away by Warren's oratory.

Just before sunset on June 26 Warren and Pepperrell were informed that an officer from Louisbourg, under cover of a flag of truce, was carrying a letter to them from Du Chambon.[108] Du Chambon was now willing to begin to negotiate regarding the capitulation of Louisbourg. He wrote:

> Desirous of putting a stop to acts of hostility and prevent the effusion of blood on one side and on the other, I send you an officer of the garrison...in order to desire of you a suspension of arms, for so long a time as shall be needful for me to make proposals to you, upon the conditions of which I shall determine to deliver up to you, the place which the King my master has entrusted me with.[109]

It was half-past eight in the evening when Pepperrell and Warren sent their brief reply to Du Chambon:

> We have yours of the date proposing a suspension of hostilities for such a time as shall be necessary for you to determine

> upon the conditions of delivering up the garrison of Louis-
> bourg, which arrived at a happy juncture to prevent the Effu-
> sion of Christian blood as we were together and had just de-
> termined upon a general attack. We shall comply with your
> desire until eight of the clock to-morrow, and if in the mean-
> time you surrender yourselves prisoners of war, You may de-
> pend upon honour and generous treatment.[110]

The hard bargaining had begun. Unfortunately for Du Chambon,
Pepperrell and Warren possessed almost all of the good cards.

The sending of Du Chambon's letter brought the cannonading
on both sides to an end. The French in the Island Battery were
without question the ones to benefit most from the lull. For the
large mortar at the Lighthouse Battery had driven them to despair:

> they having but little to shelter them from the Shot, that
> ranged quite through their Barracks, so terrified them, that
> many of them left the Fort, and ran into the Water for
> Refuge.[111]

Du Chambon was unable to get very much sleep on the evening
of June 26 as he wrestled with the problem of drawing up terms of
capitulation. Being a shrewd bargainer, he decided to ask for far
more than he expected to receive from his enemies. The "Articles
of Capitulation," as finally drawn up by Du Chambon, consisted of
no less than seventeen clauses.[112] The first six clauses were particularly concerned with the civil inhabitants of Louisbourg and their
possessions. Du Chambon demanded that they should be free to
sail to France, New France, or the French West Indies in vessels
supplied by Warren, and to take with them all their possessions.
Furthermore, if they so wished, they were to be permitted to remain in Cape Breton where they were to have freedom of worship.
The remaining clauses dealt with the French troops. Du Chambon
insisted that his troops should be unmolested and properly fed and
housed by the invaders in Louisbourg until British vessels were
ready to carry them to France. In a rather fascinating clause, Du
Chambon claimed the right to be supplied with "*deux chariots cou-
verts*"[113] in which he could place whatever he wished, and also demanded permission for any of his troops to mask themselves until
their return to France.

At 8 o'clock in the morning on June 27, Du Chambon's "Articles of Capitulation" were presented to Pepperrell and to Warren
by the governor's envoy, Captain Bonnaventure.[114] It was perhaps of
some symbolic importance that June 27 was the New England Sabbath. It did not take Pepperrell and Warren long to draft a reply to

Du Chambon. Their counter-proposals accepted many of Du Chambon's articles. "Desirous to treat [the French] in a generous manner," Pepperrell and Warren reiterated the terms of surrender proposed by them on May 18:

> that all the subjects of the French king, now in said city and territory, shall be treated with utmost humanity, have their personal estate secured to them and have leave to transport themselves and said effects to any part of the French king's dominions in Europe.

But they were not to be free to remain in North America. In addition to their May 18 proposal, Pepperrell and Warren put forward six new clauses, all of which were contained in Du Chambon's "Articles":

> *First.* That if your vessels shall be found insufficient for the transportation of your persons and proposed effects to France, we will provide such a farther number of vessels as may be sufficient for that purpose, also any provisions necessary for the voyage that you cannot furnish yourselves with.
>
> *Secondly.* That all commission officers belonging to the garrison, and the inhabitants of the town, may remain in their houses with their families and enjoy the free exercise of their religion, and no person shall be suffered to molest or misuse any of them till such time as they can conveniently be transported to France.
>
> *Thirdly.* That the non-commission officers and soldiers shall, immediately upon the surrender of the town and fortresses, be put on board some of his Britannic Majesty's ships till they can also be transported to France.
>
> *Fourthly.* That all your sick and wounded shall be taken tender care of in the same manner with our own.
>
> *Fifthly.* That the commander in chief now in the garrison shall have liberty to send off two covered wagons, to be inspected only by one officer of ours, that no warlike stores may be contained therein.
>
> *Sixthly.* That if there are any persons in the town or garrison which you shall desire may not be seen by us, they shall be permitted to go off masked.

Pepperrell and Warren stressed that they would grant these generous terms only if Du Chambon promised, first, to surrender the Island Battery by six in the afternoon and permit the entry of Warren's vessels; second, to swear that no inhabitant of Louisbourg "shall take up arms against his Britannic majesty" until after a period of one year; and third, to free immediately the New England prisoners.[115]

After Bonnaventure's return to Louisbourg with Pepperrell's and Warren's proposals, Warren returned to the *Superbe*, so that he would be able to lead his fleet into Louisbourg harbour at six that evening. Du Chambon and his officers were willing to accept the terms offered them, but they requested one further concession that their "troops may march out of the garrison with their arms and colours flying, to be there delivered [to the invaders] till the said troop's arrival in France, at which time to have them returned to them."[116] At three in the afternoon Du Chambon sent two of his officers under cover of a flag of truce, one to Pepperrell and the other to Warren, with copies of Du Chambon's letter requesting the full honours of war for his troops. Pepperrell immediately accepted Du Chambon's demand and informed Warren of his decision.[117] The French officer remained with Pepperrell as a hostage and Pepperrell sent one of his officers, Captain Mason, into Louisbourg to act in the same capacity.[118] Warren's response to Du Chambon's request was similar to that of Pepperrell. Warren wrote to Pepperrell:

> I received your favour by Col Moore, and am glad our sentiments agree, with regard to allowing the troops the honours of war which they desired, the uncertainty of our affairs that depends so much on wind and weather, made it necessary not to stickle at trifles.[119]

Captain Philip Durell of the *Eltham* was chosen by Warren to be his emissary and hostage in Louisbourg.[120] Durell carried with him more than just a letter from Warren accepting Du Chambon's demand, for he had been instructed to attempt to convince Du Chambon to surrender to Warren rather than to Pepperrell. Warren urged Du Chambon:

> ...to march to my Boats at the Beach, with their musquets, and Bayonets, and colours flying, there to deliver them to the officers of his Brittanic Majesty whom I shall appoint for that purpose, to be kept in my custody till they shall be landed in the French King's Dominions.... That all the ships of war and other vessels do enter the Harbour without molestation at any time after daylight to-morrow morning, and that the keys of the town be delivered to such officers and troops as I shall appoint to receive them, and that all the cannon, warlike and other King's stores in the town be also delivered up to the said officer.[121]

Durrell further argued that if Du Chambon surrendered to Pepperrell, the New Englanders would pillage the town and rape the
women. Only Warren, as the representative of the British Crown,
could ensure good order and discipline.[122] "L'Habitant De Louisbourg" commented:

> All this shows very little co-operation between the two gener-
> als, and sufficiently confirms the remark which I have already
> made; in fact one could never have told that these troops be-
> longed to the same nation and obeyed the same prince.[123]

By six in the afternoon both Pepperrell and Warren had been
informed that Du Chambon and his officers had agreed to capitulate. The Island Battery was occupied before nightfall by a few of
Warren's men. Pepperrell expected that when the New Englanders
marched into Louisbourg the following day, he would receive the
keys to the city. On the other hand, Warren believed that when his
fleet sailed into Louisbourg harbour the following day, Du Chambon would surrender to him rather than to Pepperrell.

While preparations were being made that evening both inside
and outside of Louisbourg for the surrender of the fortress on
June 28, Marin's force was encamped near Tatamagouche harbour
on Northumberland Strait. The previous day his flotilla of canoes,
schooners and sloops on its way to Louisbourg had encountered
the three New England vessels, the *Tartar*, the *Bonetta*, and the *Resolution*, and had been forced to take refuge in Tatamagouche harbour. The presence of the New England vessels discouraged the Indians from going any further.[124]

Most of the New England volunteers regarded the terms of capitulation with considerable scorn. There was soon "a great Noys
and hubbub a mungst the Solders about the Plonder."[125] Feeling
that they had been cheated out of what was rightfully theirs, many
New Englanders wanted to return to their homes immediately.
They wanted to sing:

> Faire Well Cape: Britton
> faire well all you fases
> that Bread such Dis:greases
> a gainst Solders that are True to their King
> for I Boldely Do Say
> If they once git a way
> You will be hard Poot to it to Catch them agin.[126]

Even before the articles of capitulation had been properly rati-
fied, Pepperrell was planning to enter Louisbourg. He was ignorant of military niceties and had only one thing in mind, to enter

Louisbourg as quickly as possible. He wrote to Du Chambon on the morning of June 28:

> I desire the favour that your officers and families, with the inhabitants and their families, may repair to their own houses as soon as possible where they may depend they shall not meet with the least bad treatment, nor any person suffered to give them the least disturbance, and that your troops' arms may be put by themselves in a magazine, where they shall be safe, and delivered to you the day they are to march out of town. I shall send Col. Bradstreet with a detachment at four o'clock this afternoon to take possession of the town and fort, to whom I desire you will deliver them up with all warlike stores, and keys.[127]

When Warren heard about Pepperrell's letter, he denounced the New Englander for violating the accepted rules of warfare and for showing "a kind of jealousy."[128] Warren had reacted violently to being unexpectedly outmanoeuvred by a military novice. He saw sinister motives in almost everything now being contemplated by Pepperrell. But as far as Pepperrell, who was not aware of Warren's machinations, was concerned, Du Chambon had no other choice but to surrender to the New Englanders. For had not the expedition originated in New England and had not the New Englanders alone been responsible for besieging the fortress? Warren had helped, of course, but in Pepperrell's eyes the naval role was a secondary one.

In the early afternoon Warren's ships began to sail slowly into Louisbourg harbour. At 4 o'clock, before Warren's Marines were landed, Pepperrell ordered his men to march to the Maurepas Bastion and to enter Louisbourg by way of the South Gate:

> ...the Colours were flying the Drums Beating Trumpets Sounding Flutes & Viols Playing Col Bradstreet att ye Head of the Army The Genl. Lt. Genl. and Gentry in ye Rear.[129]

On entering Louisbourg they turned to the left and proceeded to the parade ground near the Citadel, where the New Englanders received the keys to the fortress.[130]

With the landing of Warren's Marines, bickering began in earnest between the New Englanders and the British regarding who was in fact directly responsible for the fall of Louisbourg.[131] Both groups should have realized that "Neither would have succeeded alone,"[132] and that, furthermore, as Lord Selkirk commented concerning another military episode: "There would appear in this celebrated campaign fully as much guid luck as guid guiding."[133]

Most of the New Englanders tended to equate "guid luck" with "God's Wonder-working Providence for New-England."[134] They saw their God's hand at work at every important stage in the development of the expedition and the siege. How else could they explain their assault landing at Gabarus Bay, their capture of the Grand Battery, the unexpected arrival of naval reinforcements, the exceptionally fine weather throughout most of the siege?

A long and complex chain of events had led to the fall of Louisbourg. There was the vital role played by Vaughan, Bradstreet, Shirley and Pepperrell in organizing the expedition. There was also Warren's gamble in deciding to sail to Louisbourg and the unexpected enthusiasm of the British admiralty for the expedition. And finally there were the strategic weaknesses of the fortress and the blunders committed by Du Chambon before and during the siege. But too much criticism should not be heaped upon Du Chambon. With British naval supremacy assured in the North Atlantic because of the weakness of the French navy, Du Chambon's task was virtually an impossible one. For Louisbourg without a powerful naval force to defend it was an easy prey for an invader supported by naval strength. Furthermore, Du Chambon was not responsible for the military weaknesses of the fortress itself. Some of the walls were crumbling before the New England bombardment began; the Grand and Island Batteries were dominated by neighbouring heights of land; and the landward defences of the fortress were inadequate. What is remarkable is that under these circumstances the French were still able to conduct a reasonably vigorous defence.

Louisbourg, France's key stronghold in the New World, had now become New England's northeastern outpost and Britain's steppingstone into the St. Lawrence region. It is noteworthy that the siege proper took so few lives. Only fifty-three French troops and 101 New Englanders[135] were killed. The capture of Louisbourg in 1745, which one New Englander thought "can scarce be parallel'd in History,"[136] showed what could be accomplished by a combined British and American force and by a combined sea and land force. But it also demonstrated that there was a widening chasm developing between Britain and its New England colonies. During the months following the capture of Louisbourg this chasm widened dangerously.

12

Epilogue

THE NEWS OF THE CAPTURE of Louisbourg set off wild and unprecedented celebrations throughout New England.[1] Never before had the inhabitants seen such brilliant displays of fireworks, such "universal and unaffected joy," such vast supplies "of good Liquor for all that would drink."[2] And in Great Britain the victory-starved inhabitants heaped praise upon the New England troops:

> Hail, heroes born for action, not for show!
> Who leave toupees and powder to the beau,
> To war's dull pedants tedious rules of art,
> And know to conquer by a dauntless heart,
> Rough *English* virtue gives your deeds to fame.
> And o'er the *Old* exalts *New England's* name.[3]

In France, as would be expected, the news brought about a temporary mood of gloom. But Maurepas was undaunted. He vowed to recapture Louisbourg as soon as a powerful enough expedition could be organized.[4]

The capture of Louisbourg convinced the vast majority of New Englanders of the validity of at least two of their most cherished beliefs. First, they were now certain that "ye God of Heaven" was "ye God of New England"[5] since "The finger of God has been so conspicuous in every circumstance of this expedition."[6] Ministers and laymen alike hammered away on this theme during the weeks and months following their being informed of the fall of Louisbourg. In the spring of 1745 some of these same men had had serious doubts as to whether their God was pleased with developments in New England. The Great Awakening had come to an abrupt stop and New Lights and Old Lights were at each other's throats. However, Louisbourg's capture was felt by both extremes to be proof of the fact that the Almighty, in order to show his extreme pleasure with New England, had made all the necessary arrangements for victory. The Reverend Charles Chauncy of Boston, in his "Thanksgiving Sermon for the Reduction of Cape Breton" declared:

> I scarce know of a Conquest, since the days of Joshua and the Judges, wherein the Finger of God is more visible.... The Lord hath *done great things* for us. The God of Jeshurun *hath rode upon the Heaven in our help, and in his Excellency on the Skie.* And this wonderful Appearance of God for us, should excite our love, warm our Devotion, confirm our Faith and encourage our Hope.[7]

Secondly, the capture of Louisbourg strengthened the view widely held in New England of the superiority of the American citizen soldier over European regulars. The Almighty may have been directly responsible for the capture of Louisbourg, but it was argued that the "Supreme Contriver, Mover and Director"[8] used the best instruments available—the New England volunteers—to defeat the French. The Louisbourg expedition did much to strengthen what Daniel Boorstin has referred to as the "long-standing American myth of a constantly prepared citizenry."[9] The New Englanders became supremely confident in their military ability. They were as proud as peacocks when they read the frequently reprinted paragraph from the British publication, *The Craftsman*:

> But while I contemplate the virtues of the *New Englishmen*, I grieve and blush at the reproach of the *Old*, and I cannot conclude this paper without observing, that if a neglect of public *justice* prevails much longer in this land, we may possibly have reason to think this country no safe abode, and may find it necessary to seek a refuge in *New England*, where *justice* and *industry seem to have taken their residence.*[10]

Furthermore, they could not forget the memorable pronouncement made by Morpain, Louisbourg's Port Captain:

> That he thot the n England men were Cowards—but now he thot that if they had a pick Ax and Spade—they would dig their way to Hell and storm it.[11]

Taking into account this cocky mood which at times blurred into a kind of chauvinistic arrogance, it is not surprising that the New Englanders violently objected to the attempt made by Warren "to take upon himself the chief command on shoar"[12] and to give the impression that his naval force was responsible for Louisbourg's surrender. As far as William Shirley was concerned, and he was speaking for all of New England, Warren's policy was "an unwarrantable usurpation."[13] Eventually Pepperrell, who was disturbed because of the powerful anti-Warren movement, especially in Massachusetts, endeavoured to pour oil on the troubled waters by explaining that in spite of Warren's indiscretions "these disputes are all over, as we both aim at ye good & security of this place."[14] But the New Englanders found it difficult to forgive Warren and his officers for their effrontery and for their brazen attempt to steal the spotlight from Pepperrell's volunteers.

In Great Britain news of the unexpected capture of Louisbourg was received with unbounded enthusiasm by the ordinary man in the street, but the news embarrassed and annoyed the government led by Henry Pelham and his brother the Duke of Newcastle. The popular acclaim which greeted the victory was undoubtedly—at first, anyway—"the spontaneous outburst of a nation which had waited long for anything to celebrate."[15] Writing to the British Minister in Holland in August 1745, the Earl of Chesterfield described the popular mood.

> One, almost insurmountable, difficulty I foresee in any negotiation with France, is our new acquisition of Cape Breton, which is become the darling object of the whole nation; it is ten times more so than ever Gibraltar was.[16]

The Pelhams found themselves in a perplexing situation for while Pepperrell and Warren were capturing Louisbourg, the Pelhams were endeavouring to negotiate an early peace with France. Not only were the peace negotiations with the French undermined, but the Pelhams found themselves threatened by a Cabinet faction, encouraged by Louisbourg's capture, now demanding a more aggressive British military policy both in Europe and in North America. In order to retain political power, Newcastle was forced to agree not only to utilize Louisbourg in a large-scale assault upon New France but also to prosecute the war on the Continent with some vigour. Probably never before had a North American event exerted such a profound impact upon both the political and the diplomatic policies of a British government.[17]

Newcastle did not hesitate to reward Warren, Pepperrell and Shirley. Warren was promoted to the rank of rear-admiral and appointed Governor of Louisbourg. Pepperrell was granted a baronetcy and he and Shirley secured potentially profitable regimental commissions. Moreover, it was understood that in due course the British government would reimburse the various colonial governments for most of the expenses incurred in carrying out the Louisbourg expedition.

In July, August, and September 1745, while many inhabitants in New England and in Britain were joyously celebrating Louisbourg's capture, the New England troops in Louisbourg were on the verge of mutiny. There were four main reasons for their discontent. First, there was little plunder for the volunteers who, instead of sharing the not inconsiderable French property as they had been originally promised, were "forst to Stand att there Dores to gard them."[18] This was a humiliating experience. Second, to make matters even more serious as far as the New Englanders were concerned, Warren's ships in August had little difficulty in capturing three French vessels loaded with exotic goods and precious metals on their way home from the East Indies. It was estimated that the total value of these vessels was £600,000 sterling.[19] And the New Englanders received not one shilling of prize money. They were furious. Thomas Waldron complained to his father:

> ...'tis Galling...that the army should both fight for and afterwards Guard The City and yet they have none of the [Plunder] Prizes which Cost the Men of War nothing more than go and meet them which we could do was the City afloat.[20]

And what made the New Englanders even more furious was the fact that Warren's men, when on shore, strutted about Louisbourg arrogantly explaining to all within earshot that the navy had alone been responsible for the capture of Louisbourg. The third reason for the discontent among the volunteers was that they were receiving inadequate food rations and that most of them were "barefootd & their cloths tore almost in pieces."[21] Finally, many of the New Englanders were just plain homesick and wanted desperately to return to their homes and families. The troops had had enough excitement and disappointment to last them a lifetime.

To deal with the serious situation Pepperrell urged Shirley to come to Louisbourg and he also increased the rum ration to his troops.[22] In addition, he permitted a surprisingly large number of his men to return to their homes. He hoped thus to get rid of the worst troublemakers. By mid-September, 1,238 of the original volunteers had returned to New England, leaving only 1,912 to defend Louisbourg. But reinforcements increased this number to 2,250 in November and 2,623 in December 1745.[23]

Shirley, who had arrived in Louisbourg harbour on August 27, did not leave for Boston until December. By increasing the monthly salaries of the Massachusetts troops and by promising all those who would winter in Louisbourg adequate clothing and food supplies as well as their discharges as soon as British troops arrived in 1746, Shirley "quite appeased the late spirit of discontent."[24] He had performed a most useful service, for there is every indication that if he had not visited Louisbourg, the fortress would have witnessed its second mutiny within less than a year.

It was a disastrous winter in Louisbourg. Pepperrell noted to Shirley on February 8, 1746:

> ...that from ye last of Nov. to this date we have buried 561 men, and have at this time 1100 sick. We flatter ourselves from ye burials of three or four days past not amountg to more than 3, 4, & 5, of a day, w^n before were generally from 14 to 17, that the distemper abates.[25]

The epidemic, which fed upon the low resistance of the men, brought about by excessive drinking and inadequate housing, did not, however, abate in February. For Pepperrell had to admit in June 1746 that "about 1200"[26] troops had died. When the British regulars arrived in May 1746, those New Englanders who had not enlisted in Pepperrell's and Shirley's regiments sailed for home. They had had more than enough of the foggy, desolate death-trap. Some 450 New Englanders remained in Louisbourg and they were soon reinforced by 480 colonial recruits.[27]

Maurepas was not interested only in the recapture of Louisbourg; he also wanted to drive the British out of Nova Scotia and then ravage the New England coast, razing Boston. However, it was not until June 22, 1746, that his expedition was able to sail from France. It consisted of ten ships of the line, three frigates, three bomb vessels, and approximately sixty transports carrying 3,500 regular troops.[28] The expedition was under the command of the Duc d'Anville.

It was not until September 15, 1746, that d'Anville's fleet sighted Nova Scotia and a few days later most of his ships lay anchored in the commodious Chebucto harbour. What d'Anville saw disheartened him. At least two of his frigates had been forced to return to France; a terrible epidemic was sweeping the remaining ships, most of which had been badly battered by unusually severe Atlantic storms. It has been estimated that by the end of September, 2,300 soldiers and sailors had died from scurvy and from smallpox.[29] D'Anville himself died, probably from apoplexy. He was replaced by d'Estourmelles, the commanding officer of the *Trident*, who because of sickness and attempted suicide was replaced by La Jonquière. The latter sent four warships to destroy Annapolis Royal. But another Atlantic storm was responsible for the return of these ships to Chebucto harbour without even sighting Annapolis. La Jonquière had no choice but to lead his shattered expedition to Brest. Maurepas had no word of criticism for La Jonquière. Instead the Minister of Marine maintained:

> When fate intervenes it might diminish the commander's glory but it neither diminishes his labour nor his merit.[30]

New England was terror-stricken when information first arrived of d'Anville's fleet.[31] Thomas Hutchinson observed that "England was not more alarmed with the Spanish Armada in 1588 than Boston and the other North American sea-ports were with the arrival of this fleet in their neighbourhood."[32] Pious men dropped to their knees to petition the Almighty to destroy the French armada, while more practical men improved the coastal defences. Some 6,500 volunteers from the interior were rushed to the coast to repulse the anticipated French assault.[33] When in the middle of October the New Englanders were informed of the withdrawal of the French fleet there was another outburst of relief and joy. The New Englanders once again "saw the immediate hand of divine providence in the protection, or rather rescue, of the British Colonies."[34] The Almighty was certainly making it abundantly clear to the New Englanders that He was the God of New England.

The Louisbourg expedition had driven the Massachusetts government close to bankruptcy. Because of inadequate accounts and because of a difference of opinion concerning the actual value, in terms of sterling, of the Massachusetts paper money used to pay for the expedition, it was not until 1748 that the British government decided on the actual sums to be reimbursed to the various New England colonies. Massachusetts received £183,649/2/7; New Hampshire £16,355/13/4; Connecticut £28,863/19/1; Rhode Island £16,322/12/10.[35]

Undoubtedly the British government hoped that the money sent to the New England colonies in 1749 would temper somewhat their disappointment at seeing Louisbourg returned to France.[36] For the Treaty of Aix-la-Chapelle of October 1748 returned "New England's conquest" to the French. The New Englanders were not taken by surprise by this development. Throughout 1748 their newspapers had prepared them for the shock.[37] A poem published in May 1749 in the *Boston Weekly News-Letter* accurately reflected the New England response to the peace treaty:

> Vanquish'd by Peace, that Heros like withstood,
> Loud thund'ring Cannons, mix'd with Streams of Blood.

Epilogue

The Gallics triumph—their Recess so short
Joyful return, to that late conquer'd Fort,
Where Monuments of English Arms will shew,
When Time may serve, ye shall our Claims renew,
New England's Fate insult! The Day is Yours,
Constrain'd, we yield the Conquest that was ours.[38]

There was no public outcry in New England. The practical New Englanders realized that they could not change the peace. But many, though not all, felt betrayed and insulted. New Englanders would not respond so enthusiastically in another war with France. In such a war, Louisbourg, of course, would have to be recaptured, and as far as most of the New Englanders were concerned "the lobster backs could jolly well do the job themselves."[39] It was clear that the New England grasp of military and commercial realities was far more sophisticated and long-sighted than that of the Pelhams. The New Englanders, together with a small minority in Britain led by William Pitt, realized that Louisbourg was the base from which successful assaults could be launched against the French Empire in North America. With Louisbourg back in French hands the British settlements in North America were once again threatened by French aggrandizement.

But a few New Englanders, especially those merchants who had vociferously opposed the expedition in early 1745, were pleased with the return of Louisbourg. Before the capture of the French fortress there had been a valuable illicit trade between New England and Louisbourg. Through Louisbourg the New England merchants had been able to penetrate the valuable French West Indies market. With Louisbourg once again under French control such a trade could be resumed in earnest.

The Louisbourg episode had driven the New England colonies further away from Great Britain. Moreover, the expedition had strengthened New England's sense of mission. As far as Jeremy Belknap was concerned: "Never was the hand of divine Providence more visible."[40] Convinced that they were the Almighty's special instruments in the New World, the New Englanders became increasingly confident in their superior abilities and in their superior way of life.

Bibliographical Note

THIS BOOK is largely based upon contemporary documents both in manuscript form and in print. Relevant primary sources from various archives and libraries in the United States and in Canada have been carefully examined in the hope of obtaining a balanced approach to the problem of New England-Louisbourg relations in the 1740's. The work of six historians, interested in various aspects of Louisbourg's development, has influenced the way in which this primary material has been interpreted. These studies are Francis Parkman, *A Half Century of Conflict*, Vol. II (Boston, 1892); J. S. McLennan, *Louisbourg from its Foundation to its Fall, 1713-1758* (London, 1918); Guy Frégault, *François Bigot, administrateur français*, Vol. I (Montreal, 1948); Gerald Graham, *Empire of the North Atlantic* (London, 1950); Byron Fairchild, *Messrs. William Pepperrell: Merchants at Piscataqua* (Ithaca, 1954); and J. A. Schutz, *William Shirley: King's Governor of Massachusetts* (Chapel Hill, 1961).

The vast collection of French and British documents at the Public Archives of Canada provided much valuable information for this volume. Especially significant were letters and journals from the *Archives des Colonies* Series B, the correspondence of the Minister of Marine to the Louisbourg officials, Series C[11]B, general correspondence from Louisbourg to the Minister of Marine, Series E, *Dossiers Personnels* of various Louisbourg inhabitants. Relevant series from the *Archives de la Marine* and the *Archives de la Guerre* as well as various volumes from the British Admiralty Papers, the British Museum Additional Manuscripts, the Anson Papers, the Colonial Office C.O. 5 and C.O. 217 series dealing with New England and Nova Scotia respectively, and the Louisbourg Map Collection were also extensively used.

In the United States the impressive manuscript holdings, especially of the Massachusetts Historical Society and to a lesser extent of the New Hampshire Historical Society and the Clements Library, University of Michigan, proved to be most valuable. At the Massachusetts Historical Society are to be found the Belknap, Pepperrell, Davis, French, Louisbourg, Saunders, Parkman, and Shirley Papers; at the New Hampshire Historical Society the Vaughan and Waldron Papers; and at the Clements Library the Louisbourg and Warren Papers. In addition the Maurepas papers at the University of Rochester were examined. Of lesser importance were the Bastide Letters at the Boston Public Library, the Jonathan Law Papers and the Roger Wolcott Papers at the Connecticut Historical Society, the Massachusetts Court Records at the Massachusetts State Archives, the Lennox Papers at the New York Public Library, and the Accounts of Rhode Island Agents in London at the Rhode Island Archives.

Of the printed sources the Massachusetts Historical Society *Collections* 1st Series, I, and 6th Series, X, "Pepperrell Papers" are indispensible as is G. M. Wrong (ed.), *Louisbourg in 1745: The Anonymous Lettre D'Un Habitant De Louisbourg* (New York, 1897). L. E. DeForest, *Louisbourg Journals 1745* (New York, 1932) is a fine collection of ten pertinent journals and other important documents. There are numerous available printed journals written by some of those involved in the Louisbourg expedition. The best of these are E. M. Bidwell (ed.), "Journal of the Rev. Adonijah Bidwell," *New England Historical and Genealogical Register* (1873), Vol. XXVII, 153-160; "Benjamin Cleaves's Journal," *ibid* (1912), Vol. LXVI, 113-124; L. E. DeForest (ed.) *The Journals and Papers of Seth Pomeroy* (New Haven, 1926); James Gibson, *A Journal of the Late Siege by the Troops from North America Against the French at Cape Breton* (London, 1747); "Journal Kept by Lieut. Daniel Giddings of Ipswich During the Expedition Against Cape Breton in 1744-5," Essex Institute Historical *Collections* (Oct., 1912), Vol. XLVIII, 293-304; S. A. Green (ed.), *Three Military Diaries Kept by Groton Soldiers in Different Wars* (Groton, 1901); C. H. Lincoln (ed.) *The Journal of Sir William Pepperrell Kept During the Expedition Against Louisbourg, Mar. 24-Aug. 22, 1745* (Worcester, 1910); William Pepperrell, *An Accurate Journal and Account of the Proceedings of the New England Land-Forces During the Late Expedition Against the French Settlements on Cape Breton* (London, 1746); William Shirley, *A Letter from William Shirley Esq., Governor of Massachusett's Bay, to his Grace the Duke of Newcastle: With a Journal of the Siege of Louisbourg* (London, 1748); W. P. Upham (ed.), "Craft's Journal of the Siege of Louisbourg," Essex Institute Historical *Collections* (1864), Vol. VI, 180-194; and "Journal of Roger Wolcott at the Siege of Louisbourg," Connecticut Historical Society *Collections* (1860), Vol. I, 131-162.

There are also some important printed volumes of private letters and government documents available. J. B. Akins (ed.), *Selections from the Public Documents of the Province of Nova Scotia* (Halifax, 1869); N. Bouton (ed.), *Documents and Records Relating to the Province of New Hampshire from 1738-1749* (Nashua, 1871); Vol. V, Connecticut Historical Society *Collections* (1907); Vol. XI, *ibid,* "Law Papers"; C. J. Hoadley, *The Public Records of the Colony of Connecticut from May, 1744 to November, 1750 Inclusive* (Hartford, 1876), Vol. IX; *Journals of the House of Representatives of Massachusetts, 1744-1745* (Boston, 1946), Vol. XXI; and C. H. Lincoln (ed.), *The Correspondence of William Shirley* (New York, 1912), Vol. I.

Soon after the Louisbourg expedition historians began to write about the episode. William Douglass, *A Summary, Historical and Political, of the First Planting, Progressive Improvements, and Present State of the British Settlements in North America* (London, 1760), Thomas Hutchinson, *The History of the Province of Massachusetts Bay...1691-1750* (Boston, 1767) and Jeremy Belknap, *A History of New Hampshire* (Boston, 1791) each contain enlightening descriptions of the expedition. Belknap and Hutchinson are particularly impressive.

It was not until 1891 that the work of these two scholars was in any effective manner superseded. In that year Francis Parkman published three brilliant articles in the *Atlantic Monthly* on the "Capture of Louisbourg by the New England Militia." Parkman owed a great deal to Belknap and Hutchinson but he also plowed virgin soil by making extensive use of some of the French sources. H. M. Burrage, *Maine at Louisbourg in 1745* (Augusta, 1910) added nothing of consequence to Parkman and in many respects was quite unreliable. But J. S. McLennan, *Louisbourg from its Foundation to its Fall* (London, 1918), though somewhat lacking in literary style, made noteworthy use of the available French and British sources and became the widely accepted authorized study on the general subject of Louisbourg. William Wood, *The Great Fortress: A Chronicle of Louisbourg, 1720-1760* (Toronto, 1928), is superficial and flimsy when compared to McLennan.

Of more recent historians, these mentioned earlier in the note, Frégault, *François Bigot,* Graham, *Empire of the North Atlantic,* Fairchild, *Messrs. William Pepperrell,* and Schutz, *William Shirley,* added considerable depth to McLennan's rather restrictive approach to

New England and Louisbourg in the 1740's. But Fairfax Downey, *Louisbourg: Key to a Continent* (Englewood Cliffs, 1965) makes little use of twentieth century scholarship and in addition is inadequately researched. Downey's *Louisbourg* is inferior to McLennan's *Louisbourg* as a general study of the French fortress.

Footnotes

INTRODUCTION

1 J. B. Brebner, *New England's Outpost* (New York, 1927), 15.
2 R. W. Van Alstyne, *The Rising American Empire* (Oxford, 1960), 26.
3 H. Pirenne, *Economic and Social History of Medieval Europe* (New York, 1964), 26.
4 J. S. McLennan, *Louisbourg from its Foundation to its Fall—1713-1758* (Toronto, 1918), 223.
5 J. S. McLennan, "Louisbourg," *Canadian Geographical Journal*, III, No. 3 (Oct. 1931), 260.
6 J. S. McLennan, *Louisbourg, 1713-1758*, 222.
7 See A. H. Clark, "New England's Role in the Underdevelopment of Cape Breton Island During the French Régime, 1713-1758," *Canadian Geographer*, IX, No. 1, 1965, 1-12.
8 L. E. DeForest, *Louisbourg Journals 1745* (New York, 1932), xv.

Chapter 1
THE FRENCH ATTACKS UPON CANSO AND ANNAPOLIS ROYAL

1 "New style" dates will be used throughout even though it was not until 1752 that the British adopted the Gregorian reform of the calendar.
2 Public Archives of Canada (P.A.C.), Archives Coloniales (A.C.), C¹¹B, Vol. 26, Du Quesnel & Bigot to Maurepas, May 9, 1744.
3 G. M. Wrong (ed.), *Louisbourg in 1745: The Anonymous Lettre D'Un Habitant De Louisbourg* (New York, 1897), 15. On the whole, the anonymous author of this most significant document was quite accurate regarding events in Louisbourg in 1744 and 1745.
4 P.A.C., A.C., C¹¹B, Vol. 26, Du Quesnel & Bigot to Maurepas, May 9, 1744.
5 *Ibid.*
6 *Ibid.*
7 *Ibid.*
8 *Ibid.*, A.C., B, Vol. 78, Maurepas to Du Quesnel & Bigot, March 18, 1744. (The Author has made this and later translations from the French.)
9 G. S. Kimball (ed.), *The Correspondence of the Colonial Governors of Rhode Island, 1723-1775* (Boston, 1902), I, 258-9, Gov. Clinton to Gov. Greene, May 28, 1744.
10 P.A.C., A.C., C¹¹B, Vol. 26, Du Quesnel & Bigot to Maurepas, May 9, 1744.
11 *Ibid.*, Du Chambon & Bigot to Maurepas, Nov. 4, 1744.

12 *Ibid.*, A.C., B, Vol. 78, Maurepas to Du Quesnel & Bigot, March 18, 1744.
13 *Ibid.*
14 *Ibid.*, Maurepas to Bigot, March 13, 1744.
15 *Ibid.*, Maurepas to Bigot, March 3, 1744.
16 P.A.C. Public Record Office (P.R.O.), A 26, Hibbert Newton, Collector of the Customs at Canso, to Capt. Robert Young, Sept. 1, 1743.
17 *Ibid.*, Capt. Young of the *Kinsale* to the Lords of Trade, Dec. 6, 1743.
18 No historian has explained adequately why Du Quesnel decided to attempt to capture Canso. Francis Parkman argued that Du Quesnel simply "thought he saw an opportunity to strike an unexpected blow for the profit of France and his own great honour." William Wood and J. G. Bourinot maintained that in attacking Canso, Du Quesnel was not only acting "contrary to the orders of the government of France," but also against the wishes of his subordinates. J. S. McLennan does not even discuss the general question of why Du Quesnel decided to attack Canso when he did. See Francis Parkman, *A Half-Century of Conflict* (Boston, 1899), II, 60; William Wood, *The Great Fortress: A Chronicle of Louisbourg, 1720-1760* (Toronto, 1928), 25; J. G. Bourinot, "Cape Breton and its Memorials of the French Regime," Royal Society of Canada *Proceedings & Transactions* (1891), Vol. IV, Section II, 205; McLennan, *Louisbourg*, 110.
19 P.A.C., A.C., B, Vol. 78, Maurepas to DuQuesnel, Apr. 17, 1744. "As to the pretension of the English regarding the Canceaux fishery, the best way to put an end to it would be to repossess this post."
20 *Ibid.*,Vol. 70, Maurepas to Du Quesnel, Sept. 18, 1740.
21 R. Rumilly, *Histoire des Acadiens* (Montreal, 1955), I, 296.
22 P.A.C., A.C., C¹¹B, Vol. 26, DuChambon & Bigot to Maurepas, Nov. 4, 1744.
23 *Ibid.*, Du Chambon to Maurepas, Nov. 10, 1744.
24 G. D. B. Beaumont, *Les Derniers Jours de L'Acadie (1748-58)* (Paris, 1899), 287, De La Boularderie to De Surlaville, Sept. 1, 1755.
25 *Ibid.*, 288.
26 P.A.C., A.C., F 3, Vol. 50, Pt. II, Moreau St. Méry Papers, "Description of the Canso Armament," [1744]. Other historians have argued that the force consisted of almost 1,000 men. See especially Brebner, *New England's Outpost*, 110. It would seem, however, that Brebner's estimate, based largely upon exaggerated New England sources, is far wide of the mark.
27 *Ibid.*, P.R.O., A 26, Mascarene to King Gould, June 14, 1744.
28 *Ibid.*, Captain Young of the *Kinsale* to the Lords of Trade, Dec. 6, 1743. See also H. A. Innis, "Cape Breton and the French Régime," Royal Society of Canada *Transactions*, XXIX, Sec. II (1935), 68-76.
29 *Ibid.*, Admiralty Papers, II, 483, T. Corbett (Secretary to the Admiralty) to John Scrope, May 31, 1744.
30 W. Douglass, *A Summary, Historical and Political, of the First Planting, Progressive Improvements, and Present State of the British Settlements in North America* (London, 1760), I, 302.
31 P.A.C., P.R.O., A 26, Mascarene to King Gould, June 14, 1744.
32 T.B. Akins, Selections from the Public Documents of The Province of Nova Scotia (Halifax, 1869), 129, Mascarene to the Secretary of State, Dec. 1, 1743.
33 *Ibid.*
34 P.A.C., P.R.O., A 26, Mascarene to King Gould, June 14, 1744.
35 *Ibid.*
36 *Pennsylvania Journal or Weekly Advertiser,* July 4, 1744.
37 *Collection de Manuscrits Contenant Lettres, Mémoires, et Autres Documents Historique Relatifs à La Nouvelle-France* (Quebec, 1884), III, 201, "Capitulation of Canso, May 24, 1744."
38 P.A.C., A.C., C¹¹B, Vol. 26, "Statement made by Messrs. Garrerot, Sabatier and

Footnotes

Bigot concerning the booty taken at Canso, June 20, 1744."

[39] *Ibid.*, P.R.O., A 26, Mascarene to Shirley, June 9, 1744.

[40] *Ibid.*, A.C., C¹¹B, Vol. 26, Bigot to Maurepas, Nov. 16, 1744.

[41] *Ibid.*, P.R.O., A 26, Troops at Louisbourg to John Bradstreet, June 10, 1744.

[42] *Ibid.*, Shirley to Du Quesnel, Sept. 22, 1744.

[43] *Ibid.*

[44] *Boston Weekly News-Letter*, Sept. 20, 1744.

[45] P.A.C., P.R.O., A 26, Shirley to Du Quesnel, July 26, 1744.

[46] B. Murdock, *A History of Nova Scotia or Acadie* (Halifax, 1865), I, 509-510, "Du Vivier's Memoir on Acadia, 1609-1735" [1735].

[47] *Ibid.*, I, 510.

[48] P.A.C., A.C., C¹¹B, Vol. 21, Forant to Maurepas, Nov. 14, 1739.

[49] "Le Loutre's Autobiography," in J. C. Webster, *The Career of Abbé Le Loutre* (Shediac, 1933), 35. See also N. McL. Rogers, "The Abbé Le Loutre," *Canadian Historical Review* (C.H.R.) XI, 2 (June, 1930), 112.

[50] P.A.C., P.R.O., A 26, Mascarene to Shirley, July 2, 1744.

[51] F. Parkman, *Montcalm and Wolfe* (Boston, 1885), 114.

[52] Rogers, "The Abbé Le Loutre," 111-112.

[53] C. H. Lincoln (ed.), *The Correspondence of William Shirley* (New York, 1912), I, 134, Shirley to the Lords of Trade, July 25, 1744.

[54] Parkman, *A Half-Century of Conflict*, II, 61.

[55] P.A.C., Manuscript Group 18, Pre Conquest Papers, Mascarene Letter Book from the Public Archives of Nova Scotia (M.G. 18 F 8), Mascarene to Henry Bastide, May 26, 1744.

[56] See *ibid.* for an excellent description of the actual repairs that took place from October 1743 to May 1744.

[57] Akins, *N. S. Documents*, 129, Mascarene to the Secretary of State, Dec. 1, 1743.

[58] Brebner, New *England's Outpost*, 104.

[59] *Ibid.*, 105.

[60] Akins, *N. S. Documents*, 140, Mascarene to Shirley, Dec. 1744: "On the 18th of May, I found a sudden pannick had seiz'd the whole lower Town where several Officers and Soldiers familys were quarter'd, every body removing their goods to the Fort. Upon enquiry I found a rumour had spread that one Morpain a famous commander of a privateer in the last Warr, was up the River with five hundred French and Indians. Whatever inquiry I could make, I could not find the author of this report, and tho' We were assur'd the next day that this piece of news was false, the impression it had made would not however be taken off from most peoples minds."

[61] P.A.C., M.G. 18 F 8, Mascarene to King Gould, May 21, 1744.

[62] *Ibid.*, June 4, 1744.

[63] *Ibid.*, P.R.O., A 26, Mascarene to Shirley, July 4, 1744.

[64] *Ibid.*

[65] *Ibid.* For a detailed account of the first siege of Annapolis Royal, see Atkins, *N. S. Documents*, 140-142, Mascarene to Shirley, Dec. 1744.

[66] Murdoch, *History of Nova Scotia*, II, 30, Mascarene to the Indians, July 3, 1744.

[67] P.A.C., Admiralty Papers, I, 3817, Mascarene to Peter Warren, Oct. 22, 1744.

[68] *Pennsylvania Journal*, July 26, 1744.

[69] P.A.C., A.C., B, Vol. 78(2), Maurepas to Du Quesnel & Bigot, March 29, 1744. Also see *ibid.*, Maurepas to Du Quesnel, April 30, 1744.

[70] *Ibid.*, A.M., B4, Vol. 56, M. Meschin, Commander of *L'Ardent*, to Maurepas, Dec. 26, 1744.

[71] *Ibid.*, A.C., E 169, Du Vivier's "Journal of the Annapolis Royal Expedition, May 16, 1745."

[72] *Ibid.*

[73] *Ibid.*

[74] *Ibid.*

[75] Akins, *N. S. Documents*, 147, Mascarene to ———— , Dec., 1744: "As soon as the French and Indians had left our River the Deputies of the Inhabitants came before me in Council and represented the dread they had been kept under by the French Commander, producing his written orders threatening with Death those who should disobey."

[76] *Ibid.*, 134, Du Vivier's "Order to the inhabitants of Mines, Piziquid, River Conard and Cobequid, Aug. 27, 1744."

[77] P.A.C., A.C., E 169, Du Vivier's "Journal."

[78] *Ibid.*

[79] The missionary priest Maillard from Isle Royale accompanied the expedition. He led the Isle Royale Micmacs, but had little if any influence on the "Nova Scotia" Micmacs.

[80] P.A.C., A.C., E 169, Du Vivier's "Journal."

[81] *Ibid.*, B, Vol. 81, Maurepas to the Bishop of Quebec, May 12, 1745.

[82] *Ibid.*, E 169, Du Vivier's "Journal."

[83] *Ibid.*

[84] Akins, *N. S. Documents*, 143, Mascarene to Shirley, Dec. 1744.

[85] *Ibid.*

[86] Lincoln, *Shirley Correspondence*, I, 135, Shirley to the Lords of Trade, July 25, 1744.

[87] *Boston Weekly News-Letter*, Nov. 15, 1744.

[88] Akins, *N. S. Documents*, 143, Mascarene to Shirley, Dec. 1744.

[89] P.A.C., A.C., E 169, Du Vivier's "Journal."

[90] Akins, *N. S. Documents*, Mascarene to Shirley, Dec. 1744.

[91] For a hitherto untapped source of information regarding the correspondence between Du Vivier and Mascarene during the capitulation negotiations see P.A.C., A.C., G 2, Vol. 29.

[92] Akins, *N. S. Documents*, 144, Mascarene to Shirley, Dec. 1744.

[93] P.A.C., A.C., C^{11}B, Vol. 26, De Gannes to Maurepas, Nov. 28, 1744 .

[94] *Ibid.*, E 169, Du Vivier's "Journal."

[95] Akins, *N. S. Documents*, 145, Mascarene to Shirley, Dec. 1744.

[96] *Ibid.*

[97] P.A.C., A.C., E 169, Du Vivier's "Journal."

[98] *Ibid.*

[99] *Ibid.*, and *ibid.*, C^{11}B, Vol. 26, Du Chambon to Maurepas, Nov. 18, 1744.

[100] *Ibid.*, A.M., B4, Vol. 56, Meschin to Maurepas, Dec. 26, 1744.

[101] *Ibid.*

[102] *Ibid.*, A.C., E 197, Du Quesnel to De Gannes, Sept. 8, 1744.

[103] *Ibid.*, B, Vol. 78(2), Maurepas to Du Quesnel, Apr. 30, 1744.

[104] *Ibid.*, C^{11}B, Vol. 26, Du Chambon and Bigot to Maurepas, Nov. 20, 1744.

[105] *Ibid.*, De Gannes to Maurepas, Nov. 28, 1744.

[106] *Ibid.*, Du Chambon to Maurepas, Nov. 10, 1744.

[107] *Boston Weekly News-Letter*, Nov. 15, 1744.

[108] P.A.C., A.C., C^{11}B, Vol. 26, Du Chambon to Maurepas, Nov. 18, 1744.

[109] Akins, *N. S. Documents*, 135, "The inhabitants of Mines...to De Gannes, Oct 10, 1744."

Chapter 2
MASSACHUSETTS RESPONSE TO FRENCH AGGRESSION

[1] Kimball, *The Correspondence of the Colonial Governors of Rhode Island*, I, 258-9, Governor Clinton to Governor Greene, May 28, 1744.

[2] V. Parsons, *The Life of Sir William Pepperrell, Bart.* (Boston, 1856), 41-2, Shirley to

Footnotes

Pepperrell, Oct. 10, 1743.

[3] G. A. Wood, *William Shirley: Governor of Massachusetts, 1741-1756* (New York, 1920), 114-131.

[4] For an excellent account of Shirley's successful drive for the control of patronage see J. A. Schutz, *William Shirley: King's Governor of Massachusetts* (Chapel Hill, 1961), 80-85.

[5] *Journals of the House of Representatives of Massachusetts, 1744-1745* (Boston, 1946), Vol. XXI, 8-11.

[6] *Ibid.*, 10.

[7] *Pennsylvania Journal*, June 28, 1744.

[8] *Mass. House Journals*, XXI, 15-16.

[9] J. R. Bartlett (ed.), *Records of the Colony of Rhode Island and Providence Plantations in New England, 1741 to 1756* (Providence, 1860), V, 87-94; N. Bouton (ed.), *Documents and Records Relating to the Province of New Hampshire from 1738 to 1749* (Nashua, 1871), V, 232-235.

[10] *Mass. House Journals*, XXI, 31: "On the Report of the Committee upon Defence, Voted, That the Captain General be desired with all possible Speed to give Order to raise five Hundred effective Men, to be disposed of for the further Defence both of the Eastern and Western Frontier Towns of the Province, in Addition to the five Hundred Men now to be raised, be continued in the Pay of the Province till the 15th day of October next, and no longer."

[11] Lincoln, *Shirley Correspondence*, I, 138-9, Shirley to the Lords of Trade, Aug. 10, 1744.

[12] *Ibid.*, 150-1, Shirley to the Lords of Trade, Oct. 16, 1744.

[13] *Mass. House Journals*, XXI, 36.

[14] *Ibid.*, 28.

[15] P.A.C., A.C., C^{11}B, Vol. 26, Du Quesnel & Bigot to Maurepas, May 9, 1744.

[16] This information can be found in the valuable "Amirauté et Conseil des Prises," P.A.C., Archives Nationale (A.N.), G.5, Vol. 253, Carton 258.

[17] *Ibid.* See also the *Pennsylvania Journal*, June 28, 1744, to August 2, 1744, and also the *Boston Weekly News-Letter* for the same period.

[18] See especially the report from Boston in the *Pennsylvania Journal*, July 4, 1744.

[19] *Ibid.*

[20] P.A.C., A.N., G 5, Vol. 253, Carton 258, "Amirauté et Conseil des Prises."

[21] *Pennsylvania Journal*, July 11, 1744.

[22] H. M. Chapin, *Rhode Island Privateers in King George's War 1739-1748* (Providence, 1926),11.

[23] *Pennsylvania Journal*, Nov. 1, 1744.

[24] Chapin, *Rhode Island Privateers*, 11.

[25] P.A.C., A.C., C^{11}B, Vol. 21, Du Chambon & Bigot to Maurepas, Nov. 4, 1744.

[26] *Pennsylvania Journal*, Nov. 1, 1744.

[27] P.A.C., A.C., C^{11}A, Vol. 89, Hocquart to Maurepas, Oct. 9, 1744.

[28] *Ibid.*, A.N., G 5, Vol. 253, Carton 258, "Amirauté et Conseil des Prises."

[29] A careful reading of contemporary newspapers makes it clear that the Rhode Island privateers were especially numerous, active and successful during the 1744 privateering war with France.

[30] It should probably be pointed out that if one takes into consideration the total number and value of prizes taken by the French and British privateers in North Atlantic waters in the latter half of 1744, the British privateers were more successful. However, for the purpose of this book only shipping directly concerned with Cape Breton and Massachusetts or New England has been considered.

[31] Lincoln, *Shirley Correspondence*, I, 126.

[32] *Pennsylvania Journal*, June 14, June 21, 1744.

[33] Lincoln, *Shirley Correspondence*, I, 137, Shirley to the Lords of Trade, July 25, 1744.

34 *Mass. House Journals*, XXI, 29.
35 Old tenor refers to paper money circulated by the Massachusetts government before 1743. New tenor refers to the paper currency circulated in 1743. See Lincoln, *Shirley Correspondence*, I, 95-98, Shirley to the Lords of Trade, Jan. 24, 1742 (3).
36 Bouton, *N. H. Documents*, V, 235, "Establishment of the Officers' Pay in Massachusetts on the Expedition Against Louisbourg."
37 P.A.C., P.R.O., A 26, Mascarene to Shirley, June 8, 1744: "The heavy Loss His Majesty's Service has sustain'd by the Surprise of Canso and the Troops being carried to Louisbourg, where we hear they are to remain Prisoners of War for one year, whereby we are utterly deprived of all hopes of their Assistance, and as the weak Condition of This Garrison and the ill State of the Fortification make it highly probable that the Enemy will immediately make some vigorous attempts against us before the Garrison is reinforced from England, and the Works thoroughly repaired; We think it our indispensible Duty to Apply to your Excellency the Honourable Council and the Honourable Gentlemen of the Assembly for your aid and assistance in this dangerous conjuncture, and that you'll please immediately order a Body of at least 200 men well armed to be transported hither under their proper officers victuall'd for the Time you'll think proper to leave them for our Security, to help us to Defend this important Fort."
38 *Mass. House Journals*, XXI, 39-40.
39 *Ibid.*, 42.
40 *Ibid.*, 47.
41 *Ibid.*, 49.
42 *Ibid.*, 58.
43 P.A.C., P.R.O., A 26, Mascarene to Shirley, July 7, 1744.
44 Lincoln, *Shirley Correspondence*, I, 135, Shirley to the Lords of Trade, July 25, 1744.
45 *Mass. House Journals*, XXI, 57.
46 P.A.C., P.R.O., A 26, Mascarene to Shirley, June 9, 1744.
47 *Mass. House Journals*, XXI, 57.
48 Akins, *N. S. Documents*, 146, Mascarene to Shirley, Dec. 1744.
49 Lincoln, *Shirley Correspondence*, I, 143, "Royal Order Approving Conduct of William Shirley, Sept. 6, 1744."
50 *Mass. House Journals*, XXI, 85.

Chapter 3
PLANS FOR THE CAPTURE OF LOUISBOURG

1 Lincoln, *Shirley Correspondence*, I, 153, Shirley to Jonathan Law, Nov. 19, 1744.
2 P.A.C., Admiralty Papers, I, 3817, Shirley to the Lords of the Admiralty, Dec. 7, 1744.
3 Lincoln, *Shirley Correspondence*, I, 146, Shirley to the Duke of Newcastle, Sept. 22, 1744.
4 P.A.C., C¹¹B, 26, Du Chambon & Bigot to Maurepas, Nov. 20, 1744.
5 *Ibid.*, Du Chambon & Bigot to Maurepas, Nov. 23, 1744.
6 *Collection de Manuscrits*, III, 213-215, "Mémoire Sur La Nouvelle Angleterre Par Monsieur Doloboratz, November 19, 1744."
7 Lincoln, *Shirley Correspondence*, I, 159, Shirley to the Duke of Newcastle, Jan. 5, 1745.
8 P.A.C., Admiralty Papers, I, 3817, Shirley to the Lords of the Admiralty, Nov. 14, 1744.
9 Clements Library (Cl.L.), George Clinton Papers, Newcastle to Clinton, Jan. 3, 1745. See also Lincoln, *Shirley Correspondence*, I, 155-6, Newcastle to Shirley, Jan. 3,

Footnotes

1745.

[10] *Ibid.*, I, 152, Shirley to Benning Wentworth, Nov. 10, 1744.

[11] P.A.C., Admiralty Papers, I, 3817, Shirley to the Lords of the Admiralty, Dec. 7, 1744.

[12] *Ibid.*

[13] E. B. O'Callaghan (ed.), *Documents Relative to the Colonial History of the State of New York* (Albany, 1855), VI, 182-184, Lieutenant-Governor Clarke to Newcastle, Apr. 22, 1744.

[14] *Ibid.*, 229, Clarke to Newcastle, June or July, 1743.

[15] *Ibid.*, 183, Clarke to Newcastle, Apr. 22, 1744.

[16] P.A.C., Admiralty Papers, I, 3817, Shirley to the Lords of the Admiralty, Dec. 4, 1744.

[17] Massachusetts Historical Society *Collections*, 1st Ser. (1798), V, 202-205, "The Importance of Cape-Breton to the Nation—Humbly represented by Robert Auchmuty, Judge of His Majesty's Court of Vice-Admiralty for the Provinces of the Massachusetts-Bay and New Hampshire, in New England, April 9, 1744."

[18] *Ibid.*, 205.

[19] P.A.C., P.R.O., A 26, Christopher Kilby to Newcastle, Oct. 8, 1744.

[20] See P.A.C., Admiralty Papers, I, 2655, for the description of Louisbourg made by Kilby's "kinsman."

[21] P.A.C., P.R.O., A 26, Kilby to Newcastle, Oct. 8, 1744.

[22] P.R.O., C.O., 5, 884, Kilby to the Board of Trade, Apr. 3, 1744, quoted in Wood, *William Shirley*, 227.

[23] *Ibid.*

[24] P.A.C., P.R.O., A 26, Kilby to Newcastle, Oct. 8, 1744.

[25] P.A.C., P.R.O., C.O., 5900, Kilby to Earl of Harrington, Apr. 22, 1745.

[26] *Ibid.*

[27] P.A.C., Admiralty Papers, I, 3819, Shirley to the Lords of the Admiralty, Dec. 7, 1744.

[28] *Dictionary of American Biography* (New York, 1929), II, 578.

[29] *Ibid.*

[30] DeForest, *Louisbourg Journals*, 171, "Colonel John Bradstreet's Journal."

[31] W. Goold, "Col. William Vaughan, Of Matinicus and Damariscotta," Maine Historical Society *Proceedings* (Portland, 1881), VIII, 295, 302.

[32] New Hampshire Historical Society (N.H.H.S.), Vaughan Papers, "The Memorial of William Vaughan of Damariscotta" sent to King in 1745. See also, McLennan, *Louisbourg*, 361-5.

[33] J. Belknap, *The History of New Hampshire* (Boston, 1813), II, 154.

[34] *Ibid.*

[35] McLennan, *Louisbourg*, 366, J. T. Mason to Newcastle, Oct. 25, 1745.

[36] Douglass, *A Summary, Historical and Political*, I, 348.

[37] Belknap, *History of New Hampshire*, I, 155.

[38] McLennan, *Louisbourg*, 366, J. T. Mason to Newcastle, Oct. 25, 1745.

[39] *Ibid.*, 362, "Memorial of William Vaughan."

[40] For Vaughan's claim see *ibid.*, 361-2:

"That your Memorialist's Design in thus quitting his Settlement was to travel through the Provinces of Massachusetts Bay and New Hampshire to enquire into the strength and Circumstances of Louisburgh, & the other French Settlemants on, or adjoining to the Island of Cape Breton: & this he performed with infinite Fatigue & Hazard during the last Winter.

That your Memorialist met with several intelligent Men who had been Prisoners there the Summer before & were good Pilots; from whom he learnt the Strength (or rather Weakness) of the Enemy & such other Particulars as might encourage an Undertaking against them.

That your Memorialist likewise calculated the Force that might be raised to attack them, & having digested the whole into a regular Scheme, about the first of December last he waited on their Excellencies William Shirley & Benning Wentworth."

For Bradstreet's claim see DeForest, *Louisbourg Journals*, 171, "Colonel John Bradstreet's Journal":

"I was an Officer in the late Lieut.-General Philipps's Regiment, taken by the French at Canso in June 1744, and carry'd to Louisbourg, where I had an opportunity of informing myself of the State and Condition of the Said Place, and of Laying a Plan for the attacking thereof; which I communicated to Governor Shirley at Boston in December following."

[41] As far as Shirley was concerned Vaughan first proposed the plan to attack Louisbourg. McLennan, *Louisbourg*, 365, Shirley to Newcastle, Mar. 23, 1745.

[42] *Ibid.*

[43] Lincoln, *Shirley Correspondence*, I, 159-160, Shirley to the General Court, Jan. 9, 1745.

[44] G. W. Wood deprecated the view that Vaughan was instrumental in persuading Shirley to advocate a New England attack upon Louisbourg. Rather, Wood was of the opinion that Shirley already had the idea and cleverly "made use of [Vaughan's] proposals and his energy...to promote interest in and sentiment for the Louisbourg expenditure."

Wood, *William Shirley*, 245. Wood's interpretation, now widely accepted, appears to be based upon not only a misreading of Shirley's mind but also upon a misreading of contemporary documents.

[45] T. Hutchinson, *The History of the Province of Massachusetts Bay...1691-1750* (Boston, 1767), II, 408.

[46] Massachusetts State Archives (M.S.A.), "Court Records for Massachusetts, January 9, 1744-5."

[47] Hutchinson, *History of Massachusetts Bay*, II, 408-410.

[48] *Ibid.*

[49] M.S.A., "Court Records for Massachusetts, January 12, 1744-5."

[50] *Ibid.*

[51] Lincoln, *Shirley Correspondence*, I, 163, Shirley to Newcastle, Jan. 15, 1745.

[52] *Ibid.*, 164-165.

[53] McLennan, *Louisbourg*, 360, Vaughan to Shirley, Jan. 14, 1745.

[54] *Ibid.*

[55] *Ibid.*

[56] Rhode Island Archives (R.I.A.), "Memorandum for an Attack upon Louisbourg," enclosed in Shirley's letter to Governor Greene, Jan. 29, 1745; N.H.H.S., "Cape Breton Expedition—Plan of Operations—February 1, 1745." It is interesting to note that Shirley had serious reservations regarding certain features of the plan. He referred to it as "a rough, inaccurate and imperfect scheme." P.R.O., Admiralty Papers, I, 3817, quoted in Wood, *William Shirley*, 246.

[57] R.I.A.., "Memorandum for an Attack upon Louisbourg," and N.H.H.S., "Cape Breton Expedition—Plan of Operations."

[58] *Ibid.*

[59] M.S.A., "Court Records for Massachusetts, January 19, 1744/5."

[60] *Ibid.*

[61] *Ibid.*, "Court Records for Massachusetts, January 23, 1744/5."

[62] *Ibid.*

[63] *Ibid.*, "Court Records for Massachusetts, January 25, 1744/5."

[64] Hutchinson, *History of Massachusetts Bay*, II, 411; Douglass, *A Summary, Historical and Political*, I, 349; T. Prince, *Extraordinary Events the Doings of God, and Marvellous in pious Eyes* (Boston, 1747), 22; Kimball, *R. I. Correspondence*, I, 364, Governor

Footnotes

Wanton to Richard Partridge, July 26, 1745.

In his circular letter sent to the various colonial governors, Shirley maintained that the vote on the committee's report was "a cheerfull and almost unanimous resolution of the Court to undertake this Important Business." See Connecticut Historical Society *Collections*, XI, 254, Shirley to Law, Jan. 29, 1745, and R.I.A., Shirley to Greene, Jan. 29, 1745. Wood unquestionably accepted Shirley's veracity and totally disregarded various contemporary accounts which clearly contradict Shirley's statement. (Wood, *William Shirley*, 255.) Wood's position is entirely untenable. Shirley could not expect very much support from the other colonies if they seriously doubted Massachusetts enthusiasm for the projected expedition. Consequently he did not hesitate to distort the facts.

[65] Belknap, *History of New Hampshire*, II, 155.

Chapter 4
ORGANIZING THE EXPEDITION

[1] Lincoln, *Shirley Correspondence*, I, 169-170, "Massachusetts General Court Action on the Cape Breton Expedition."

[2] *Ibid.*

[3] M.S.A., "Massachusetts Court Records, January 25, 1744/5."

[4] *Ibid.*

[5] Belknap, *History of New Hampshire*, II, 158.

[6] McLennan, *Louisbourg*, 360, Vaughan to Shirley, Jan. 14, 1744/5.

[7] Douglass, *A Summary, Historical and Political*, I, 348.

[8] Schutz, *William Shirley*, 31, 33. For a disappointing biographical sketch of Waldo see J. Williamson, "Brigadier General Samuel Waldo, 1696-1759," Maine Historical Society *Collections*, IX (Portland, 1887), 75-93.

[9] P.A.C., C.O. 5, 753, "The humble Petition of Wyndham Beawes of London and Samuel Waldo of Boston, n.d." See also *ibid.*, "The Case of Samuel Waldo of Boston in the Province of Massachusetts Bay in New England [n.d.]." In this memoir Waldo maintained that:

"In the year 1740: War having been declared between Great Britain and Spain, and a Rupture with France being greatly apprehended; Mr. Waldo then in England thought it his Duty as one well acquainted with American affairs, to lay before his Grace the Duke of Newcastle...a Plan for the Reduction of Cape Breton, and the French Territories on Canada River to be put in Execution as soon as a war with that Crown should happen.

In the year 1741 Mr. Waldo embark'd for New England; and soon after his arrival there communicated to Mr. Shirley His Majesty's Governor of the Massachusetts Bay, the said Plan, and gave him a Copy thereof, which he was pleas'd to approve of."

In spite of Waldo's claims, he did little if anything to bring about the actual expedition. However, it must be emphasized that he laboured diligently "to encourage and facilitate the Enlistment of Men."

[10] Schutz, *William Shirley*, 92.

[11] Bouton, *N. H. Documents*, V, 936, Shirley to Wentworth, Feb. 16, 1745.

[12] DeForest, *Louisbourg Journals*, 171, "John Bradstreet's Journal."

[13] *Ibid.*

[14] B. Fairchild, *Messrs. William Pepperrell: Merchants at Piscataqua* (Ithaca, 1954), 174-5.

[15] DeForest, *Louisbourg Journals*, 172, "John Bradstreet's Journal."

[16] Belknap, *History of New Hampshire*, II, 158.

[17] Fairchild, *Messrs. William Pepperrell*, 174.

[18] Massachusetts Historical Society *Collections*, 6th Ser. (1899), X, 392. Pepperrell

to Silas Hooper, Nov. 9, 1745.

[19] *Ibid.*

[20] *Ibid.*, "Ye Govr, Council & Speaker of ye Lower House told me there would be no expedition without I would head ye forces." See also, W. Pepperrell, *An Accurate Journal and Account of the Proceedings of the New England Land-Forces During the Late Expedition Against the French Settlements on Cape Breton* (London, 1746), 3, Pepperrell to Captain Henry Stafford, Nov. 4, 1745.

[21] M.H.S. *Colls.*, 6th Ser., X, 392, Pepperrell to Silas Hooper, Nov. 9, 1745.

[22] Pepperrell, *An Accurate Journal*, 4, Pepperrell to Henry Stafford, Nov. 4, 1745.

[23] *Boston Gazette*, Jan. 22, 1745.

[24] L. Tyerman, *The Life of The Reverend George Whitefield* (New York, 1877), II, 150, Whitefield to ———, July 29, 1745.

[25] *Ibid.*

[26] Schutz, *William Shirley*, 92.

[27] *Ibid.* "Honours aside, the colonelcies were enviable posts, for deductions were allowed colonels in the purchase of clothes and handling of soldier pay in addition to the privileges of selling certain luxuries to enlisted men and of taking spoils from enemy territory."

[28] McLennan, *Louisbourg*, 365-7, Shirley to Newcastle, Mar. 23, 1745; Mason to Newcastle, Oct. 25, 1745.

[29] J. Eliot, *God's Marvellous Kindness* (New London, 1745), 19. See also H. M. Burrage, *Maine at Louisbourg in 1745* (Augusta, 1910), 14-15, Jonathan Edwards to a friend in Scotland, [n.d.]:
"The state of the place [Louisbourg] was strangely concealed from us, which if it had been known, would have effectually prevented the design....
It was unaccountable that so many, that had been conversant there, should be kept in such ignorance. If one-half of the strength of the place had been known, the expedition had never been thought of."

[30] From a careful examination of most, if not all, available journals and letters written by the Louisbourg volunteers, it seems that the desire for plunder was by far the most important motivating factor as far as enlisting in the expedition was concerned.

[31] Tyerman, *George Whitefield*, II, 151, Whitefield to ———, July 29, 1745.

[32] John Carter Brown Library (J.C.B.L.), "Moses pleading with God for Israel...With a Word to our Brethren gone and going out on the present Expedition against Cape-Breton, 1745."

[33] M.H.S. *Colls.*, 6th Ser., X, 106, John Gray to William Pepperrell, Feb. 25, 1744/5.

[34] See especially W. McClenachan, *The Christian Warriour* (Boston, 1745), and Prince, *Extraordinary Events*.

[35] *Ibid.*, 34.

[36] M.H.S. *Colls.*, 6th Ser., X, 99, Alexander Bulman to Pepperrell, Feb. 4, 1745.

[37] *Ibid.*, 102, A. Le Mercier to Pepperrell, Feb. 8, 1745.

[38] N.H.H.S., Waldron Papers, R. Waldron to Pepperrell, Mar. 19, 1745.

[39] M.H.S., Belknap Papers, "Shirley's Beating Orders, Feb. 5, 1745."

[40] M.H.S. *Colls.*, 6th Ser., X, 99-100, Bulman to Pepperrell, Feb. 4, 1745.

[41] J. Gibson, *A Journal of the Late Siege by the Troops from North America Against the French at Cape Breton* (London, 1747), v.

[42] Bouton, N. H. *Documents*, V, 937, Shirley to Wentworth, Mar. 1, 1745.

[43] M.H.S. *Colls.*, 6th Ser., X, 104, Ammi Cutter to Pepperrell, Feb. 20, 1745.

[44] H. L. Osgood, *The American Colonies in the Eighteenth Century* (New York, 1924), III, 498-9.

[45] DeForest, *Louisbourg Journals*, 2, "First Journal, Anonymous."

[46] M.H.S., Belknap Papers, "Establishment of Wages for the Expedition, Feb.,

Footnotes

1745."

[47] *Ibid.*, "Incouragement for the Soldiers, February, 1745."

[48] Bouton, *N. H. Documents*, V, 234-5, "Establishment of the Officers Pay in Massachusetts...Incouragement for the men that Inlist."

[49] M.H.S. *Colls.*, 6th Ser., X, 106, John Gray to Pepperrell, Feb. 25, 1745.

[50] *Mass. House Journals*, XXI, 197.

[51] *Ibid.*, 185.

[52] M.H.S. Belknap Papers, Waldo to Pepperrell, Feb. 19, 1744.

[53] There were others who favoured "waiting for ships from abroad and troops" before sending any expedition from Massachusetts. See M.H.S. *Colls.*, 6th Ser., X, 109, Jothan Odiorne Jr. to Pepperrell, Feb. 27, 1745.

[54] Lincoln, *Shirley Correspondence*, I, 196, Shirley to Newcastle, Mar. 27, 1745; and H. M. Chapin, *New England Vessels in the Expedition Against Louisbourg 1745* (Boston, 1923), 3-8.

[55] Lincoln, *Shirley Correspondence*, I, 196, Shirley to Newcastle, Mar. 27, 1745.

[56] McLennan, *Louisbourg*, 360, Vaughan to Shirley, Jan. 14, 1745.

[57] *Mass. House Journals*, XXI, 198.

[58] *Ibid.*, 200.

[59] Lincoln, *Shirley Correspondence*, I, 171-2, Shirley to Law, Jan. 29, 1744/5.

[60] M.S.A., "Court Records for Massachusetts, Jan. 30, 1745."

[61] Wood, *William Shirley*, 270.

[62] L. W. Labaree (ed.), *The Papers of Benjamin Franklin* (New Haven, 1961), III, 15, "Notes on Assembly Debates."

[63] *Colonial Records of Pennsylvania* (1851), IV, 754.

[64] Labaree, *Franklin Papers*, III, 15, "Notes on Assembly Debates."

[65] *Ibid.*, III, 16.

[66] *Ibid.*, III, 26, Franklin to John Franklin, 1745.

[67] *Colonial Records of Pennsylvania*, IV, 755.

[68] O'Callaghan, *New York Documents*, VI, 284, Clinton to Newcastle, Nov. 18, 1745.

[69] Cl.L., George Clinton Papers, Clinton to Board of Trade, Mar. 27, 1745.

[70] Hutchinson, *History of Massachusetts Bay*, II, 413.

[71] Kimball, *R. I. Correspondence*, I, 322, Shirley to Greene, Mar. 4, 1745.

[72] *Records of the Colony of Rhode Island* (Providence, 1860), V, 100.

[73] Kimball, *R. I. Correspondence*, I, 312, Governor Greene to Shirley, Feb. 8, 1745.

[74] *R. I. Records*, V, 101.

[75] Kimball, *R. I. Correspondence*, I, 364-5, Governor Wanton to Richard Partridge, July 26, 1745.

[76] Chapin, *New England Vessels in the Expedition Against Louisbourg*, 4.

[77] Kimball, *R. I. Correspondence*, 1, 320-322, Shirley to Greene, Mar. 4, 1745.

[78] *Ibid.*, 322.

[79] *R. I. Records*, V, 102-6.

[80] Kimball, *R. I. Correspondence*, I, 316, Richard Partridge to Greene, Dec. 14, 1744. Partridge was Rhode Island's agent in London.

[81] *Ibid.*, 324, Greene to Governor Law of Connecticut, Mar. 11, 1745.

[82] *Ibid.*, 367-8, Wanton to Partridge, July 26, 1745.

[83] Chapin, *Rhode Island Privateers*, 191-195.

[84] Kimball, *R. I. Correspondence*, I, 368, Wanton to Partridge, July 21, 1745. See also *R. I. Records*, V, 113-4.

[85] Kimball, *R. I. Correspondence*, I, 321, Shirley to Greene, Mar. 4, 1745. Shirley was particularly concerned with the "Characteristick Difference between the Spirit of the Old Charter Governments and those commonly distinquished by the Name of the King's Governments that the former have less Duty to his Majesty and Zeal for the Publick Service in proportion to the privileges and Indulgence they enjoy under his Government."

86 B. Trumbull, *A Complete History of Connecticut* (New Haven, 1818), II, 275.
87 C. J. Hoadley, (ed.), *The Public Records of the Colony of Connecticut* (Hartford, 1867), IX, 83-4, 93.
88 Connecticut Historical Society (C.H.S), Wolcott Papers, Pepperrell to Wolcott, Mar. 8, 1745.
89 *Ibid.*, Shirley to Wolcott, Mar. 8, 1745.
90 Hoadley, *Public Records of Connecticut*, IX, 96.
91 C.H.S., Law Papers, Wolcott to Mrs. Wolcott, Apr. 10, 1745.
92 *Ibid.*; see also Hoadley, *Public Records of Connecticut*, IX, 96-99.
93 C.H.S., Law Papers, Gurdon Saltonstall to Jonathan Law, Apr. 17, 1745.
94 *Ibid.*
95 Bouton, *N. H. Documents*, V, 272.
96 *Ibid.*, 276.
97 *Ibid.*, 277.
98 *Mass. House Journals.* XXI, 181.
99 Bouton, *N. H. Documents*, V, 279, Wentworth to the House of Representatives, Feb. 5, 1745.
100 *Ibid.*, V, 280, The House of Representatives to Wentworth, Feb. 6, 1745.
101 Lincoln, *Shirley Correspondence*, I, 184, Shirley to Pepperrell, Feb. 14, 1745.
102 Bouton, *N. H. Documents*, V, 933, Shirley to Wentworth, Feb. 2, 1745.
103 McLennan, *Louisbourg*, 261-2, "The Memorial of William Vaughan of Damariscotta."
104 Bouton, *N. H. Documents*, V, 287-8, "Journal Of The House."
105 *Ibid.*, 286-7, Petition of T. Packer, G. Mitchell, J. Wentworth, N. Peirce, J. Newmarch, J. Ayers, J. T. Mason, N. Meserve, J. Pierce to Wentworth, Feb. 11, 1745.
106 *Ibid.*, 289-291, "Journal Of The House."
107 *Ibid.*, 282-3.
108 *Ibid.*, 937, Shirley to Wentworth, Feb. 27, 1745.
109 *Ibid.*, 943. "Copy of the Muster Roll...sent by...Pepperrell from Canso." Belknap was of the opinion that "New Hampshire employed 500 men; about 1/8th part of the whole land force." Belknap, *History of New Hampshire*, II, 165.
110 Bouton, *N. H. Documents*, V, 300-301, Wentworth to Pepperrell, Mar. 23, 1745.
111 P.A.C., Admiralty Papers, I, 233, Shirley to Ogle, Jan. 1744. *Ibid.*, I, 3817, Shirley to Warren, Jan. 29, 1745.
112 *Ibid.*, I, 233, Shirley to Ogle, Jan. 1744/5.
113 *Ibid.*, Ogle to Davers, Mar. 14, 1745.
114 H. W. Richmond, *The Navy in the War of 1739-48* (Cambridge, 1920), II, 204.
115 P.A.C., Admiralty Papers, II, 487, Secretary of the Lords of the Admiralty to Warren, Mar. 18, 1745.
116 Richmond, *The Navy in the War of 1739-48*, II, 205.
117 Cl.L., Warren Papers, see letters written in 1744 and 1745.
118 Lincoln, *Shirley Correspondence*, I, 197, Shirley to Newcastle, Mar. 27, 1745.
119 P.A.C., Admiralty Papers, I, 3817, Shirley to Warren, Jan. 29, 1745.
120 Lincoln, *Shirley Correspondence*, I, 197, Shirley to Newcastle, Mar. 27, 1745.
121 Richmond, *The Navy in the War of 1739-48*, II, 207.
122 Lincoln, *Shirley Correspondence*, I, 156, Newcastle to Shirley, Jan. 3, 1745.
123 Richmond, *The Navy in the War of 1739-48*, II, 207-8.
124 *Ibid.*
125 *Ibid.*, 209.
126 Lincoln, *Shirley Correspondence*, I, 196-9, Shirley to Newcastle, Mar. 27, 1745.
127 *Journals and Letters of the Late Samuel Curwen An American Refugee in England from 1775 to 1784* (New York, 1842), 12.
128 Lincoln, *Shirley Correspondence*, I, 196, Shirley to Newcastle, Mar. 27, 1745.
129 Chapin, *New England Vessels in the Expedition Against Louisbourg*, 4-5.

Footnotes

[130] The *Caesar* and *Fame* were owned by Rhode Islanders.

[131] Chapin, *New England Vessels in the Expedition Against Louisbourg*, 6.

[132] *Ibid.*

[133] Chapin was of the opinion that the second contingent sailed on April 6. *Ibid.* See also DeForest, *Louisbourg Journals*, 2, "First Anonymous Journal." However, in his letter to Newcastle written on Apr. 7, Shirley stated: "2800...have already taken their departure and the remainder are embark'd, and will I hope sail from this place tomorrow." Lincoln, *Shirley Correspondence*, I, 196, Shirley to Newcastle, Mar. 27, 1745. It appears that Shirley had mixed up his dates.

[134] Labaree, *Franklin Papers*, III, 26-7, Benjamin Franklin to John Franklin, 1745.

Chapter 5
CANSO

[1] M.H.S. *Colls.*, 1st Ser., I, 13, Pepperrell to Shirley, Mar. 27, 1745.

[2] *Ibid.*

[3] *Ibid.*, 5-12, Shirley to Pepperrell, Mar. 19, 1745, and Mar. 22, 1745.

[4] M.H.S., Miscellaneous Papers, J. H. Bastide to the Board of Trade, Feb. 1, 1745.

[5] M.H.S. *Colls.*, 1st Ser., I, 5-8, Shirley to Pepperrell, Mar. 19, 1745.

[6] Shirley, Bastide and Durelle failed to realize that there were a few French inhabitants residing in the Gabarus Bay area. These inhabitants, unless they were all deaf, blind and crippled, were bound to notice in one way or another the arrival of a large invading fleet and to carry word of it to the Louisbourg officials.

[7] M.H.S. *Colls.*, 1st Ser., I, 8, Shirley to Pepperrell, Mar. 19, 1745.

[8] *Ibid.*, 10. See also *ibid.*, 12, Shirley to Pepperrell, Mar. 22, 1745: "As Capt. Bosch is an armed sloop, and you have another also from Piscataqua, with their forces, it won't be amiss to employ them; but if affairs should encourage you to spare a detachment, with four or six whale boats, to destroy the fishery at St. Esprit, Tourchet, Lourembecque, Niganish, St. Anns, and other small harbours in your neighbourhood; those two vessels, with such a number of boats, may be very well employed."

[9] *Ibid.*, 11, Shirley to Pepperrell, Mar. 19, 1745.

[10] *Ibid.*, 13, Shirley to Pepperrell, Mar. 22, 1745

[11] *Ibid.*, 15, Pepperrell to Shirley, Mar. 27, 1745.

[12] C. H. Lincoln (ed.), *The Journal of Sir William Pepperrell Kept During the Expedition Against Louisbourg, Mar. 24-Aug. 22, 1745* (Worcester, 1910), 10.

[13] L. E. DeForest (ed.), *The Journals and Papers of Seth Pomeroy* (New Haven, 1926), 15.

[14] DeForest, *Louisbourg Journals*, 3, "First Journal, Anonymous."

[15] *Ibid.*

[16] DeForest, *Pomeroy Journals*, 15.

[17] J. C. L. Clark (ed), "Benjamin Stearns's Diary, 11 March-2 August, 1745," *Acadiensis* (Saint John, N.B., 1908) VIII, 318.

[18] *Ibid.*

[19] *Ibid.* See also DeForest, *Pomeroy Journals*, 15.

[20] Lincoln, *Pepperrell Journal*, 11.

[21] *Ibid.*

[22] M.H.S. *Colls.*, 6th Ser., X, 124-5, Pepperrell to Osborne, Apr. 10, 1745.

[23] Clark, "Benjamin Stearns's Diary," *Acadiensis*, VIII, 318.

[24] DeForest, *Louisbourg Journals*, 5, "First Journal, Anonymous."

[25] *Ibid.*

[26] Lincoln, *Pepperrell Journal*, 11, 15.

[27] Essex Institute Historical *Collections* (1861), III, 187, "Extracts From Letters

Written By Capt. Geo. Curwen...While On The Expedition Against Louisbourg,"
George Curwen to Mrs. Curwen, Apr. 22, 1745.

28 W. Shirley, *A Letter From William Shirley, Esq; Governor of Massachusetts Bay, To his Grace the Duke of Newcastle: With a Journal of the Siege of Louisbourg* (London, 1748), 17.
29 M.H.S. *Colls.*, 1st Ser., I, 15, Pepperrell to Shirley, Apr. 10, 1745.
30 *Ibid.*
31 Bouton, *N. H. Documents*, V, 943, "List of New Hampshire men in Col Samuel Moore's Regiment."
32 M.H.S. *Colls.*, 1st Ser., I, 15, Pepperrell to Shirley, Apr. 10, 1745.
33 *Ibid.*, I, 14.
34 *Ibid.* It is interesting to note that on April 16 the council of war: "Advised unanimously, that notwithstanding the train of artillery and some part of the troops are not yet arrived at Canso, those now there proceed with the first favourable wind and weather to Chapeaurouge Bay, and endeavour to take possession of the field; at least after their having been review'd and completely furnish'd wth ye necessary accountrements, provided that upon examination it shall appear that a sufficiency of ammunition and other stores for them be also arrived." *Ibid.*, 6th Ser., X, 4, "Records Of The Councils Of War."
35 *Ibid.*, 1st Ser., I, 14-5, Pepperrell to Shirley, Apr. 10, 1745.
36 Lincoln, *Pepperrell Journal*, 12.
37 *Ibid.*, 13.
38 DeForest, *Louisbourg Journals*, 6, "First Journal, Anonymous."
39 Lincoln, *Pepperrell Journal*, 13.
40 M.H.S. *Colls.*, 1st Ser., I, 18, Captain Snelling to Pepperrell, Apr. 16, 1745.
41 *Ibid.*, I, 22, Pepperrell to Shirley, Apr. 28, 1745.
42 *Ibid.*, 23.
43 *Ibid.*, 24.
44 W. P. Upham (ed.), "Craft's Journal of the Siege of Louisbourg," Essex Institute Historical *Collections* (1864) VI, 183.
45 Essex Institute Historical *Collections*, III, 187, George Curwen to Mrs. Curwen, Apr. 22, 1745.
46 Lincoln, *Pepperrell Journal*, 14-5.
47 *Ibid.*, 15.
48 M.H.S. *Colls.*, 1st Ser., I, 27, Pepperrell to Shirley, May 11, 1745.
49 Richmond, *The Navy in the War of 1739-48*, II, 210-11.
50 *Ibid.*, 211.
51 P.A.C., B.M. Add. M.S. 15957, Anson Papers, Warren to Anson, Apr. 2, 1745. In this lengthy memoir Warren clearly stated his ideas regarding the military importance of Louisbourg.
52 DeForest, *Louisbourg Journals*, 184, Warren to Pepperrell, Apr. 23, 1745.
53 Essex Institute Historical *Collections* (1912), XLVIII, 298, "Journal Kept by Lieut. Daniel Giddings of Ipswich During the Expedition Against Cape Breton in 1744-5."
54 Shirley, *Letter to Newcastle*, 19.

Chapter 6
LOUISBOURG

1 *Pennsylvania Journal*, Jan. 1, 1744/5.
2 P.A.C., A.C., C11B, Vol. 26, Du Chambon to Maurepas, Nov. 10, 1744.
3 *Ibid.*
4 *Ibid.*
5 *Ibid.*, Du Chambon & Bigot to Maurepas, Nov. 18, 1744.

Footnotes

6 *Ibid.*

7 *Ibid.*, Du Chambon to Maurepas, Nov. 10, 1744.

8 *Collection de Manuscrits*, III, 217, "Extrait En Forme De Journal De Ce Qui S'Est Passé D'Intéressant Dans La Nouvelle-France Pendant Les Années 1745, 1746, 1747, 1748."

9 P.A.C., A C., C¹¹B, Vol. 25, Du Chambon & Bigot to Maurepas, Nov. 14, 1744. See also *ibid.*, Du Chambon & Bigot to Maurepas, Nov. 14, 1744, "Projet pour prendre le fort de port Royal à l'acadie."

10 *Ibid.*, "Projet pur prendre...port Royal."

11 *Ibid.*, Vol. 26, Du Chambon & Bigot to Maurepas, Nov. 23, 1744. At first Du Chambon and Bigot believed that 600 troops would be enough. *Ibid.*, Vol. 25, Du Chambon & Bigot to Maurepas, Nov. 14, 1744, "Projet pour prendre...port Royal." But because of rumours of reinforcements being sent to Annapolis Royal by the British it was decided that 200 more French troops would be needed.

12 *Ibid.*, "Projet pour prendre...port Royal."

13 *Ibid.*, Vol. 26, Du Chambon to Maurepas. Nov. 27, 1744.

14 *Ibid.*, Vol. 25, Du Chambon & Bigot to Maurepas, Nov. 19, 1744, "Projet pour prendre...port Royal."

15 *Ibid.*

16 *Ibid.*, Du Chambon & Bigot to Maurepas, Nov. 14, 1744.

17 *Ibid.*

18 University of Rochester [U.R.], Maurepas Papers, "Plans To Retake Acadia and Newfoundland and to Defend the Isle Royale, Jan. 1745."

19 P.A.C., Archives De La Guerre [A.G.], Vol. 3127, "Mémoire dont l'original est de la main de M. le Ct. de Maurepas Sur la Marine et le Commerce, remis au feu Roi par ce Ministre à la fin de l'année 1745."

20 U.R., Maurepas Papers, "Plans to Retake Acadia...1745."

21 G. Lacour-Gayet, *La Marine-Militaire De La France Sous Le Règne De Louis XV* (Paris, 1910), 97-8.

22 P.A.C., A.G., Vol. 3127, "Maurepas Memoir, 1745."

23 U.R., Maurepas Papers, "Plans To Retake Acadia...1745."

24 *Ibid.*

25 P.A.C., A.G., Vol. 3127, "Maurepas Memoir, 1745."

26 P.A.C., Archives De La Marine [A.M.], B 4, Vol. 57, "Resumé of Captain Kersaint's Expedition, n.d."

27 *Ibid.*, B 2, Vol. 155, Maurepas to de Camilly, Mar. 17, 1745. See also *ibid.*, A.C., B, Vol. 81, Maurepas to Beauharnois, Mar. 31, 1745.

28 *Ibid.*, Maurepas to de Clarambault, Feb. 22, 1745.

29 *Ibid.*, A.M., B 4, Vol. 57, "Resumé of Captain Kersaint's Expedition."

30 *Ibid.*, A.M., B 2, Vol. 155, Maurepas to de Camilly, Mar. 17, 1745.

31 *Ibid.*, A.C., B, Vol. 81, Maurepas to Du Vivier, May 27, 1745.

32 *Ibid.*, A.C., C¹¹A, Vol. 93, Hocquart to Maurepas, May 19, 1745.

33 *Ibid.*, A.C., C¹¹B, Vol. 21, Forant to Maurepas, Sept. 27, 1739. Translation from McLennan, *Louisbourg*, 95.

34 For the best firsthand accounts of the revolt see Wrong, *Louisbourg In 1745*, 33-5; P.A.C., A.C., C¹¹B, Vol. 27, "Mémoire Touchant la révolte des soldats de Louisbourg, le [2]7, Dec. 1744," 1745; *ibid.*, A.C., E 157, "Trial of Abraham Du Pacquier, Nov. 25, 1745." For Bigot's detailed and often inaccurate account, written years after the event, see the relevant quotations from the *Mémoire pour Messire François Bigot* (Paris, 1763), I, and G. Frégault, *François Bigot, administrateur français* (Montreal, 1948), I, 208-211.

35 Prince, *Extraordinary Events*, 21.

36 An excellent description of their living conditions is to be found in Frégault, *François Bigot*, I, 207.

37 Wrong, *Louisbourg In 1745*, 34.
38 D. A. De Ulloa, *A Voyage to South America* (London, 1758), II, 384.
39 P.A.C., A.C., C¹¹B, Vol. 27, "Mémoire Touchant la révolte."
40 *Ibid.*, A.C.E., 157, "Trials of Abraham Du Paquier, Nov. 25, 1745"; see also *ibid.*, E., 233, "Trail of Christopher Jout, Dec. 2, 1745."
41 *Ibid.*, A.C.E., 157, "Trial of Abraham Du Paquier, Nov. 25, 1745"; *ibid.*, A.C.B., Vol. 82(2), Maurepas to Karrer, Dec. 10, 1745.
42 *Ibid.*, A.C.E., 157, "Trial of Abraham Du Paquier, Nov. 25, 1745."
43 *Ibid.*
44 *Ibid.*
45 Wrong, *Louisbourg In 1745*, 33.
46 De Ulloa, *A Voyage To South America*, II, 384.
47 P.A.C., A.C., C¹¹B, Vol. 27, "Mémoire Touchant la révolte."
48 *Ibid.*
49 *Ibid.*
50 Wrong, *Louisbourg In 1745*, 33.
51 P.A.C., A.C., C¹¹B, Vol. 27, "Mémoire Touchant la Révolte."
52 *Ibid.*, A.C., B, Vol. 82(2), Maurepas to de Barrailh, Dec. 1745.
53 *Mémoire pour Messire François Bigot*, I, 8.
54 Wrong, *Louisbourg In 1745*, 34-5.
55 P.A.C. , A.C., C¹¹B, Vol. 27, "Mémoire Touchant la révolte."
56 Frégault is of the opinion that the soldiers terrorized the merchants throughout the winter months. See Frégault, *François Bigot*, I, 211. He appears, however, to be far too dependent upon Bigot's highly coloured accounts, written years after the event and intended to serve Bigot's interests. The "Habitant de Louisbourg," on the other hand, maintained that at the close of December the matter ended "without the bloodshed that had been feared."
See Wrong, *Louisbourg In 1745*, 35. In all likelihood, in January Louisbourg returned to its usual somnolent winter state with the soldiers quite content to live off the laurels of their December victories.
57 P.A.C., A.C., C¹¹B, Vol. 27, "Mémoire Touchant la révolte," 1745.
58 *Ibid.*, A.C., B, Vol. 81, Maurepas to Beauharnois and Hocquart, June 9, 1745.
59 *Ibid.*, Maurepas to Du Vivier, May 27, 1745.
60 Wrong, *Louisbourg In 1745*, 24: "We had the whole winter before us—more time than was necessary to put ourselves in a state of defense. We were, however, overcome with fear. Councils were held, but the outcome was only absurd and childish. Meanwhile the time slipped away; we were losing precious moments in useless discussions and in forming resolutions abandoned as soon as made. Some things begun required completion; it was necessary to strengthen here, to enlarge there, to provide for some posts, to visit all those on the island, to see where a descent could be made most easily, to find out the numbers of persons in a condition to bear arms, to assign to each his place; in a word, to show all the care and activity usual in such a situation. Nothing of all this was done, and the result is that we were taken by surprise, as if the enemy had pounced upon us unawares.... Negligence and fatuity conspired to make us lose our unhappy island."
61 P.A.C., A.C., F 3, Moreau St. Méry Papers, Vol. 50 (Pt. 1), Du Chambon to Maurepas, Sept. 2, 1745.
62 *Ibid.*
63 Chapin, *New England Vessels in the Expedition Against Louisbourg*, 4-5. Apparently the New England vessels, *Prince of Orange, Boston Packet, Fame, Molineux, Caesar,* and the *Massachusetts* arrived in Louisbourg waters by March 31. But because of bad weather and other circumstances they were not sighted until April 9. It must be kept in mind that because of weather conditions the ships found it very difficult to work in concert. The official blockade of Louisbourg did not really start until

the arrival of Warren's warships in May. Until then, the New Englanders were as much dependent on the coastal ice as on their guns to keep French ships from entering Louisbourg harbour. In fact during April there were some days when the so-called New England blockading vessels were not to be found in the general vicinity of Louisbourg. These vessels were not considered to be any significant threat by the Louisbourg officials.

[64] P.A.C., A.N. Archives d'Outre-Mer, Dépôt des Fortifications des Colonies, Amérique Septentrionale [D.F.A.S.] F 557, "Raport du Nommé Gerard La Croix de ce qui s'est passé d'Intéressant à Louisbourg avant et pendant Le Siège de cette place qui s'est rendue au Roy, d'Angleterre par Capitulation Le 28 Juin, 1745," n.d.

[65] *Ibid.*, A.C., F 3, Vol. 50 (Pt 1), Du Chambon to Maurepas, Sept. 2, 1745.

[66] DeForest. *Louisbourg Journals*, 8, "First Journal, Anonymous."

[67] M.H.S. *Colls.*, 1st Ser., I, 25, Pepperrell to Shirley, Apr. 28, 1745.

[68] Chapin, *New England Vessels in the Expedition Against Louisbourg*, 8-9; E. M. Bidwell (ed.), "Journal of the Rev. Adonijah Bidwell," *New England Historical and Genealogical Register* (Boston, 1873), XXVII, 153.

[69] P.A.C., A.M., B 4, Vol. 57, "Resumé of Captain Kersaint's Expedition."

[70] *Ibid.*, D.F.A.S., F 557, "Raport du Nommé Girard La Croix."

[71] *Ibid.*

[72] See especially *ibid.*, A.C., F 3, Vol. 50(1), Du Chambon to Maurepas, Sept. 2, 1745.

Chapter 7
THE GABARUS BAY LANDING

[1] P.A.C., D.F.A.S., F 557, "Raport du Nommé Girard La Croix."

[2] Parkman, *A Half-Century of Conflict*, II, 289, Du Chambon to Maurepas, Sept. 2, 1745.

[3] *Ibid.*

[4] *Ibid.*, 289-290.

[5] *Ibid.*, 290.

[6] P.A.C., D.F.A.S., F 557, "Raport du Nommé Girard La Croix." La Croix maintained that a land force made up of twenty-five men was sent to Gabarus. But Du Chambon informed Maurepas that only twenty men were sent. It is difficult to know who was the more accurate.

See Parkman, *A Half-Century of Conflict*, II, 290, Du Chambon to Maurepas, Sept. 2, 1745.

[7] *Ibid.*, II, 290, Du Chambon to Maurpas, Sept. 2, 1745. But La Croix noted that forty-five men were sent under Daccarrette. To complicate matters still further, Bigot reported that only forty men in all were sent to Gabarus. See U.R., Maurepas Papers, Bigot to Maurepas, Aug. 15, 1745.

[8] Parkman, *A Half-Century of Conflict*, II, 290, Du Chambon to Maurepas, Sept. 2, 1745. See also P.A.C., D.F.A.S., F 557, "Raport du Nommé Girard La Croix."

[9] *Ibid.*

[10] *Ibid.*

[11] Parkman, *A Half-Century of Conflict*, II, 290, Du Chambon to Maurepas, Sept. 2, 1745.

[12] C. W. Elliot, "Mighty Man of Kittery: Sir William Pepperrell: A Hemisphere Defence Campaign of 200 Years Ago," *Infantry Journal*, XLVII, 4 (July-Aug., 1940), 348.

[13] Pepperrell, *An Accurate Journal*, 10.

[14] *Ibid.* See also DeForest, *Louisbourg Journals*, 182.

[15] Lincoln, *Pepperrell Journal*, 16.

16 Upham, "Craft's Journal," Essex Institute Historical *Collections*, VI, 184.

17 DeForest, *Louisbourg Journals*, 9, "First Journal, Anonymous."

18 Lincoln, *Pepperrell Journal*, 16.

19 M.H.S. *Colls.*, 1st Ser., I, 6, Shirley to Pepperrell, Mar. 19, 1745.

20 *Ibid.*, I , 26, Pepperrell to Shirley, May 11, 1745

21 M.H.S., Belknap Papers, Warren to his Officers, Apr. 29, 1745.

22 Cl.L., Louisbourg Papers, T. W. Waldron to his father, July 26, 1745.

23 *Ibid.*

24 *Ibid.*, Waldron to his father, July 8, 1745.

25 See U.R., Maurepas Papers, Bigot to Maurepas, Aug. 15, 1745; P.A.C., D.F.A.S, F 557, "Rapart du Nommé Girard La Croix"; Parkman, *A Half-Century of Conflict*, II, 291, Du Chambon to Maurepas, Sept. 2, 1745.

26 P.A.C., D.F.A.S., F 557, "Raport du Nommé Girard La Croix."

27 M.H.S. *Colls.*, 1st Ser., I. 27, Pepperrell to Shirley, May 11, 1745.

28 *Ibid.*

29 U.R., Maurepas Papers, Bigot to Maurepas, Aug. 15, 1745.

30 Pepperrell, *An Accurate Journal*, 10. See also DeForest, *Louisbourg Journals*, 67, "Fourth Journal, Anonymous."

31 *Ibid.*, 10, "First Journal, Anonymous."

32 Pepperrell, *An Accurate Journal*, 10.

33 J. Sewell, *The Lamb slain, worthy to be praised, as the most powerful, rich, wise, and strong* (Boston, 1745), 30.

34 De Beaumont, *Les Derniers Jours*, 288, De La Boularderie to De Surlaville, Sept. 1, 1755; P.A.C., A.C., C11B, Vol. 27, Morpain to Maurepas, Feb. 4, 1746; *ibid.*, A.C.E., 240, De La Boularderie to the Secretary of State for War and Marine, n.d.

35 *Ibid.*, A.C., C11B, Vol. 27, Morpain to Maurepas, Feb 4. 1746.

36 *Ibid.*

37 De Beaumont, *Les Derniers Jours*, 288, De La Boularderie to De Surlaville, Sept. 1, 1755.

38 P.A.C., A.C.E., 240, De La Boularderie to Maurepas, n.d.

39 De Ulloa, *A Voyage to South America*, II, 389.

40 DeForest, *Louisbourg Journals*, 10, "First Journal, Anonymous."

41 G. T. Bates, "John Gorham, 1709-1751," Nova Scotia Historical Society *Collections* (Halifax, 1954), Vol. 30, 34-5. See also *Pennsylvania Journal*, May 30, 1745,—— to ——, May 4, 1745.

42 Lincoln, *Pepperrell Journal*, 17.

43 Parkman, *A Half-Century of Conflict*, II, 291, Du Chambon to Maurepas, Sept. 2, 1745.

44 DeForest, *Louisbourg Journals*, 10, "First Journal, Anonymous."

45 Lincoln, *Pepperrell Journal*, 17; Shirley, *Letter to Newcastle*, 20; Gibson, *A Journal of the Siege of Louisbourg*, 9; M.H.S. *Colls.*, 1st Ser., I, 26, Pepperrell to Shirley, May 11, 1745.

46 *Ibid.*, Shirley to Pepperrell, Mar. 19, 1745.

47 Shirley, *Letter to Newcastle*, 20.

48 P.A.C., Admiralty Papers, I, 3817, Pepperrell to Shirley, May 12, 1745.

49 J. M. Hitsman with C. C. J. Bond, "The Assault Landing at Louisbourg, 1758," *C.H.R.*, XXXV, 4 (Dec. 1954), 323.

50 DeForest, *Louisbourg Journals*, 68, "Fourth Journal, Anonymous."

51 Parkman, *A Half-Century of Conflict*, II, 290, Du Chambon to Maurepas, Sept. 2, 1745.

52 De Beaumont, *Les Derniers Jours*, 288, De La Boularderie to De Surlaville, Sept. 1, 1755.

53 P.A.C., A.C., C11B, Vol. 27, Morpain to Maurepas, Feb. 4, 1746.

54 There is a sharp difference of opinion regarding the size of the contingent

sent under Morpain. Bigot maintained that eighty men were sent (U.R., Maurepas Papers, Bigot to Maurepas, Aug. 15, 1745). On the other hand, Du Chambon informed Maurepas that eighty civilians *and* thirty soldiers were dispatched to Gabarus Bay (Parkman, *A Half-Century of Conflict*, II, 291, Du Chambon to Maurepas, Sept. 2, 1745). But De La Boularderie noted that only eighty men in all were sent (De Beaumont, *Les Derniers Jours*, 288-9, De La Boularderie to De Surlaville, Sept. 1, 1755). Finally, Morpain observed that fifty civilians, twenty-four soldiers and twelve men under De La Boularderie, in addition to De La Boularderie, the governor's son and himself, marched against the New Englanders (P.A.C., A.C., C¹¹B, Vol. 27, Morpain to Maurepas, Feb. 4 , 1746).

[55] *Ibid.*, A.C., C¹¹B, Vol. 27, Morpain to Maurepas, Feb. 4, 1746.

[56] *Ibid.*

[57] De Beaumount, *Les Derniers Jours*, 289, De La Boularderie to De Surlaville, Sept. 1, 1755.

[58] DeForest, *Louisbourg Journals*, 68, "Fourth Journal, Anonymous."

[59] S. A. Green, *Three Military Diaries kept by Groton Soldiers in Different Wars* (Groton, 1901), 13, "Dudley Bradstreet's Diary."

[60] Upham, "Craft's Journal," Essex Institute Historical *Collections*, VI, 184.

[61] De Beaumont, *Les Derniers Jours*, 289-290, De La Boularderie to De Surlaville, Sept. 1, 1755.

[62] Pepperrell, *An Accurate Journal*, 11.

[63] De Beaumont, *Les Derniers Jours*, 290, De La Boularderie to De Surlaville, Sept. 1, 1755.

[64] *Boston Evening Post*, May 20, 1745,———— to ————, May 4, 1745.

[65] De Beaumont, *Les Derniers Jours*, 290, De La Boularderie to De Surlaville, Sept.1, 1755.

[66] DeForest *Louisbourg Journals*, 84, "Sixth Journal, Anonymous."

[67] *Ibid.*, 74-5, "Fifth Journal, Anonymous."

[68] P.A.C., Admiralty Papers, I, 3817, Pepperrell to Shirley, May 12, 1745. The casualty figures vary greatly, but from a careful examination of all available records it appears that Pepperrell's statement is very close to the truth.

[69] Sewell, *The Lamb slain*, 31.

[70] Essex Insititute Historical *Collections* (Salem, 1912), Vol. 48, 298, "Journal Kept By Lieut. Daniel Giddings."

[71] Connecticut Historical Society *Collections* (Hartford, 1924), XXI, 427, "The Wylls Papers, Correspondence and Documents Chiefly of Descendants of Gov. George Wylls of Connecticut, 1590-1796," Theophilus Woodbridge to Joshua Lamb Woodbridge, May 12, 1745.

[72] Bidwell, "Journal Of The Rev. Adonijah Bidwell," *New England Historical and Genealogical Register*, Vol. 27, 154.

[73] M.H.S., Davis Papers, ? ———— ?, n.d. See also *New England Historical and Genealogical Register* (Boston, 1912), Vol. 66, 117, "Benjamin Cleaves's Journal of the Expedition to Louisbourg, 1745."

[74] DeForest, *Louisbourg Journals*, 10, "First Journal, Anonymous." See also P.A.C., D.F.A.S., F 557, "Raport du Nommé Girard La Croix."

[75] DeForest, *Louisbourg Journals*, 10, "First Journal, Anonymous."

[76] *Ibid.*, 68, "Fourth Journal, Anonymous."

[77] P.A.C., D.F.A.S., F 557, "Raport du Nommé Girard La Croix." See also Lincoln, *Pepperrell Journal*, 17.

[78] M.H.S. *Colls.*, 1ˢᵗ Ser., I, 26, Pepperrell to Shirley, May 11, 1745.

[79] P.A.C., D.F.A.S., F 557, "Raport du Nommé Girard La Croix."

[80] Parkman, *A Half-Century of Conflict*, II, 292, Du Chambon to Maurepas, Sept. 2, 1745.

[81] Essex Institute Historical *Collections*, Vol. 48, 298, "Journal Kept By Lieut. Da-

niel Giddings."

82 *New England Historical and Genealogical Register,* Vol. 66, 117, "Benjamin Cleaves's Journal"; Green, *Three Military Diaries,* 13, "Dudley Bradstreet's Diary."
83 DeForest, *Louisbourg Journals,* 10, "First Journal, Anonymous."
84 *Ibid.*
85 M.H.S., Massachusetts Broadsides, "A Brief Journal of the Taking of Cape Breton by L.G. one of the Soldiers in the Expedition."

Chapter 8
THE TAKING OF THE GRAND BATTERY

1 P.A.C., Moreau St. Méry Papers, A.C., F 3, Vol. 50, Pt. I, Chassin de Thierry to Du Chambon, May 11, 1745. See also M.H.S., Parkman Papers, Bigot to Maurepas, Aug. 1, 1745, and Parkman, *A Half-Century of Conflict,* II, 292, Du Chambon to Maurepas, Sept. 2, 1745.
2 P.A.C., A.C., C¹¹B, Vol. 27, Verrier to Maurepas, Aug. 22, 1745; *ibid.,* D.F.A.S., F 557, Verrier to Maurepas, Nov. 18, 1744.
3 *Ibid.,* Du Chambon & Bigot to Maurepas, Nov. 22, 1744.
4 Wrong, *Louisbourg In 1745,* 39.
5 P.A.C., D.F.A.S., F 557, Verrier to Maurepas, Nov. 18, 1744.
6 M.H.S. *Colls.,* 1st Ser., I, 7, Shirley to Pepperrell, Mar. 19, 1745.
7 DeForest, *Louisbourg Journals,* 174, "Bradstreet's Journal."
8 Pepperrell, *An Accurate Journal,* 12.
9 *Ibid.*
10 F. Downey, "Yankee Gunners at Louisbourg," *American Heritage* (Feb. 1955), 51.
11 Douglass, *A Summary, Historical and Political,* I, 341.
12 Hutchinson, *History of Massachusetts Bay,* II, 413.
13 Wrong, *Louisbourg In 1745,* 38.
14 M.H.S., Parkman Papers, "État des soldats, habitants, matelots et pêcheurs...au commencement du siège dans la ville de Louisbourg," 1745.
15 Wrong, *Louisbourg In 1745,* 39.
16 Parkman, *A Half-Century of Conflict,* II, 292, Du Chambon to Maurepas, Sept. 2, 1745; U.R., Maurepas Papers, Bigot to Maurepas, Aug. 15, 1745.
17 Wrong, *Louisbourg In 1745,* 39.
18 Parkman, *A Half-Century of Conflict,* II, 193, Du Chambon to Maurepas, Sept. 2, 1745; M.H.S., Parkman Papers, Bigot to Maurepas, Aug. 1, 1745 .
19 P.A.C., A. C., C¹¹B, Vol. 26, Verrier to Maurepas, Feb. 8, 1744.
20 U.R., Maurepas Papers, Bigot to Maurepas, Aug. 15, 1745.
21 Parkman, *A Half-Century of Conflict,* II, 293, Du Chambon to Maurepas, Sept. 2, 1745; M.H.S., Parkman Papers, Bigot to Maurepas, Aug. 1, 1745.
22 P.A.C., A.C., F 3, Pt. I, Du Chambon to Chassin de Thierry, May 11, 1745.
23 M.H.S. *Colls.,* 1st Ser., I, 26, Pepperrell to Shirley, May 11, 1745; M.H.S., Parkman Papers, Waldo to Shirley, May 12, 1745.
24 Parkman, *A Half-Century of Conflict,* II, 293, Du Chambon to Maurepas, Sept. 2, 1745.
25 Wrong, *Louisbourg In 1745,* 38-40.
26 P.A.C., A.C., C¹¹B, Vol. 27, Morpain to Maurepas, Feb. 4, 1746.
27 *Ibid.,* D.F.A.S, F 557, "Raport du Nommé Girard La Croix."
28 Green, *Three Military Diaries,* 14, "Dudley Bradstreet's Diary."
29 DeForest, *Louisbourg Journals,* 68-9, "Fourth Journal, Anonymous."
30 *Ibid.,* 69.
31 *Ibid.*
32 *Boston Evening Post,* May 20, 1745, ? ——— ? , May 4, 1745.

[33] DeForest, *Louisbourg Journals*, 11, "First Journal, Anonymous."

[34] *Ibid.*, 84, "Sixth Journal, Anonymous."

[35] *New England Historical and Genealogical Register*, Vol. 66, 117, "Benjamin Cleaves's Journal."

[36] Clark, "Benjamin Stearns's Diary," *Acadiensis*, VIII, 320-1.

[37] Upham, "Craft's Journal," Essex Institute Historical *Collections*, VI, 184.

[38] Lincoln, *Pepperrell Journal*, 18.

[39] McLennan, *Louisbourg*, 363, Vaughan to King George II, 1745.

[40] Parkman, *A Half-Century of Conflict*, II, 293, Du Chambon to Maurepas, Sept. 2, 1745.

[41] Wrong, *Louisbourg In 1745*, 40.

[42] Upham, "Craft's Journal," Essex Institute Historical *Collections*, VI, 184.

[43] Parkman, *A Half-Century of Conflict*, II, 293, Du Chambon to Maurepas, Sept. 2, 1745; DeForest, *Pomeroy Journals*, 23-4.

[44] P.A.C., A.C., C^{11}B, Vol. 27, Morpain to Maurepas, Feb. 4, 1746.

[45] Pepperrell, *An Accurate Journal*, 12.

[46] DeForest, *Louisbourg Journals*, 11, "First Journal, Anonymous." See also Green, *Three Military Diaries*, 14, "Dudley Bradstreet's Diary."

[47] Lincoln, *Pepperrell Journal*, 18.

[48] DeForest, *Louisbourg Journals*, 11, "First Journal, Anonymous."

[49] McLennan, *Louisbourg*, 363, Vaughan to King George II, 1745.

[50] Belknap, *History of New Hampshire*, II, 168.

[51] *Ibid.*; P.A.C., Admiralty Papers, I, 3817, Waldo to Shirley, May 12, 1745.

[52] McLennan, *Louisbourg*, 363, Vaughan to King George II, 1745.

[53] Pepperrell, *An Accurate Journal*, 12.

[54] Belknap, *History of New Hampshire*, II, 168-9.

[55] M.H.S. *Colls.*, 6th Ser., X, 138, Vaughan to Pepperrell, May 2, 1745.

[56] McLennan, *Louisbourg*, 363, Vaughan to King George II, 1745.

[57] Lincoln, *Pepperrell Journal*, 18.

[58] McLennan, *Louisbourg*, 363, Vaughan to King George 11, 1745; *ibid.*, 366-7, J. T. Mason to T. De Veil, Oct. 25, 1745; *ibid.*, D. Woaster to T. De Veil, Oct. 28, 1745.

[59] *Ibid.*, 363, Vaughan to King George II, 1745.

[60] *Ibid.*

[61] Pepperrell, *An Accurate Journal*, 12.

[62] McLennan, *Louisbourg*, 363, Vaughan to King George II, 1745.

[63] Parkman, *A Half-Century of Conflict*, II, 293, Du Chambon to Maurepas, Sept. 2, 1745.

[64] *Ibid.*

[65] M.H.S., Parkman Papers, Waldo to Shirley, May 12, 1745.

[66] *New England Historical and Genealogical Register*, Vol. 66, 118, "Benjamin Cleaves's Journal."

[67] M.H.S., Parkman Papers, Waldo to Shirley, May 12, 1745.

[68] *Ibid.*, "On my march towards the Royal Battery I found this pretended Sally was only a Feignt of the Enemy which and the fire of their Cannon both from The Town and Island on this Defenceless Battery, they Imagined would oblige us to quit that advantageous Post."

[69] DeForest, *Louisbourg Journals*, 174, "John Bradstreet's Journal."

[70] M.H.S. *Colls.*, 6th Ser., X, 138, Bradstreet to Pepperrell, May 2, 1745.

[71] DeForest, *Pomeroy Journals*, 61, Pomeroy to Mary Pomeroy, May 8, 1745.

[72] M.H.S., Belknap Papers, Vaughan to Pepperrell, May 7 (?), 1745.

[73] Wrong, *Louisbourg In 1745*, 41.

[74] *Boston Evening Post*, May 20, 1745, ? to ?, May 4, 1745.

[75] Hutchinson, *History of Massachusetts Bay*, II, 416; DeForest, *Louisbourg Journals*,

11, "First Journal, Anonymous."

[76] J. Sewell, *The Lamb slain*, 34.

[77] T. Prentice, *When the People, and the Rulers among them, willingly offer themselves to a Military Expedition against their unrighteous Enemies* (Boston, 1745), 33.

[78] Parkman, *A Half-Century of Conflict*, II, 102; "The English occupation of the Grand Battery may be called the decisive event of the siege. There seems no doubt that the French could have averted the disaster long enough to make it of little help to the invaders."

Chapter 9
SIEGE PRELIMINARIES

[1] E. Eis, *The Forts of Folly* (London, 1959), 221.

[2] Douglass, *A Summary, Historical and Political*, I, 352.

[3] Belknap, *History of New Hampshire*, II, 170.

[4] M.H.S., Belknap Papers, Vaughan to Pepperrell, May 7, 1745.

[5] M.H.S. *Colls.*, 6th Ser., X, 141, Waldo to Pepperrell, May 3, 1745.

[6] DeForest, *Pomeroy Journals*, 22.

[7] Shirley, *Letter to Newcastle*, 21.

[8] M.H.S., Belknap Papers, Vaughan to Pepperrell, May 7, 1745.

[9] DeForest, *Louisbourg Journals*, 12, "First Journal, Anonymous."

[10] *Ibid.*

[11] S. Niles, *A Brief and Plain Essay On God's Wonder-working Providence For New England In the Reduction of Louisbourg, and Fortresses thereto belonging on Cape-Breton* (London, 1747), 12.

[12] Downey, "Yankee Gunners at Louisbourg," *American Heritage* (Feb. 1955), 54.

[13] M.H.S., Belknap Papers, Waldo to Pepperrell, May 15, 1745.

[14] M.H.S. *Colls.*, 6th Ser., X, 147, Pepperrell to Warren, May 4, 1745.

[15] *Ibid.*

[16] P.A.N.S., Vol. 19, Warren to Newcastle, June 18, 1745.

[17] M.H.S. *Colls.*, 6th Ser., X, 142-3, Waldo to Pepperrell, May 3, 1745.

[18] *Ibid.*, 150, Waldo to Pepperrell, May 4, 1745.

[19] *Ibid.*, "You must be sensible, Sir, that the four barrells of powder sent us yesterday & the last night will make out but 24 charges, that unless a further supply, it will be to little purpose for us to show the proposed forwardness. The rum sent is all expended without any waiste, I think, & the other provisions will soon be gone, and as I doubt not you will at all hazards support this post, will it not be best to give a more liberall supply, that you may not so often be troubled with applications that interfere with more weighty affairs, as well as your repose." See also DeForest, *Louisbourg Journals*, 12, "First Journal, Anonymous."

[20] M.H.S. *Colls.*, 1st Ser., I, 9, Shirley to Pepperrell, Mar. 19, 1745.

[21] *Ibid.*, 6th Ser., X, 145, Warren to Pepperrell, May 4, 1745.

[22] *Ibid.*, 147, Pepperrell to Warren, May 4, 1745.

[23] Bidwell, " Journal Of The Rev. Adonijah Bidwell," *New England Historical and Genealogical Register*, Vol. 27, 154. See also Chapin, *New England Vessels in the Expedition Against Louisbourg*, 14.

[24] Bidwell, "Journal Of The Rev. Adonijah Bidwell," *New England Historical and Genealogical Register*, Vol. 27, 154-5.

[25] M.H.S. *Colls.*, 1st Ser., I, 12, Shirley to Pepperrell, Mar. 22, 1745.

[26] M.H.S., Davis Papers, ? to ?, n.d.

[27] *Ibid.*

[28] *Ibid.* See also *ibid.*, Thomas Saunders Papers, John Kinselagh to Thomas Saunders, May 2, 1745.

[29] P.A.C., H 3/240, "A Plan of the City and Harbour of Louisbourg; shewing that

Footnotes

part of Gabarus Bay in which the English landed, also their Encampment during the Siege in 1745." See also the map in Parkman, *A Half-Century of Conflict*, II, 94-95.

30 DeForest, *Louisbourg Journals*, 114, "Eighth Journal, Anonymous."

31 M.H.S. *Colls.*, 1st Ser., I, 10, Shirley to Pepperrell, Mar. 19, 1745.

32 *Ibid.*

33 *Ibid.*, 6th Ser., X, 11-12, "Records Of The Councils Of War."

34 *Ibid.*, 12.

35 *Ibid.*, 141-2, Waldo to Pepperrell, May 3, 1745.

36 *Ibid.*, 142.

37 DeForest, *Louisbourg Journals*, 189, Warren to Pepperrell, May 2, 1745: "if wee cou'd once get possession, of the Island Battery, nothing from Sea, of the Enemy, cou'd gett in, and they must starve in the town."

38 M.H.S. *Colls.*, 6th Ser., X, 148, Pepperrell to Warren, May 4, 1745.

39 Shirley, *Letter to Newcastle*, 22.

40 M.H.S. *Colls.*, 6th Ser., X, 12, "Records Of The Councils Of War."

41 DeForest, *Louisbourg Journals*, 114, "Eighty Journal, Anonymous."

42 Niles, *A Brief and Plain Essay*, 12.

43 Shirley, *Letter to Newcastle*, 23.

44 DeForest, *Louisbourg Journals*, 114, "Eighth Journal, Anonymous."

45 *Ibid.*, 85, "Sixth Journal, Anonymous."

46 Lincoln, *Pepperrell Journal*, 19.

47 *Ibid.*

48 M.H.S. *Colls.*, 6th Ser., X, 155, Samuel Rhodes to Pepperrell, May 7, 1745.

49 DeForest, *Louisbourg Journals*, 190-193, Warren to Pepperrell, May 4, 1745.

50 *Ibid.*

51 M.H.S. *Colls.*, 6th Ser., X, 14, "Records Of The Councils Of War."

52 M.H.S., Davis Papers, W. Clarke's Account of the Louisbourg Siege (?), Dec. 13, 1745.

53 Wrong, *Louisbourg In 1745*, 41.

54 M.H.S. *Colls.*, 6th Ser., X, 13, "Records of the Councils Of War."

55 Shirley, *Letter to Newcastle*, 23-4.

56 M.H.S. *Colls.*, 6th Ser., X, 14, "Records Of The Councils Of War."

57 Lincoln, *Pepperrell Journal*, 19.

58 DeForest, *Louisbourg Journals*, 15, "First Journal, Anonymous."

59 M.H.S. *Colls.*, 6th Ser., X, 14, "Records Of The Councils Of War."

60 Connecticut Historical Society *Collections* (Hartford, 1860), I, 137, "Journal of Roger Wolcott at the Siege of Louisbourg." See also M.H.S. *Colls.*, 6th Ser., X, 14-15, "Records Of The Councils Of War."

61 *New England Historical and Genealogical Register*, Vol. 66, 118, "Benjamin Cleaves's Journal."

62 Gibson, *Cape Breton Journal*, 10.

63 Douglass, *A Summary, Historical and Political*, I, 350; see also Belknap, *History of New Hampshire*, II, 169.

64 Pepperrell, *An Accurate Journal*, 15-16.

65 DeForest, *Louisbourg Journals*, 70, "Fourth Journal, Anonymous." See also *ibid.*, 115, "Eighth Journal, Anonymous."

66 Lincoln, *Pepperrell Journal*, 20.

67 *Ibid.* See also the *New England Historical and Genealogical Register*, Vol. 66, 118, "Benjamin Cleaves's Journal," and Essex Institute Historical *Collections*, Vol. 48, 298, "Journal Kept By Lieut. Daniel Giddings."

68 Lincoln, *Pepperrell Journal*, 20.

69 *New England Historical and Genealogical Register*, Vol. 66, 118, "Benjamin Cleaves's Journal."

70 P.A.C., D.F.A.S., F 557, "Raport du Nommé Girard La Croix."

[71] Wrong, *Louisbourg In 1745*, 49-50.

[72] P.A.N.S., Vol. 17, Mascarene to Newcastle, Apr. 29, 1745; *ibid.*, Dec. 9, 1745; New York Public Library, Lennox Papers, Nova Scotia, 1745-1817, "Representation of the State of his Majesty's Province of Nova Scotia and Fort and Garrison of Annapolis Royal; Drawn up by a Committee of Council and Approved in Council Nov. 8, 1745."

[73] M.H.S., Parkman Papers, Du Chambon to Marin, May 16, 1745. See also Wrong, *Louisbourg In 1745*, 41-44, and Parkman, *A Half-Century of Conflict*, II, 294, Du Chambon to Maurepas, Sept. 2, 1745: "On the 16th, I sent a messenger in a small boat to take a letter to Mr. Marin, an officer from Canada, who commanded a detachment of Canadians and Indians in Acadie, with an order to leave for Louisbourg immediately with his troops; this was a trip that took at most 20 to 25 days, if he had been at Mines as I was assured he was; but before the messenger arrived the detachment had already left for Port Royal."

[74] M.H.S., Parkman Papers, Du Chambon to Marin, May 16, 1745.

[75] P.A.N.S., Vol. 17, Mascarene to Newcastle, Dec. 9, 1745; Mascarene was of the opinion that there were "6 or 700 men to attack this place." But Mascarene tended to exaggerate the numbers of the various besieging forces. Captain William Pote, who was captured by some of the Indians in Marin's force and taken by them to Quebec, estimated that there were at least 700 of them. See V. H. Paltsits (ed.), *The Journal of Captain William Pote, Jr. During His Captivity in the French and Indian War From May, 1745, to August, 1747* (New York, 1896), 16-17.

[76] Paltsits, *The Journal of Captain William Pote, Jr.*, 16.

[77] See especially Wrong, *Louisbourg In 1745*, 53-4. Of course it is always dangerous to discuss the "ifs" of history. However, after a careful examination of the sources, it seems that "L'Habitant de Louisbourg" was right.

[78] *Collection de Manuscrits*, III, 221, Du Chambon to Pepperrell & Warren, May 18, 1745. See also C.H.S. *Colls.*, I, 137-8, "Wolcott's Journal."

[79] Wrong, *Louisbourg In 1745*, 50; and P.A.C., D.F.A.S., F 557, "Raport du Nommé Girard La Croix."

[80] Lincoln, *Pepperrell Journal*, 20.

[81] C.H.S. *Colls.*, I, 138, "Wolcott's Journal."

[82] M.H.S. *Colls.*, 6th Ser., X, 15, "Records of The Councils of War."

[83] Lincoln, *Pepperrell Journal*, 20.

[84] C.H.S. *Colls.*, XXI, 427, Theophilus Woodbridge to Joshua Lamb Woodbridge, May 12, 1745.

[85] Lincoln, *Pepperrell Journal*, 20.

[86] C.H.S. *Colls.*, XXI, 427, T. Woodbridge to J. L. Woodbridge, May 12, 1745.

[87] M.H.S., Belknap Papers, Waldo to Pepperrell, May 7, 1745.

[88] C.H.S. *Colls.*, XXI, 427, Woodbridge to J. L. Woodbridge, May 12, 1745.

[89] *New England Historical and Genealogical Register*, Vol. 66, 118, "Benjamin Cleaves's Journal."

[90] C.H.S. *Colls.*, XXI, 428, T. Woodbridge to J. L. Woodbridge, May 12, 1745.

[91] Lincoln, *Pepperrell Journal*, 20.

[92] DeForest, *Louisbourg Journals*, 76, "Fifth Journal, Anonymous." See also *New England Historical and Genealogical Register*, Vol. 66, 118, "Benjamin Cleaves's Journal."

[93] Lincoln, *Pepperrell Journal*, 20-21.

[94] M.H.S. *Colls.*, 6th Ser., X, 16, "Records Of The Councils Of War."

[95] C.H.S. *Colls.*, XXI, 428, T. Woodbridge to J. L. Woodbridge, May 12, 1745.

[96] Lincoln, *Pepperrell Journal*, 21; DeForest, *Louisbourg Journals*, 70, "Fourth Journal, Anonymous"; *ibid.*, 76, "Fifth Journal, Anonymous."

[97] C.H.S. *Colls.*, XXI, 428, T. Woodbridge to J. L. Woodbridge, May 12, 1745.

[98] P.A.C., Admiralty Papers, I, 3817, Warren to Shirley, May 12, 1745.

[99] M.H.S. *Colls.*, 6th Ser., X, 16, "Records Of The Councils Of War."

[100] DeForest, *Louisbourg Journals*, 15, "First Journal, Anonymous."

[101] *Ibid.*

[102] Green, *Three Military Diaries*, 16, "Dudley Bradstreet's Diary."

[103] DeForest, *Louisbourg Journals*, 15, "First Journal, Anonymous."

[104] *Ibid.* The quotations are referred to by the anonymous writer who throughout his journal is amazingly accurate.

[105] M.H.S. *Colls.*, 6th Ser., X, 17, "Records Of The Councils Of War."

[106] P.A.N.S., Vol. 19, Warren to Newcastle, June 18, 1745.

[107] Lincoln, *Pepperrell Journal*, 21. It seems that after the abandonment of the frontal attack scheme late on May 20, there was "Another att. on Isl. Batt but [it] did not proceed."

Chapter 10
SIEGE AND BLOCKADE

[1] M.H.S. *Colls.*, 6th Ser., X, 162, Warren to Pepperrell, May 11, 1745.

[2] *Ibid.*, 330, Pepperrell to Shirley, July 17, 1745.

[3] *Ibid.*, 162, Warren to Pepperrell, May 11, 1745; *ibid.*, 164, Pepperrell to Warren, May 12, 1745; *ibid.*, 168, Warren to Pepperrell, May 13, 1745; *ibid.*, 174-5, Warren to Pepperrell, May 16, 1745. Se also DeForest, *Louisbourg Journals*, 195, Warren to Pepperrell, May 18, 1745.

[4] M.H.S. *Colls.*, 6th Ser., X, 17-23, "Records Of The Councils Of War." See also P.A.C., Admiralty Papers, I, 3817, Pepperrell to Shirley, May 12, 1745.

[5] M.H.S. *Colls.*, 6th Ser., X, 162, Warren to Pepperrell, May 11, 1745.

[6] DeForest, *Louisbourg Journals*, 76, "Fifth Journal, Anonymous." See also Lincoln, *Pepperrell Journal*, 21.

[7] M.H.S., Davis Papers, ? to ?, 1745. See also Pepperrell, *An Accurate Journal*, 14.

[8] DeForest, *Louisbourg Journals*, 76, "Fifth Journal, Anonymous."

[9] Green, *Three Military Diaries*, 17, "Dudley Bradstreet's Dairy."

[10] Gibson, *Cape Breton Journal*, 11. Gibson was one of the lucky ones who was able to escape. He wrote: "A small Scout of 25 Men, got to the North-East Harbour. I and four more being in a House upon Plunder, 140 French and Indians come down upon us first, and fired a Volley, with a great Noise. Two jumped out of the Window, and were shot dead. With great Difficulty the other two and myself got safe to the Grand Battery."

[11] DeForest, *Louisbourg Journals*, 86, "Sixth Journal, Anonymous."

[12] Essex Institute Historical *Collections* (1860), III, 187, "Extracts From Letters Written by Capt. Geo. Curwen of Salem, Mass., to His wife, While on the Expedition Against Louisbourg." See also P.A.C., Admiralty Papers, I, 3817, Warren to Shirley, May 12, 1745.

[13] *New England Historical and Genealogical Register*, Vol. 66, 118-119, "Benjamin Cleaves's Journal."

[14] C.H.S. *Colls.*, XXI, 428, Theophilus Woodbridge to J. L. Woodbridge, May 12, 1745.

[15] *Ibid.*

[16] Cl.L., Louisbourg Papers, Richard Waldron to T. W. Waldron, June 21, 1745.

[17] M.H.S. *Colls.*, 6th Ser., X, 19, "Records Of The Councils Of War."

[18] *Ibid.*, 162, Warren to Pepperrell, May 11, 1745.

[19] *Ibid.*, 19, "Records Of The Councils Of War." See also *ibid.*, 164-5, Pepperrell to Warren, May 12, 1745: "I have resented and taken measures to suppress the surmizes that some silly persons had propagated of Col. Bradstreet's behaviour wch am sensible was as ill grounded and prejudicial to our design here as it was injurious to him; hope shall hear no more of it."

20 Essex Institute Historical *Collections*, III, 187, "Extracts From Letters Written by Capt. Geo. Curwen."
21 *Ibid.*
22 Referred to in M.H.S. *Colls.*, 6th Ser., X, 162, Warren to Pepperrell, May 11, 1745.
23 See especially, M.H.S., Davis Papers, "W. Clarke's Account of Louisbourg Siege, Dec. 13, 1745."
24 DeForest, *Louisbourg Journals*, 76, "Fifth Journal, Anonymous."
25 Essex Institute Historical *Collections*, III, 187, "Extracts From Letters Written By Capt. Geo. Curwen."
26 Cl.L., Louisbourg Papers, T. W. Waldron to R. Waldron, June 6, 1745.
27 DeForest, *Louisbourg Journals*, 86, "Sixth Journal, Anonymous."
28 *Ibid.*, 16, "First Journal, Anonymous."
29 Green, *Three Military Diaries*, 17, "Dudley Bradstreet's Diary."
30 Cl.L, Louisbourg Papers, R. Waldron to T. W. Waldron, June 21, 1745.
31 DeForest, *Louisbourg Journals*, 76, "Fifth Journal, Anonymous."
32 Green, *Three Military Diaries*, 15, 19, "Dudley Bradstreet's Diary"; M.H.S. *Colls.*, 6th Ser., X, 167, Waldo to Pepperrell, May 13, 1745.
33 P.A.C., D.F.A.S., F 557, "Raport du Nommé Girard LaCroix."
34 M.H.S. *Colls.*, 6th Ser., X, 159, Vaughan to Pepperrell, May 11, 1745; *ibid.*, 165, Vaughan to Pepperrell, May 12, 1745.
35 P.A.C., Admiralty Papers, I, 3817, Waldo to Shirley, May 12, 1745.
36 It would just be one of many rebuffs. See Cl.L., Louisbourg Papers, Vaughan to Richard Waldron, June 19, 1745.
37 Lincoln, *Pepperrell Journal*, 21; M.H.S., Davis Papers, ? to ?, 1745; DeForest, *Louisbourg Journals*, 76, "Fifth Journal, Anonymous."
38 Lincoln, *Pepperrell Journal*, 21.
39 M.H.S. *Colls.*, 6th Ser., X, 166, Warren to Pepperrell, May 13, 1745; *ibid.*, 168, Warren to Pepperrell, May 13, 1745: "I did not know Mr Thane was come off. I will speak to him. He complain'd the people wou'd not assist him at the bomb battery."
40 *Ibid.*, 167, Waldo to Pepperrell, May 13, 1745.
41 *Ibid.*, 166-7.
42 *Ibid.*, 170, Waldo to Pepperrell, May 14, 1745.
43 P.A.C., D.F.A.S., F 557, "Raport du Nommé Girard La Croix."
44 M.H.S., Davis Papers, ? to ?, 1745.
45 Pepperrell, *An Accurate Journal*, 14.
46 *Ibid.*
47 Parkman, *A Half-Century of Conflict*, II, 296-7, Du Chambon to Maurepas, Sept. 2, 1745. See also DeForest, *Louisbourg Journals*, 70, "Fourth Journal, Anonymous."
48 Lincoln, *Pepperrell Journal*, 22.
49 M.H.S., *Colls.*, 6th Ser., X, 180-1, A. Noble to Pepperrell, May 17, 1745.
50 Shirley, *Letter to Newcastle*, 25.
51 M.H.S., Davis Papers, ? to ?, 1745.
52 P.A.C., D.F.A.S., F 557, "Raport du Nommé Girard La Croix."
53 M.H. S., Davis Papers, ? to ?, 1745.
54 Shirley, *Letter to Newcastle*, 26.
55 Lincoln, *Pepperrell Journal*, 22; and M.H.S. *Colls.*, 1st Ser., I, 31, Pepperrell to Shirley, May 20, 1745.
56 Parkman, *A Half-Century of Conflict*, II, 298, Du Chambon to Maurepas, Sept. 2, 1745.
57 *Ibid.* See also P.A.C., D.F.A.S., F 557, "Raport du Nommé Girard La Croix," and U.R., Maurepas Papers, Bigot to Maurepas, Aug. 15, 1745.
58 Upham, "Craft's Journal," Essex Institute Historical *Collections*, VI, 186; *New*

Footnotes

England Historical and Genealogical Register, Vol. 66, 119, "Benjamin Cleaves's Journal."

[59] Gibson, *Cape Breton Journal,* 13.

[60] M.H.S. *Colls.,* 6th Ser., X, 187, Pepperrell to Warren, May 19, 1745.

[61] *Ibid.,* 175-178, Warren to Pepperrell, May 16, 1745.

[62] *Ibid.,* 176-7.

[63] *Ibid.,* 20, "Records Of The Councils Of War."

[64] Parkman, *A Half-Century of Conflict,* II, 298, Du Chambon to Maurepas, Sept. 2, 1745. See also U.R., Maurepas Papers, Bigot to Maurepas, Aug. 15, 1745. Du Chambon made a mistake when he estimated that there were 500 in the force! See also P.A.C., D.F.A.S., F 557, "Raport du Nommé Girard La Croix."

[65] U.R., Maurepas Papers, Bigot to Maurepas, Aug. 15, 1745; and P.A.C., D.F.A.S., F 557, "Raport du Nommé Girard LaCroix."

[66] Parkman, *A Half-Century of Conflict,* II, 296-297, Du Chambon to Maurepas, Sept. 2, 1745: "The 20th, in the morning. I called a meeting of the company captains in order to decide on whether it was convenient to organize sorties against the enemy. It was resolved that the fortress lacked sufficient men...with the 1300 men including the 200 from the Royal Battery it was already difficult to defend the ramparts."

[67] Lincoln, *Pepperell Journal,* 22.

[68] Shirley, *Letter to Newcastle,* 25; Gibson, *Cape Breton Journal,* 13.

[69] DeForest, *Louisbourg Journals,* 17, "First Journal, Anonymous." See also Lincoln, *Pepperrell Journal,* 22.

[70] DeForest, *Louisbourg Journals,* 56, "Second Journal, Captain Joseph Sherburne."

[71] *Ibid.*

[72] N.H.H.S., Waldron Papers, T. Waldron to R. Waldron, May 20, 1745.

[73] Essex Institute Historical *Collections,* Vol. 48, 299, "Journal Kept By Lieut. Daniel Giddings."

[74] See especially P.A.C., 240, "Plan De Louisbourg Dans L'Isle Royalle, 1745, Verrier, Fils."

[75] DeForest, *Louisbourg Journals,* 56, "Second Journal, Captain Joseph Sherburne."

[76] McLennan, *Louisbourg,* 367, David Wooster to T. De Veil, Oct. 28, 1745.

[77] Niles, *A Brief and Plain Essay,* 32-33.

[78] P.A.C., H 3/240, "Plan of the City and Fortress of Louisbourg...Drawn on the Spot by Jn. Henry Bastide, 1745." See also McLennan, *Louisbourg,* 363, Vaughan to King George II, 1745.

[79] DeForest, *Louisbourg Journals,* 57, "Second Journal, Captain Joseph Sherburne."

[80] *Ibid.*

[81] Essex Institute Historical *Collections,* Vol. 48, 299, "Journal Kept By Lieut. Daniel Giddings."

[82] DeForest, *Louisbourg Journals,* 57, "Second Journal, Captain Joseph Sherburne."

[83] *Ibid.*

[84] N.H.H.S., Waldron Papers, T. Waldron to R. Waldron, May 20, 1745.

[85] DeForest, *Louisbourg Journals,* 57, "Second Journal, Captain Joseph Sherburne."

[86] For two excellent descriptions of the naval battle, see McLennan, *Louisbourg,* 156, and Chapin, *New England Vessels in the Expedition Against Louisbourg,* 17-18.

[87] M.H.S. *Colls.,* 6th Ser., X, 188, Warren to Pepperrell, May 19, 1745.

[88] P.A.C., Admiralty Papers, 51, 933, "Captain's Log of the H.M.S. *Superbe*"; *Boston Weekly News-Letter,* July 4, 1745, Captain Tyng to ?, May 23, 1745. See also McLen-

nan, *Louisbourg*, 177, "Captain's Log of the *Mermaid*"; "Captain's Log of the *Eltham*."

89 *Boston Weekly News-Letter*, July 4, 1745, Captain Tying to ?, May 23, 1745.

90 Massachusetts Historical Society *Proceedings* (Boston, 1910), 78, "Emerson's Louisbourg Journal," and Green, *Three Military Diaries*, 19, "Dudley Bradstreet's Diary." For a different view regarding the amount of powder, see P.A.C., Admiralty Papers, 51, 933, "Captain's Log of the H.M.S. *Superbe*": "40 cannon and 100 Barrels of Powder." It would seem that the 100 is a copyist's error.

91 McLennan, *Louisbourg*, 156-157.

92 As would be expected the British naval officers emphasized that the capture of the *Vigilant* was almost alone responsible for the fall of Louisbourg. See P. Durell, *A Particular Account of the Taking Cape Breton From the French by Admiral Warren and Sir William Pepperrell, the 17th of June 1745* (London, 1745), 3-4; *ibid.*, 5-6, An officer of Marines to a friend, June 21, 1745.

93 Green, *Three Military Diaries*, 18-19, "Dudley Bradstreet's Diary."

94 Wrong, *Louisbourg In 1745*, 48.

95 M.H.S., Davis Papers, ? to ?, 1745.

96 Parkman, *A Half-Century of Conflict*, II, 301, Du Chambon to Maurepas, Sept. 2, 1745.

97 Lincoln, *Pepperrell Journal*, 25.

98 DeForest, *Louisbourg Journals*, 195, Warren to Pepperrell, May 18, 1745.

99 M.H.S., Belknap Papers, N. Walter to ?, 1745.

100 M.H.S. *Colls.*, 6th Ser., X, 204, Waldo to Pepperrell, May 21, 1745.

101 *New England Historical and Genealogical Register*, Vol. 66, 119, "Benjamin Cleaves's Journal."

102 DeForest, *Louisbourg Journals*, 197, Warren to Pepperrell, May 23, 1745.

103 M.H.S. *Colls.*, 6th Ser., X, 213-4, Waldo to Pepperrell, May 23, 1745.

104 *New England Historical and Genealogical Register*, Vol. 66, 119, "Benjamin Cleaves's Journal."

105 M.H.S. *Colls.*, 6th Ser., X, 214, Waldo to Pepperrell, May 23, 1745.

106 DeForest, *Louisbourg Journals*, 77, "Fifth Journal, Anonymous."

107 M.H.S. *Colls.*, 6th Ser., X, 214, Waldo to Pepperrell, May 23, 1745.

108 DeForest, *Louisbourg Journals*, 87, "Sixth Journal, Anonymous." This estimate is probably much too high.

109 M.H.S., Cushing Papers, B. Green to Waldo, May 23, 1745.

110 DeForest, *Pomeroy Journals*, 27.

111 DeForest, *Louisbourg Journals*, 87, "Sixth Journal, Anonymous."

112 M.H.S. *Colls.*, 6th Ser., X, 21, "Records Of The Councils Of War."

113 *Ibid.*

114 Pepperrell, *An Accurate Journal*, 20.

115 Lincoln, *Shirley Correspondence*, I, 215, Shirley to Pepperrell, May 5, 1745.

116 M.H.S. *Colls.*, 6th Ser., X, 220, 223, "General Orders Of Commodore Warren...May 25, 1745."

117 *Ibid.*, 1st Ser., I, 33, Warren to Pepperrell, May 24, 1745.

118 *Ibid.*, 6th Ser., X, 22-3.

119 Lincoln, *Pepperrell Journal*, 26.

120 M.H.S., Belknap Papers, Waldo to Gorham, May 26, 1745.

121 DeForest, *Louisbourg Journals*, 58, "Second Journal, Captain Joseph Sherburne."

122 P.A.C., H 3/240, "Plan of the Town of Louisbourg."

123 Parkman, *A Half-Century of Conflict*, II, 303, Du Chambon to Maurepas, Sept. 2, 1745.

124 U.R., Maurepas Papers, Bigot to Maurepas, Aug. 15, 1745.

125 Pepperrell, *An Accurate Journal*, 26.

126 U.R., Maurepas Papers, Bigot to Maurepas, Aug. 15, 1745. Most of the New Englanders, it should be noted, were of the opinion the French were informed of the planned assault. See Green, *Three Military Diaries*, 20, "Dudley Bradstreet's Diary" and Essex Institute Historical *Collections*, Vol. 48, 300, "Journal Kept By Lieut. Daniel Giddings."
127 M.H.S., Parkman Papers, Bigot to Maurepas, Aug. 1, 1745.
128 C.H.S., *Colls.*, I, 152, "Wolcott's Journal."
129 Green, *Three Military Diaries*, 20, "Dudley Bradstreet's Diary."
130 DeForest, *Pomeroy Journals*, 28.
131 Pepperrell, *An Accurate Journal*, 21.
132 Upham, "Craft's Journal," Essex Institute Historical *Collections*, Vol. 48, 186.
133 Lincoln, *Pepperrell Journal*, 27.

Chapter 11
PEPPERRELL, WARREN AND THE FALL OF LOUISBOURG

1 M.H.S. *Proceedings* (1910), 79, "Emerson's Louisbourg Journal."
2 DeForest, *Louisbourg Journals*, 58, "Second Journal, Captain Joseph Sherburne." See also H. M. Chapin (ed.), *A Journal of the Voige in the Sloop Union, Elisha Mahew, Master, in an Expedition Against Cape Briton* (Providence, 1929), 13-14.
3 Only one day during the week, June 9, was relatively pleasant and fogfree. See DeForest, *Louisbourg Journals*, 58, "Second Journal, Captain Joseph Sherburne."
4 *Ibid.*
5 Parkman, *A Half-Century of Conflict*, II, 303, Du Chambon to Maurepas, Sept. 2, 1745.
6 DeForest, *Louisbourg Journals*, 78, "Fifth Journal, Anonymous"; Lincoln, *Pepperrell Journal*, 28.
7 See especially P.A.C., D.F.A.S., F 557, "Raport du Nommé Girard La Croix."
8 *Ibid.*
9 *Ibid.*
10 *Ibid.*
11 *Mémoire pour Messire François Bigot*, 9.
12 P.A.C., D.F.A.S., F 557, "Raport du Nommé Girard La Croix."
13 Niles, *A Brief and Plain Essay*, 16.
14 M.H.S. *Colls.*, 1st Ser., I, 34, Warren to Pepperrell, May 26, 1745.
15 Lincoln, *Shirley Correspondence*, I, 215, Shirley to Pepperrell, May 5, 1745.
16 M.H.S. *Colls.*, 6th Ser., X, 330, Pepperrell to Shirley, July 17, 1745.
17 *Ibid.*
18 *Ibid.* Pepperrell maintained that "it was of absolute necessity to keep from disputes & differences (or otherwise ye grand design might have sufferd & I have strove to my uttermost to keep things easey."
19 *Ibid.*, 1st Ser., I, 35, Pepperrell to Warren, May 28, 1745.
20 For the New England side see Lincoln, *Pepperrell Journal*, 27-8, and Gibson, *Cape Breton Journal*, 18-19. For the French side see Parkman, *A Half-Century of Conflict*, II, 299-300, Du Chambon to Maurepas, Sept. 2, 1745.
21 Lincoln, *Pepperrell Journal*, 28; and Parkman, *A Half-Century of Conflict*, II, 300, Du Chambon to Maurepas, Sept. 2, 1745.
22 M.H.S., Massachusetts Broadsides, "New England Bravery, 1745."
23 N.H.H.S., Waldron Papers, T. W. Waldron to R. Waldron, June 2, 1745: "our advance Battery is so near that we Converse with the French our People Ask'd them this morn to send out a Flag or truce they said not yet then they told them if they would come out that they would give them some of King George's bread they said they wanted None they ask'd them if they had any pretty Girls they told them they had with some other Conversation and then finish'd off with 3 or 4 showers

of bullets on both sides."

24 M.H.S. *Colls.*, 1st Ser., I, 36-8, Warren to Pepperrell, May 29, 1745.
25 *Ibid.*
26 *Ibid.*, 6th Ser., X, 233-234, Warren to Pepperrell, May 30, 1745; *ibid.*, 236-238, Warren to Pepperrell, May 31, 1745.
27 C.H.S., Wolcott Papers, Pepperrell to Warren, May 31, 1745.
28 M.H.S. *Colls.*, 6th Ser., X, 25, "Records Of The Councils Of War."
29 C.H.S., Wolcott Papers, Pepperrell to Warren, May 31, 1745.
30 M.H.S. *Colls.*, 6th Ser., X, 243, Pepperell to Shirley, June 2, 1745.
31 Tyerman, *George Whitefield*, 150.
32 M.H.S. *Colls.*, 6th Ser., X, 238, Pepperrell to Mascarene, June 2, 1745.
33 DeForest, *Louisbourg Journals*, 58, "Second Journal, Captain Joseph Sherburne"; *ibid.*, 78, "Fifth Journal, Anonymous."
34 Gibson, *Cape Breton Journal*, 20.
35 M.H.S. *Colls.*, 6th Ser., X, 256, Bastide to Warren, June 4, 1745.
36 Lincoln, *Pepperrell Journal*, 28.
37 *Ibid.*, 28.
38 M.H.S. *Colls.*, 6th Ser., X, 250, "Decision Of A Council Of War, June 3, 1745."
39 Gibson, *Cape Breton Journal*, 21.
40 M.H.S., Saunders Papers, Warren to Saunders, May 30, 1745.
41 M.H.S. *Proceedings* (1910), 80, "Emerson's Louisbourg Journal." See also Chapin, *New England Vessels in the Expedition against Louisbourg*, 20.
42 Cl.L., Sir James Douglas Papers, "Journall Kept on board His Maj. Ship *Vigilant*, Capt. James Douglass, Com., by Thos Shortland Commencing May the 23 1745."
43 C.H.S. *Colls.*, I, 132, "Wolcott's Journal."
44 *Acadiensis*, VIII, 322, "Benjamin Stearns's Journal."
45 Cl.L., Louisbourg Papers, T. W. Waldron to R. W. Waldron, June 6, 1745.
46 Green, *Three Military Diaries*, 23, "Dudley Bradstreet's Diary." See also C.H.S. *Colls.*, I, 133, "Wolcott's Journal."
47 DeForest, *Louisbourg Journals*, 24, "First Journal, Anonymous." See also *ibid.*, 78, "Fifth Journal Anonymous."
48 *Ibid.*, 89, "Sixth Journal, Anonymous." See especially Essex Institute Historical *Collections*, Vol. 48, 301, "Journal Kept By Lieut. Daniel Giddings."
49 Pepperrell, *An Accurate Journal*, 22.
50 M.H.S. *Colls.*, 1st Ser., I, 41, Warren to Pepperrell, June 7, 1745.
51 Pepperrell, *An Accurate Journal*, 22.
52 DeForest, *Pomeroy Journals*, 33.
53 C.H.S. *Colls.*, I, 132-3, "Wolcott's Journal"; DeForest, *Louisbourg Journals*, 59, "Second Journal, Captain Joseph Sherburne."
54 M.H.S. *Colls.*, 1st Ser., I, 39, Warren to Pepperrell, June 1, 1745.
55 *Ibid.*, 43, Warren to Pepperrell, June 7, 1745.
56 C.H.S. *Colls.*, I, 133, "Wolcott's Journal."
57 M.H.S. *Colls.*, 1st Ser., I, 43, de la Maisonfort to Du Chambon, June 18, 1745: "Warren...informs me, that the French have treated some English prisoners with cruelty and inhumanity; I can scarcely believe it, since it is the intention of the King our Master, that they should be well treated on every occasion. You are to know, that on the 30th of May I was taken by this squadron as I was about to enter your harbour."
58 Green, *Three Military Diaries*, 23, "Dudley Bradstreet's Diary."
59 P.A.C., A.C., F3, Vol. 50, Pt. I, Du Chambon to Warren, June 19, 1745. For the French description of this incident see Parkman, *A Half-Century of Conflict*, II, 304–305, Du Chambon to Maurepas, Sept. 2, 1745.
60 Green, *Three Military Diaries*, 23, "Dudley Bradstreet's Diary."

Footnotes

[61] Gibson, *Cape Breton Journal*, 21; and DeForest, *Pomeroy Journals*, 32.

[62] Green, *Three Military Diaries*, 23, "Dudley Bradstreet's Diary."

[63] Chapin, *A Journal of the Voige in the Sloop Union*, 21; P.A.C., D.F.A.S., F 557, "Raport du Nommé Girard La Croix."

[64] DeForest, *Pomeroy Journals*, 33.

[65] DeForest, *Louisbourg Journals*, 59, "Second Journal, Captain Joseph Sherburne."

[66] Bidwell, "Journal of the Rev. Adonijah Bidwell, " *New England Historical and Genealogical Register*, Vol. 27, 156.

[67] P.A.C., Adm. 51, 161, "Captain's Log of the H.M.S. *Canterbury*"; *ibid.*, Adm. 51, 195, "Captain's Log of the H.M.S. *Chester.*"

[68] Richmond, *The Navy in the War of 1739-48*, II, 214-215.

[69] P.A.C., A.M., B4, 57, Kersaint to Maurepas, 1745. See also *ibid.*, A.C., B, 82, Pt. I, Maurepas to de Salvert, May 15, 1745 and June 19, 1745.

[70] *Ibid.*, A.M., B4, 57, Kersaint to Maurepas, 1745.

[71] M.H.S. *Colls.*, 6th Ser., X, 267-9, Warren to Pepperrell, June 10, 1745.

[72] Gilman, *New Hampshiremen at Louisbourg*, 25, T. W. Waldron & J. Prescott to the Governor, Council and House of Representatives, Sept. 24, 1745. See also Chapin, *A Journal of the Voige in the Sloop Union*, 14.

[73] DeForest, *Pomeroy Journals*, 33.

[74] Green, *Three Military Diaries*, 24, "Dudley Bradstreet's Diary."

[75] DeForest, *Pomeroy Journals*, 34.

[76] C.H.S. *Colls.*, I, 134, "Wolcott's Journal."

[77] Pepperrell, *An Accurate Journal*, 22.

[78] DeForest, *Louisbourg Journals*, 59, "Second Journal, Captain Joseph Sherburne."

[79] M.H.S., Belknap Papers, Warren to Pepperrell, June 11, 1745.

[80] *Ibid.*, Saunders Papers, Pepperrell to Saunders, June 11, 1745.

[81] *Ibid.*, Belknap Papers, Warren to Pepperrell, June 11, 1745.

[82] Green, *Three Military Diaries*, 24, "Dudley Bradstreet's Diary."

[83] P.A.C., Adm. 51, 195, "Captain's Log of the H.M.S. *Chester.*"

[84] Chapin, *New England Vessels in the Expedition Against Louisbourg*, 20.

[85] See DeForest, *Louisbourg Journals*, 181-182, "Appendix I."

[86] M.H.S. *Colls.*, 6th Ser., X, 270, Warren to Pepperrell, June 12, 1745.

[87] *Ibid.*, 271, Warren to Pepperrell, June 12, 1745.

[88] DeForest, *Pomeroy Journals*, 34. See also C.H.S. *Colls.*, I, 135, "Wolcott's Journal."

[89] DeForest, *Louisbourg Journals*, 78, "Fifth Journal, Anonymous."

[90] *Ibid.*, 59, "Second Journal, Captain Joseph Sherburne."

[91] *Ibid.*, 78, "Fifth Journal, Anonymous."

[92] P.A.C., Adm. 51, 547, "Captain's Log of the H.M.S. *Lark.*"

[93] M.H.S. *Colls.*, 1st Ser., I, 44, Pepperrell to Warren, June 13, 1745.

[94] C.H.S. *Colls.*, I, 135, "Wolcott's Journal."

[95] M.H.S. *Colls.*, 6th Ser., X, 280, Warren to Pepperrell, June 14, 1745.

[96] *Ibid.*, 1st Ser., I, 44, Pepperrell to Warren, June 13, 1745.

[97] DeForest, *Louisbourg Journals*, 78-79, "Fifth Journal, Anonymous."

[98] *Ibid.*, 60, "Second Journal, Captain Joseph Sherburne."

[99] Parkman, *A Half-Century of Conflict*, II, 305-307, Du Chambon to Marurepas, Sept. 2, 1745.

[100] P.A.C., A.C., F 3, Vol. 50, Pt. I, Inhabitants of Louisbourg to Du Chambon, 1745.

[101] Parkman, *A Half-Century of Conflict*, II, 308, Du Chambon to Maurepas, Sept. 2, 1745.

[102] P.A.C., A. C., F 3, Vol. 50, Pt. I, Verrier to Du Chambon, June 26, 1745.

[103] *Ibid.*, Ste. Marie to Du Chambon, June 26, 1745.

[104] Lincoln, *Pepperrell Journal*, 32. See also Chapin, *A Journal of the Voige in the Sloop Union*, 23.

[105] DeForest, *Louisbourg Journals*, 26, "First Journal, Anonymous."

[106] Green, *Three Military Diaries*, 25, "Dudley Bradstreet's Diary."

[107] C.H.S. *Colls.*, I, 135, "Wolcott's Journal."

[108] DeForest, *Louisbourg Journals*, 60, "Second Journal, Captain Joseph Sherburne."

[109] M.H.S. *Colls.*, 1st Ser., I, 45, Du Chambon to Pepperrell & Warren, June 26, 1745.

[110] *Collection de Manuscrits*, III, 221, Warren & Pepperrell to Du Chambon, June 15, 1745.

[111] Pepperrell, *An Accurate Journal*, 23.

[112] C.H.S. *Colls.*, I, 137, 140-144, "Articles Of Capitulation, Proposed By Mr. Du Chambon," in "Wolcott's Journal."

[113] *Ibid.*, 141.

[114] Lincoln, *Pomeroy Journals*, 35; DeForest, *Louisbourg Journals*, 60, "Second Journal, Captain Joseph Sherburne"; Parkman, *A Half-Century of Conflict*, II, 308, Du Chambon to Maurepas, Sept. 2, 1745.

[115] C.H.S. *Colls.*, I, 144-146, Pepperrell & Warren to Du Chambon, June 16, 1745, "Wolcott's Journal."

[116] McLennan, *Louisbourg*, 179, Pepperrell to Du Chambon, June 16, 1745; see also C.H.S. *Colls.*, I, 146, Du Chambon to Warren & Pepperrell, June 27, 1745, "Wolcott's Journal."

[117] M.H.S. *Colls.*, 1st Ser., I, 45, Pepperrell to Warren, June 16, 1745.

[118] Chapin, *A Journal of the Voige in the Sloop Union*, 24.

[119] M.H.S. *Colls.*, 1st Ser., I, 45, Warren Pepperrell, June 16, 1745.

[120] *Ibid.*

[121] McLennan, *Louisbourg*, 179-180, Warren to Du Chambon, June 16, 1745.

[122] P.A.C., D.F.A.S., F 557, "Raport du Nommé Girard La Croix."

[123] Wrong, *Louisbourg In 1745*, 57-8.

[124] Paltsits, *The Journal of Captain William Pote*, 40-46.

[125] DeForest, *Louisbourg Journals*, 92, "Sixth Journal, Anonymous."

[126] *Ibid.*, 96.

[127] M.H.S. *Colls.*, 1st Ser., I, 46, Pepperrell to Du Chambon, June 17, 1745.

[128] *Ibid.*, Warren to Pepperrell, June 27, 1745.

[129] Green, *Three Military Diaries*, 26, "Dudley Bradstreet's Diary."

[130] Gibson, *Cape Breton Journal*, 25.

[131] M.H.S., Louisbourg Papers, ? to ?, n.d; *ibid.*, David Papers, "W. Clarke's Account of the Louisbourg Siege, Dec. 13, 1745."

[132] Hutchinson, *History of Massachusetts Bay*, II, 421.

[133] C. P. Stacey, *Quebec, 1759—The Siege and the Battle* (Toronto, 1959), iii, "Lord Selkirk's Diary, 1804."

[134] Niles, *A Brief and Plain Essay*, 1-34. See also T. Prince, *Extraordinary Events*; C. Chauncy, *Marvellous Things done by the right Hand and holy Arm of God in getting him the Victory* (Boston, 1745); T. Eliot, *God's Marvellous Kindness* (New London, 1745); J. Sewall, *The Lamb slain*.

[135] Prince, *Extraordinary Events*, 31.

[136] *Boston Evening Post*, July 15, 1745.

Chapter 12
EPILOGUE

[1] For interesting accounts of the celebrations in New England see *Pennsylvania Journal*, July 18, 1745, and M.H.S. *Colls.*, 6th Ser., X, 308-309, T. Hubbard to Pep-

perrell, July 4, 1745.

[2] *Pennsylvania Journal*, July 18, 1745.

[3] Dalhousie University Library, Halifax, N. S. [Dal. L.], J. G. Bourinot Transcripts of the Taking of Louisbourg in 1745 and 1758, 55, "A Poetical Essay on the Reduction of Cape Breton on June 17, 1745," from the *Gentleman's Magazine*, Vol. XVI.

[4] Lacour-Gayet, La Marine-Militaire De La France Sous Le Règne De Louis XV (1902), 181.

[5] M.H.S. *Colls.*, 6th Ser., X, 307, Benjamin Colman to Pepperrell, July 3, 1745.

[6] *Ibid.*, 308, T. Hubbard to Pepperrell, July 4, 1745.

[7] Chauncy, *Marvellous Things*, 12, 21.

[8] Prince, *Extraordinary Events*, 33.

[9] D. J. Boorstin, *The Americans: The Colonial Experience* (New York, 1964), 356.

[10] Dal. L., J. G. Bourinot Transcripts, 73, "The Virtue of the New England People," from *The Craftsman*, Aug. 3, 1745.

[11] DeForest, *Louisbourg Journals*, 130, "Ninth Journal, Chaplain Stephen Williams."

[12] M.H.S. *Colls.*, 6th Ser., X, 322, Shirley to Pepperrell, July 7, 1745.

[13] *Ibid.*, 323.

[14] *Ibid.*, 330, Pepperrell to Shirley, July 17, 1745.

[15] A. H. Buffinton, "The Canadian Expedition of 1746," *American Historical Review*, XLV, 3 (Apr., 1940), 563.

[16] Quoted in *ibid.*, Earl of Chesterfield to Robert Trevor, Aug. 13, 1745.

[17] For very good accounts of the impact of the fall of Louisbourg upon Britain's political and diplomatic policies see *ibid.*, 552-580, and J. M. Sosin, "Louisbourg and the Peace of Aix-la-Chapelle, 1748," *The William and Mary Quarterly*, 3rd Series, XIV, 4 (Oct., 1957), 516-535.

[18] DeForest, *Louisbourg Journals*, 92, "Sixth Journal, Anonymous."

[19] L. S. Mayo (ed.), T. Hutchinson, *The History of the Colony and Province of Massachusetts Bay* (Cambridge, 1936), II, 323. See also Cl.L., Papers of Sir James Douglas, "Journall Kept on board His Maj. Ship "Vigilant" Commencing May the 23, 1745," and DeForest, *Louisbourg Journals*, 35-36, "First Journal, Anonymous."

[20] Cl.L., Louisbourg Papers, T. W. Waldron to R. Waldron, July 26, 1745.

[21] M.H.S. *Colls.*, 6th Ser., X, 329, Pepperrell to Shirley, July 17, 1745.

[22] *Ibid.*, 30-31, "Records Of The Councils of War."

[23] Lincoln, *Shirley Correspondence*, I, 264, 293, Shirley to Benning Wentworth, Sept. 2, 1745, Shirley to Newcastle, Dec. 14, 1745.

[24] M.H.S. *Colls.*, 6th Ser., X, 47, "Records Of The Councils Of War."

[25] *Ibid.*, 442, Pepperrell to Shirley, Jan. 28, 1746.

[26] P.A.N.S., Vol. 19, Pepperrell to Newcastle, May 21, 1746.

[27] McLennan, *Louisbourg*, 173.

[28] Lacour-Gayet, *La Marine-Militaire*, 181. See also G. Graham, *Empire of the North Atlantic* (London, 1958), 132.

[29] Lacour-Gayet, *La Marine-Militaire*, 182-183.

[30] *Ibid.*, 184.

[31] C. L. Hanson (ed.), *A Journal for the Years 1739-1803 by Samuel Lane of Stratham, New Hampshire* (Concord, N.H., 1937), 66-67.

[32] Mayo (ed.), T. Hutchinson, *The History of the Colony and Province of Massachusetts Bay*, II, 325.

[33] Douglass, *A Summary, Historical and Political*, I, 323.

[34] Mayo (ed.), T. Hutchinson, *The History of the Colony and Province of Massachusetts Bay*, II, 328.

[35] McLennan, *Louisbourg*, 167.

[36] For an excellent analysis of the impact of the money upon the Massachusetts

economy, see M. Freiberg, "Thomas Hutchinson: the First Fifty Years (1711-1761)," *The William and Mary Quarterly*, 3rd Series, XV, 1 (Jan., 1958), 45-50.

[37] See especially the *Boston Weekly News-Letter* and *The Independent Advertiser*.
[38] *Boston Weekly News-Letter*, May 11, 1749.
[39] H. H. Peckham, *The Colonial Wars 1689-1762* (Chicago, 1964), 119.
[40] Belknap, *History of New Hampshire*, II, 232.

Index

Index

St. Ann's Bay, 101
Stearns, Benjamin, 93, 137
Ste. Marie, 145, 146
St. Francis, 16, 19
St Jean du Luz, 77
St. John River, 11
St. Malo, 1
Storer, Lt.-Col. John, 103
St. Peter's (Port Toulouse), 59, 63, 64, 65, 75, 78, 106
Subercase, 22
Sunderland, 140
Superbe, 56, 64, 81, 124, 137, 142, 143, 149
Tartar, 50, 51, 52, 124, 143, 150
Tatamagouche Harbour, 150
Thomas, Gov. George, 49
Tiddeman, Capt. Richard, 137
Titcomb's Battery, 125, 137, 144
Trident, 157
Trumble, Jonathan, 52
Tufts, William, 95, 96
Tyng, Capt., 10, 21
Utrecht, Treaty of, viii
Vauban, 98
Vaughan, William, 33, 34, 35, 38, 39, 40, 42, 44, 46, 48, 53, 58, 94, 95, 96, 103, 117, 118, 122, 123, 126, 152
Verrier, 91, 145, 146
Vigilant, 70, 71, 75, 124, 125, 126, 128, 135, 137, 138, 139, 143, 145
Waldo, Brig.-Gen. Samuel, 42, 96, 99, 100, 103, 104, 106, 109, 117, 118, 126, 127, 129, 137, 144
Waldron, Capt. Thomas Westbrook, 80, 81, 116, 122, 137, 156
Walter, Rev. Nathaniel, 126

Warren, Commodore Peter, 54; biographical sketch, 55; attitude towards the Louisbourg expedition, 55-56, 63; at Canso, 64-65; assistance in the Gabarus landing, 80-82, 100; Island Battery attack proposed, 103, 104; plan for Louisbourg attack, 105; attitude towards first summons, 106, 107, 108; Island Battery attack, 109-111; friction with Pepperell, 112-113, 115, 116, 119-120, 124, 126, 127, 128; June 4 plan to capture Louisbourg, 128-129; critical of Pepperell's indolence, 132-135, 136; plan of attack agreed upon, 137, 138, 139; attack preparations, 143-145, 146; speech to the New England troops, 146; negotiations with Du Chambon, 146-149; attempt to persuade Du Chambon to surrender to the British Navy, 149, 150; critical of Pepperell's capitulation policy, 151, 154, 155, 156
Wentworth, Lt.-Gov. Benning (Lieutenant-Governor of New Hampshire), 42, 52, 53, 54
West Gate (Dauphin Bastion), ix, 88, 96, 102, 106, 108, 113, 119, 121, 122, 123, 125, 129, 132, 134, 138, 139, 145
Whitehall, 26, 28, 50, 53
Whitefield, Rev. George, 44, 45, 136
White Point, 59, 75
Willard, Col. Samuel, 103
Williams, Rev. Elisha, 52, 104
Winchelsea, Earl of, 32
Wolcott, Major-Gen. Roger, 52, 102
Woodbridge, Theophilus, 87, 109
Young, Capt. Robert, 3

The Author

BORN IN THOROLD, ONTARIO, in 1935, George Rawlyk was one of the most distinguished historians of Maritime History. As a professor at Queen's University from 1969 until his death in 1995, and teaching at Dalhousie and Mount Allison Universities, his focus on the social and cultural history of the Maritimes in the 18th and 19th centuries had a profound influence in the field throughout the 1970s, '80s, and '90s—during the renaissance of regional history.

He is the author of many books, including *Nova Scotia's Massachusetts: A Study of Massachusetts-Nova Scotia Relations 1630-1784* (1973), and the influential *Ravished by the Spirit: Revivals, Maritime Baptists and Henry Alline* (1984). *Yankees at Louisbourg* (1967) was his first book.

ALSO AVAILABLE FROM
Breton Books

THE HIGHLAND HEART IN NOVA SCOTIA
by NEIL MacNEIL

Told with the pride and joy that only an exiled son can bring to the world of his heart and his childhood—wonderful writing about the peace and raw humour of Celtic Cape Breton's Golden Age. Raised at the turn of the century, Neil MacNeil became an editor of *The New York Times*.

$18.50

WATCHMAN AGAINST THE WORLD
by FLORA McPHERSON

The Remarkable Journey of Norman McLeod and his People from Scotland to Cape Breton Island to New Zealand

A detailed picture of the tyranny and tenderness with which an absolute leader won, held and developed a community— and a story of the desperation, vigour, and devotion of which the 19th-century Scottish exiles were capable.

$16.25

ECHOES FROM LABOR'S WARS
by DAWN FRASER

**Industrial Cape Breton in the 1920s
Echoes of World War One
Autobiography & Other Writings**
Introduction by David Frank & Don MacGillivray

Dawn Fraser's narrative verse and stories are a powerful, compelling testament to courage, peace & community. They belong in every home, in every school.

$13.00

CAPE BRETON QUARRY
by STEWART DONOVAN

A book of poetry that gravitates between rural and urban Cape Breton Island, and the experience of working away. Stewart Donovan has written a relaxed, accessible set of poems of a man's growing up and his reflections on the near and distant past of his communities. A lovely, lasting little book.

$11.00

WILD HONEY
by AARON SCHNEIDER

Stark and sensual, even sexy—funny and frightening by turns—these are poems you can read and read again, for enjoyment and for insight. By an award-winning writer, a teacher and an environmentalist who has made his life in Cape Breton.

$13.00

HIGHLAND SETTLER
by CHARLES W. DUNN

A Portrait of the Scottish Gael in Cape Breton & Eastern Nova Scotia

"This is one of the best books yet written on the culture of the Gaels of Cape Breton and one of the few good studies of a folk-culture."—*Western Folklore*.

$16.25

CASTAWAY ON CAPE BRETON
Two Great Shipwreck Narratives
1. Ensign Prenties' *Narrative* of Shipwreck at Margaree Harbour, 1780 (Edited with an Historical Setting and Notes by G. G. Campbell)
2. Samuel Burrows' *Narrative* of Shipwreck on the Cheticamp Coast, 1823 (With Notes on Acadians Who Cared for the Survivors by Charles D. Roach)

$13.00

THE CAPE BRETON GIANT
by JAMES D. GILLIS

& "Memoir of Gillis" by Thomas Raddall
A book about not one, but two singular Cape Bretoners: Giant Angus MacAskill and Author James D. Gillis.
"Informative, entertaining, outrageous...!"

$10.00

MABEL BELL:
Alexander's Silent Partner
by LILIAS M. TOWARD

The classic biography—a new edition with large, readable type and glowing photographs. Told from Mabel's letters and family papers, this is their intimate story of love and courage. With bibliography.

$18.50

• PRICES INCLUDE GST & POSTAGE IN CANADA •

CONTINUED ON NEXT PAGE